Baseball In Eau Claire

Baseball In Eau Claire

Jason Christopherson

ARCADIA
PUBLISHING

ISBN 978-0-7385-3162-5

Published by Arcadia Publishing
Charleston, South Carolina

Printed in the United States of America

Library of Congress Catalog Card Number: Applied For.

For all general information contact Arcadia Publishing at:
Telephone 843-853-2070
Fax 843-853-0044
E-mail sales@arcadiapublishing.com
For customer service and orders:
Toll-Free 1-888-313-2665

Visit us on the Internet at www.arcadiapublishing.com

Contents

ACKNOWLEDGMENTS

There are so many people to thank that I'm sure I'll miss a few, and for that I am sorry. Without further ado:

THANK YOU to:

The Chippewa Valley Museum, Eau Claire, WI, for their extensive file of photographs, and for arranging for me to be able to use them here.

All of the "Baseball Bibles," from which a lot of information was gleaned. Books such as *The Encyclopedia of Minor League Baseball, 2nd Edition* (Johnson/Wolff), *The Ballplayers* (Shatzkin/Charlton), and *Total Baseball* (Thorn, Palmer, Gershman, Pietrusga) proved to be extremely valuable.

The *Eau Claire Leader-Telegram*, for help with some photos of hard-to-find players. Jerry Poling—thanks for helping keep baseball history alive in this town.

Eunice Whipple and David Hanson, Eau Claire Cavalier "superfans" that helped me fill in the blanks with the Cavs.

Harold "Diz" Kronenberg, the first person I talked to about the history of baseball in Eau Claire. To call you a sports legend in this city is a major understatement.

Marty Appel at The Topps Company, Inc., for use of the baseball card images.

Bob Buege, author and fellow SABR-rite, for encouraging me to submit my Henry Aaron article to SABR for publication and . . .

Jeff Ruetsche, with Arcadia Publishing, for reading said article! You made a dream come true for me—thanks for trusting me to do this wonderful project.

The dozens of players (and their families), coaches, front office staff, and umpires that contributed their photos, stories, or both. You trusted a total stranger with treasured mementos from your past, and took the time to tell me more about the game we all love. I am indebted to you all forever.

My Mom, for encouraging my writing, and for always being their when writing just wasn't enough.

Les, for taking such good care of Mom!

My brother, Travis, for instilling the love of baseball into me at a very early age. Without that, this could be a book about . . . .soccer. Essch!

My children, Andrew and Camryn. As you grow up, you probably won't remember how little time I had to play with you as I was writing this book. But please know I will never forget your sacrifice of time. Thank you, too, for making me the proudest a father can be.

And finally, my wife Shelley, who is more supportive of all my endeavors that I could ever hope for. Your help with scanning all of these photos was just another example of that support. We first met at a baseball game I was playing way back in high school, which gives me all the more reason to love the game. Without your love and understanding, this book, much like my baseball playing career, would have been an unfulfilled dream. I thank you most of all.

This book is dedicated to you all, as well as to all of those involved in giving Eau Claire such a rich baseball history!

ONE

The Pioneer Era

The Eau Claire *Weekly Free Press* reported on September 5, 1867 that "Eau Claire is certainly behind the times in not having a base ball club." That apparently got someone mad enough to just go out and get a team going, because three weeks later a club known as The Clearwater Boys was organized and played a game.

"Base ball" was thus born in Eau Claire. And it wouldn't take long for it to grow up.

Numerous games were played in and around the city the following summer. One game had the West Eau Claire Crocidiles beating the Shawtown Chippewas, 97-78! The Chippewas felt cheated, though, because the Crocs had used a pitcher from Durand (though it didn't seem like this one was much of a pitcher's dual). A rivalry had begun! In October, the Crocidiles challenged the Chippewas to a rematch to determine the Championship, but the game was scheduled to be played at 1:00 p.m. the next day, which presented a problem for the Chippewas. Apparently, the Shawtown club declined because their top players were too scattered to make the early afternoon start. Oh, and they didn't have a ball. The rivalry didn't stop there, though. The "second nines" of the two clubs played instead. The Chippewas won, but didn't get the ball that they earned for the win. And, they had to go home without supper!

Though games were still being played, the local press didn't do a lot for coverage for the next few decades. In 1885, the Eau Claire Athletic Association was incorporated, and players from all around the Upper Midwest were on the team. Basically, the team was professional, but they wouldn't be affiliated with a professional league until the following year when they joined the Northwestern League. Eau Claire finished second to Duluth in 1886, playing many of the same teams they had played the previous year. In 1887, the last year of the league, Eau Claire limped to a 38-85 record, a mere 41 games out of first place. Eau Claire would not be affiliated again until 1906, when they formed the Orphans with neighboring Chippewa Falls in the Wisconsin State League.

Amateur ball, of course, was as popular as ever, and several of the city's employers had teams. Continental Clothiers and the O-Claire Box Company were the two most predominant teams in the local industrial leagues. Photos of the amateur teams began appearing around the turn of the century.

Eau Claire returned to the Wisconsin State League in 1907, but this time on their own. From 1909 to 1912, the city was represented in the Minnesota-Wisconsin League. The 1909 squad (the "Puffs") featured Len Schroeder, who pitched what is believed to be the first professional no-hitter in Eau Claire history. Dave Callahan led the Eau Claire Commissioners to the pennant in 1910. Hall of Famer Burleigh Grimes played for the club in 1912 before the entire league disbanded in July. After that unfortunate circumstance, it would be amateur and semi-pro baseball only for Eau Claire until 1933.

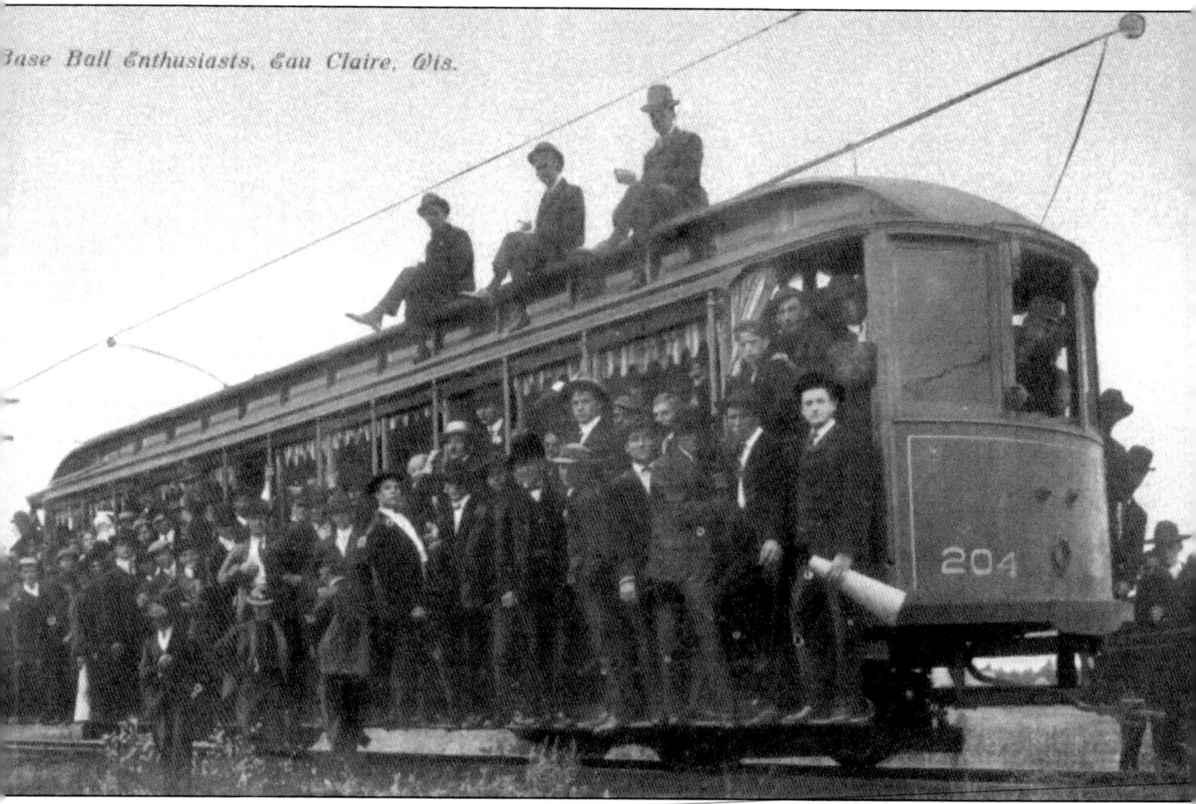

The postcard reads "Base Ball Enthusiasts, Eau Claire, Wis." Baseball (or Base Ball) has long been a popular sport with the fans in the Eau Claire area. Basketball and football probably are more popular currently, but many locals still find the ultimate way to spend a warm summer evening is at the ballpark. Of course, they don't dress as formally as they did back then. . . . (Photo courtesy of the Chippewa Valley Museum, Eau Claire, WI.)

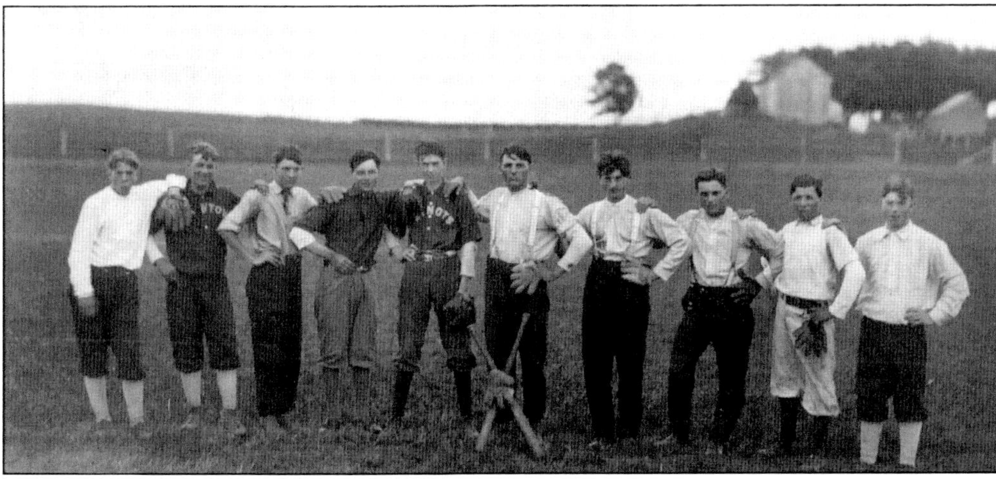

This ballgame at Johnson Grove (near Eau Claire), is estimated to have taken place in the 1890s. Like most images from that era, no player identifications are available. (Photo courtesy of the Chippewa Valley Museum, Eau Claire, WI.)

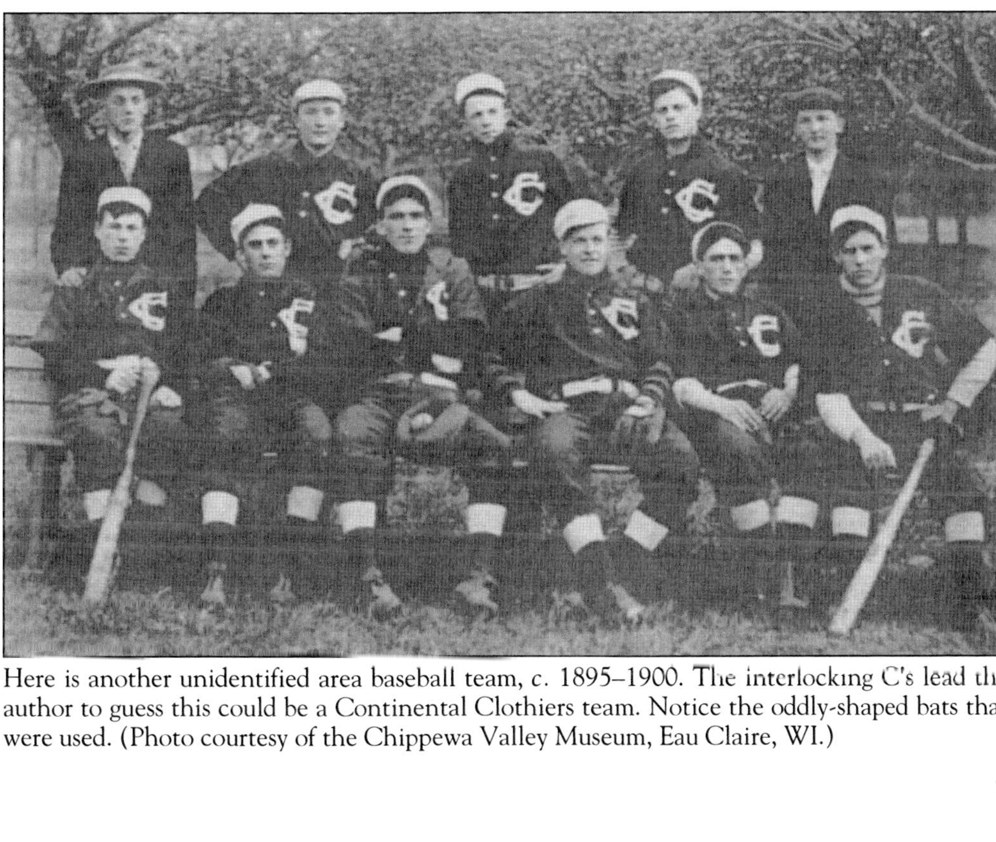

Here is another unidentified area baseball team, *c.* 1895–1900. The interlocking C's lead the author to guess this could be a Continental Clothiers team. Notice the oddly-shaped bats that were used. (Photo courtesy of the Chippewa Valley Museum, Eau Claire, WI.)

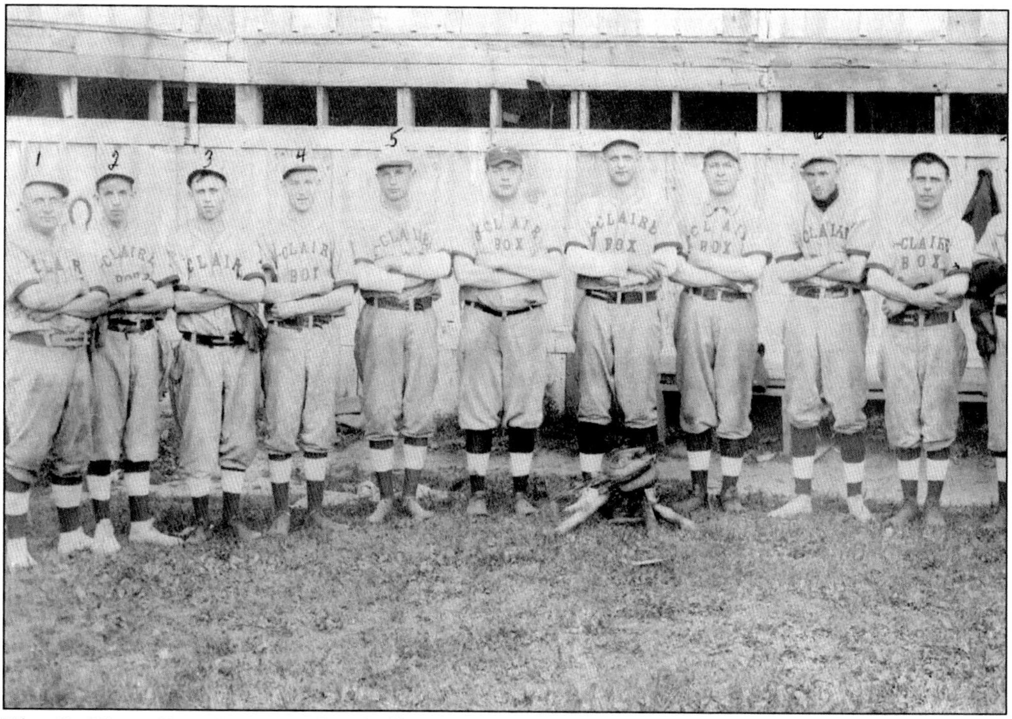

The O-Claire Box Company baseball team, captured in this turn-of-the-century photograph, would field a baseball team for several years in various local industrial leagues. Unfortunately, though there are numbers above some of the players, no player identifications were discovered. (Photo courtesy of the Chippewa Valley Museum, Eau Claire, WI.)

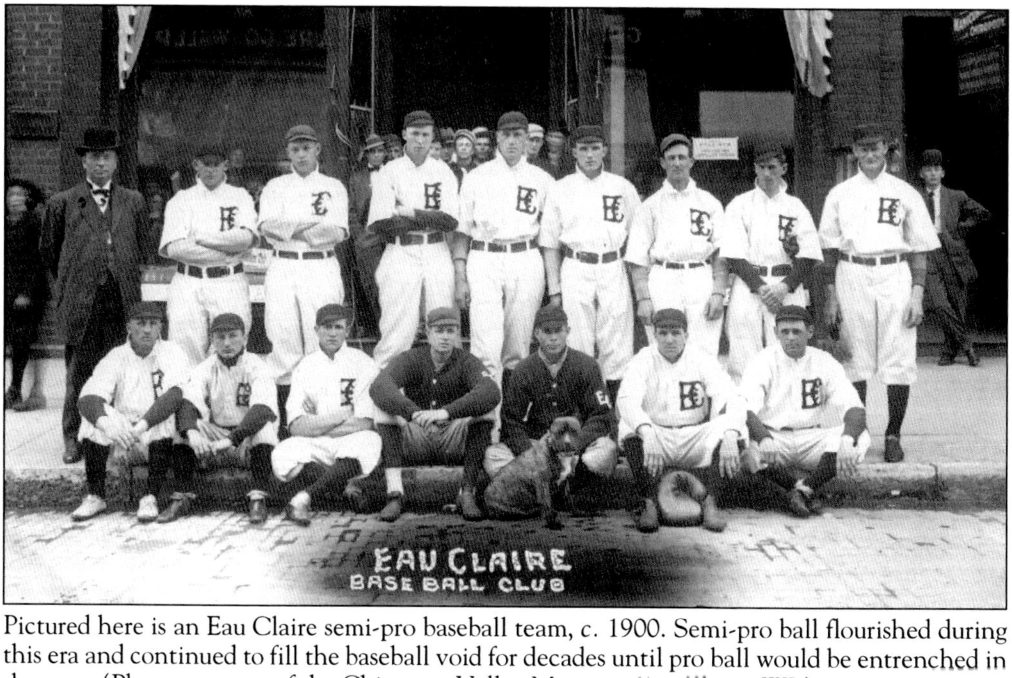

Pictured here is an Eau Claire semi-pro baseball team, *c.* 1900. Semi-pro ball flourished during this era and continued to fill the baseball void for decades until pro ball would be entrenched in the area. (Photo courtesy of the Chippewa Valley Museum, Eau Claire, WI.)

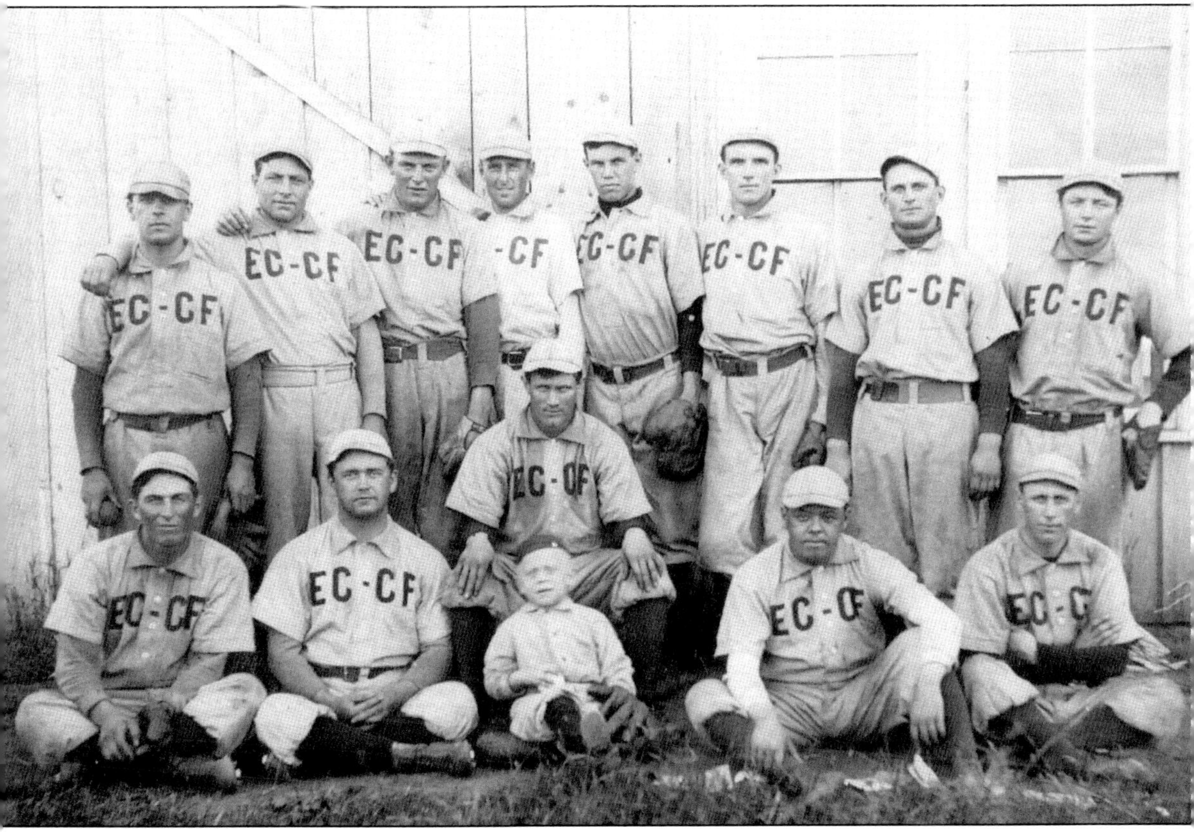

Eau Claire joined with neighboring Chippewa Falls in 1906 to get its first professional team since the city had an entry in the Northwestern League in 1886 and 1887. In late April, a reward was offered for the best team nickname. Apparently, the prize was never awarded. In May, manager Andy Porter was fired and two days later, since a new manager had not arrived yet, the local paper referred to the team as the "Orphans." The name stuck, and the Eau Claire-Chippewa Falls Orphans went through four managers, finishing in last place in the new Wisconsin State League. (Author's collection.)

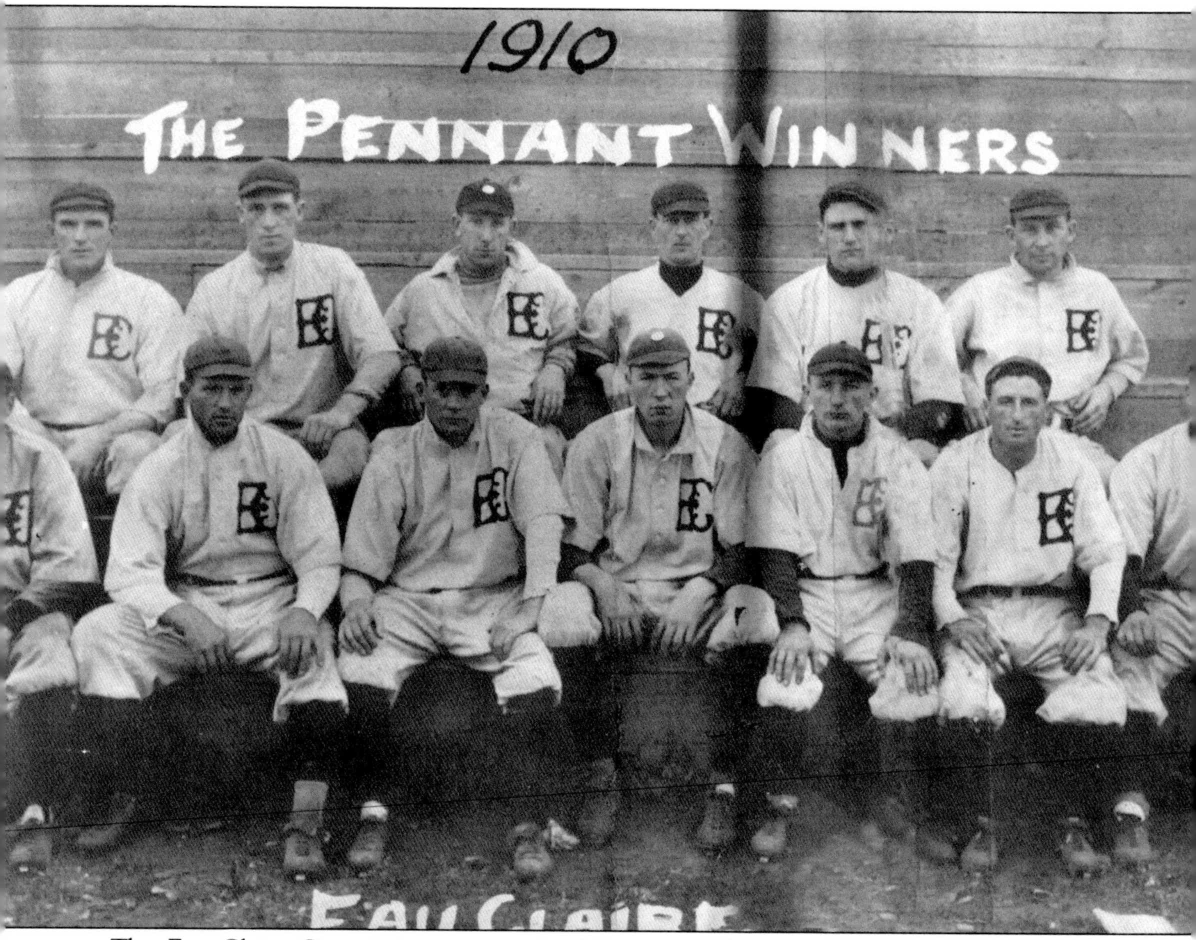

The Eau Claire Commissioners won the Minnesota-Wisconsin League pennant in 1910. Dave Callahan of Eau Claire paced the league in batting average (.365) and runs scored (92) as the Commissioners ran away from the rest of the pack. Frank Nicholson, who pitched a no-hitter for Eau Claire against second place Winona on September 6, hammered the final nail in the coffin.

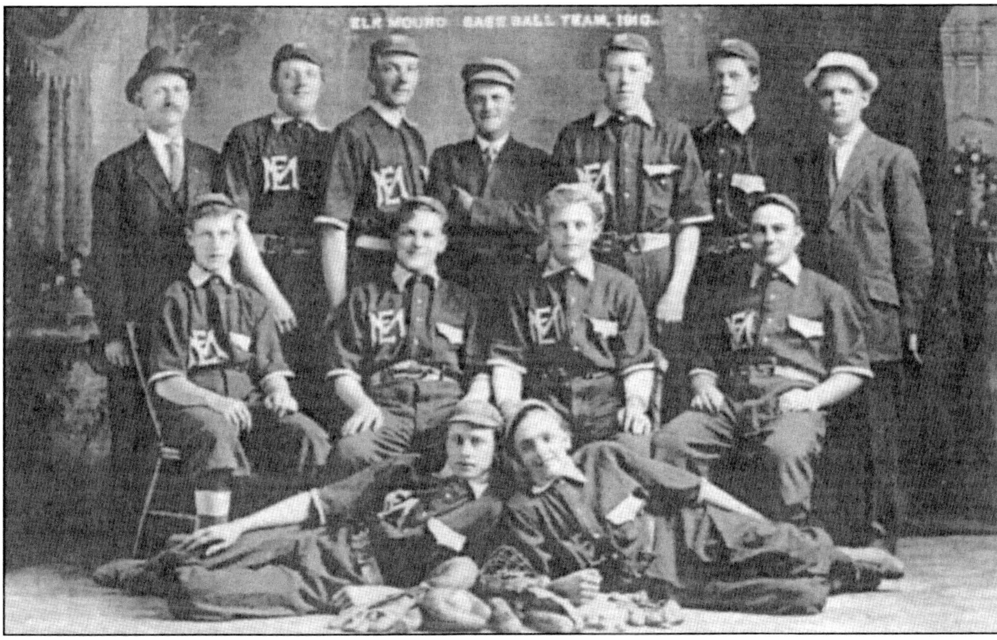

Most of the smaller towns around the Eau Claire area also fielded teams in the early twentieth century. The photos on this page show the Elk Mound team—the 1910 version (above) and the 1913 team (below). The players are not identified on the 1910 postcard, and the names written on the 1913 photo are largely illegible. Elk Mound is a community just west of Eau Claire, and small town baseball still thrives in the Chippewa Valley. The author attended a game at the Strum, Wisconsin ballpark in May of 2003, while compiling this book. The Strum team, known as the Beef River Bullfrogs, loaded the bases against the Stanley Loggers. The PA announcer put on sound effects of frogs croaking and said, "Once again, the swamp is full of frogs..." Is there anything more pure than small town baseball? (Photos courtesy of the Chippewa Valley Museum, Eau Claire, WI.)

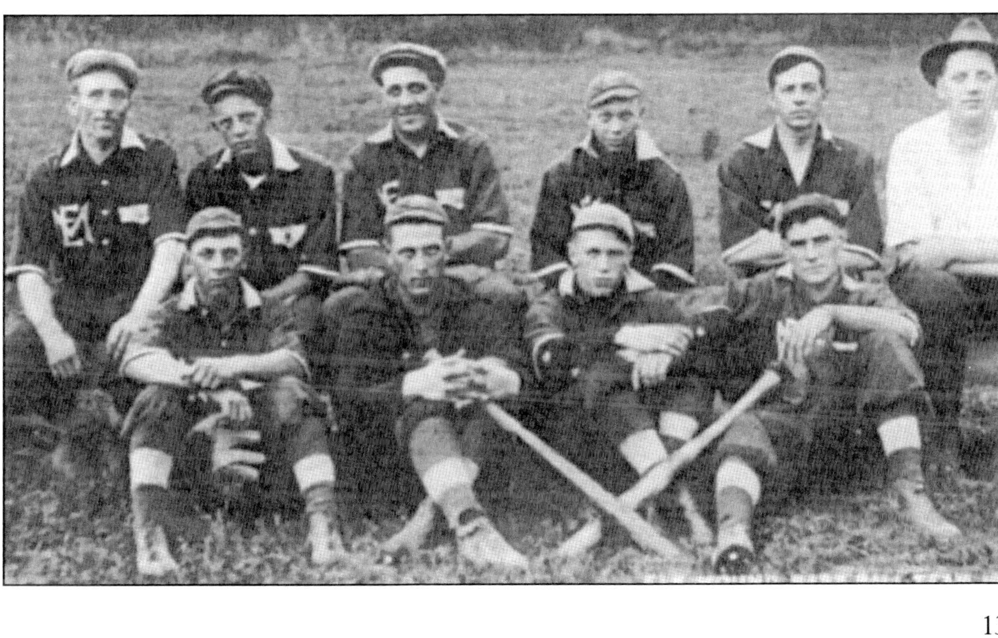

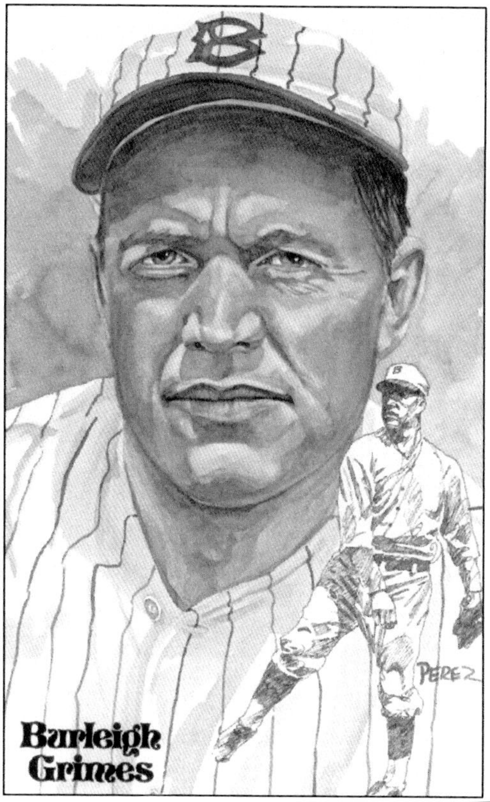

Later nicknamed "Ol' Stubblebeard," Clear Lake, Wisconsin's Burleigh Grimes was a smiling 18-year-old kid when he made his professional debut for the Eau Claire Commissioners (Class D Minnesota-Wisconsin League) in 1912. He began as an outfielder, but made his pitching debut on May 21 at the Driving Park in Eau Claire. On July 1, the Eau Claire team had to withdraw from the league due to financial difficulties stemming from poor attendance. The League was then forced to stop operations. The City would not see professional baseball for another 21 years. (Photo courtesy of Perez-Steele Galleries.)

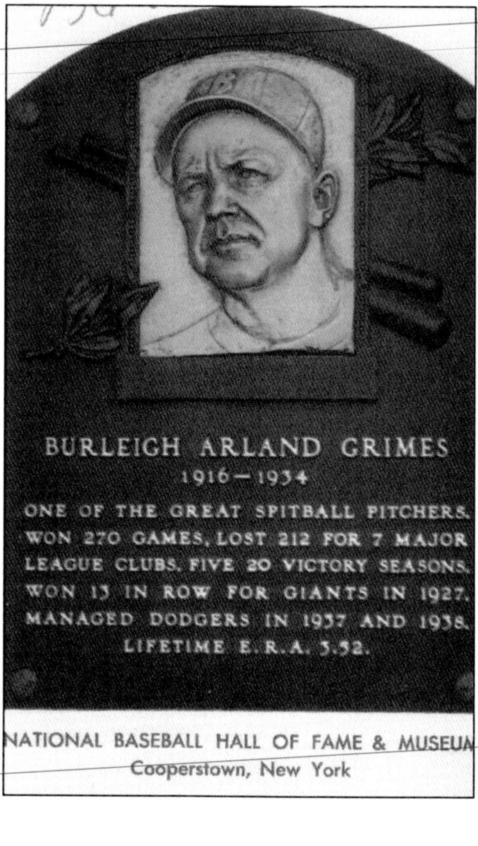

Grimes' major league playing career spanned nineteen seasons, most notably with Brooklyn from 1918 to 1926. Chewing slippery elm bark from western Wisconsin trees, Grimes' legendary "spitter" had hitters guessing until Burleigh finally retired in 1934—the last legal spitball pitcher in baseball. Grimes died in 1985 at the age of 92 in Clear Lake, his lifelong home. (Photo courtesy of the National Baseball Hall of Fame, Cooperstown, NY.)

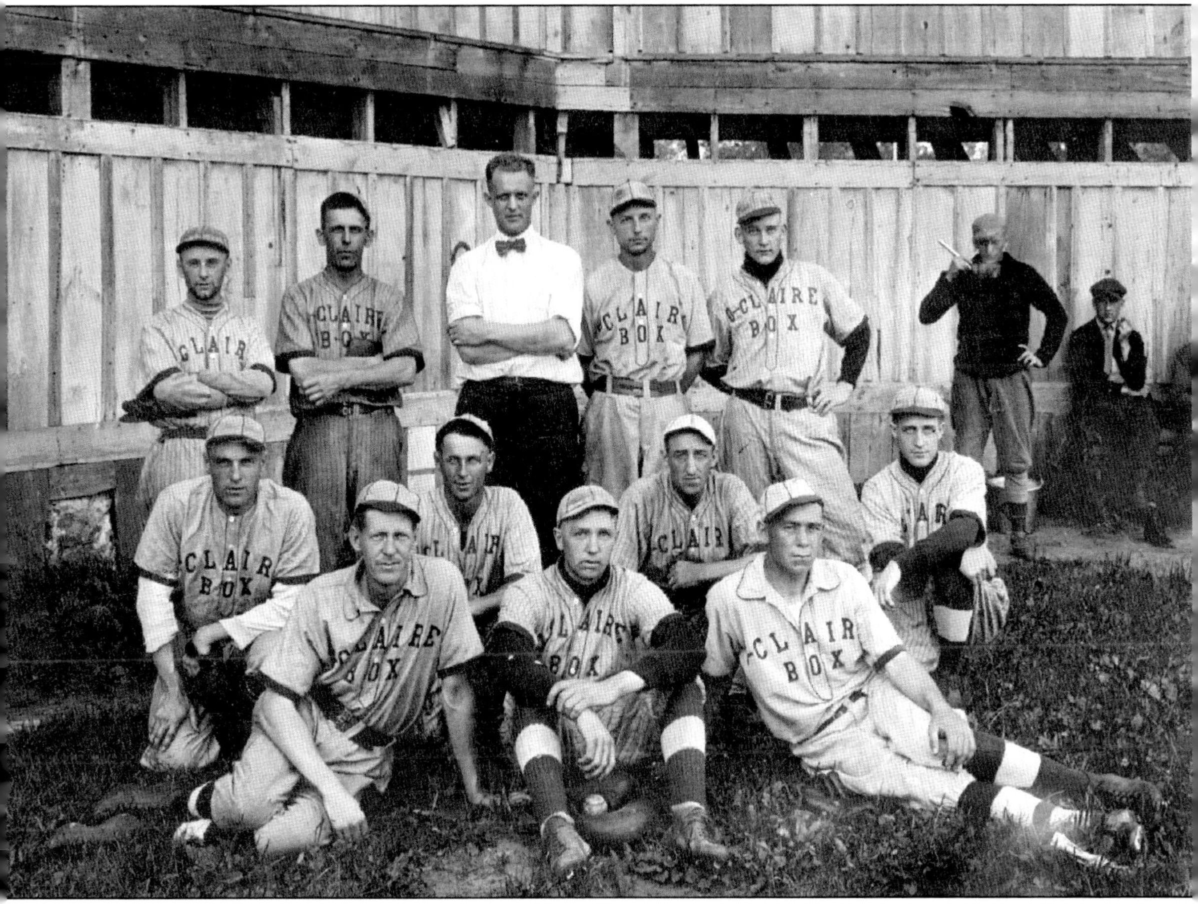

The 1914 O-Claire Box Company baseball team, from left to right: (front row) Orval Thompson, Jack Meyers, and Tom Bridges; (middle row) "Hud" Gelein, ? LaRock, Pat Baker, and Claude Lamb; (back row) Alfred Campbell, Louis DeRusha, Bob White, "Tex" Steahr, and Eddy Anderson. This photo was taken at the Driving Park in the third ward area of downtown Eau Claire. Notice the curious fellow in the background sipping water with a ladle! Gelein's family name graces a gorgeous softball field a couple of long homers from the current Carson Park baseball stadium. (Photo courtesy of the Chippewa Valley Museum, Eau Claire, WI.)

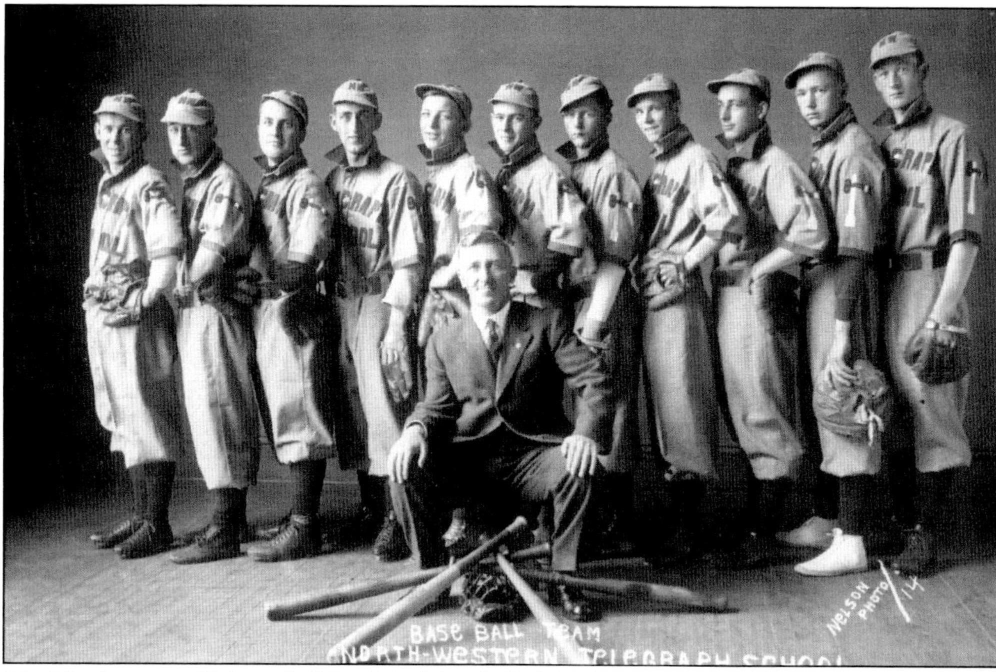

The Northwestern Telegraph School had fine ball clubs for many years. This team photo, players unidentified, is from 1914. (Photo courtesy of the Chippewa Valley Museum, Eau Claire, WI.)

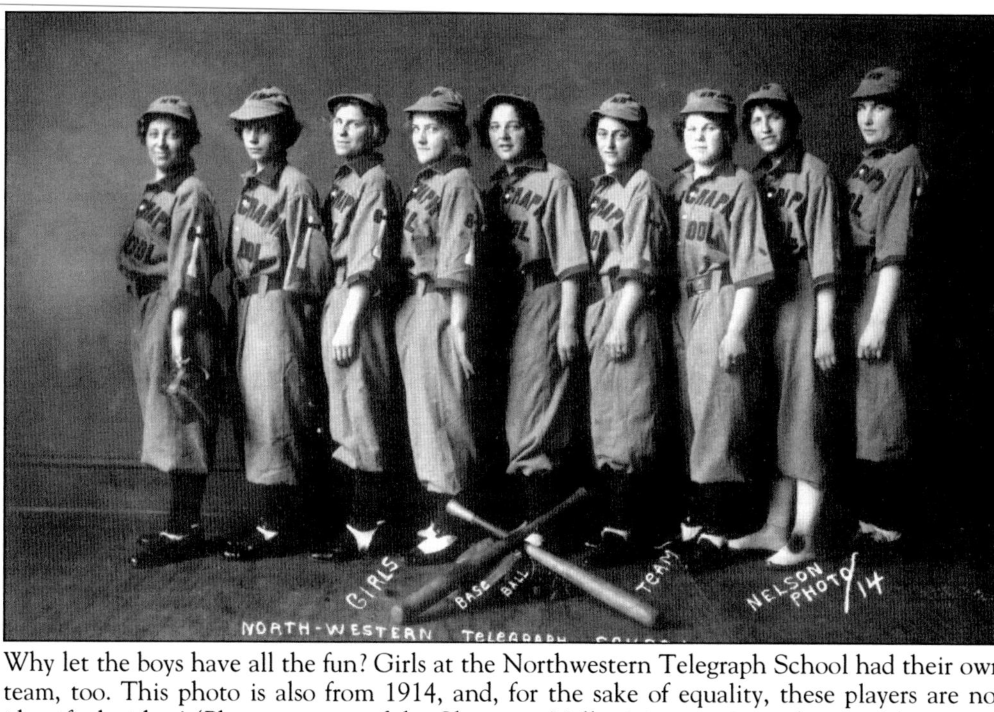

Why let the boys have all the fun? Girls at the Northwestern Telegraph School had their own team, too. This photo is also from 1914, and, for the sake of equality, these players are not identified, either! (Photo courtesy of the Chippewa Valley Museum, Eau Claire, WI.)

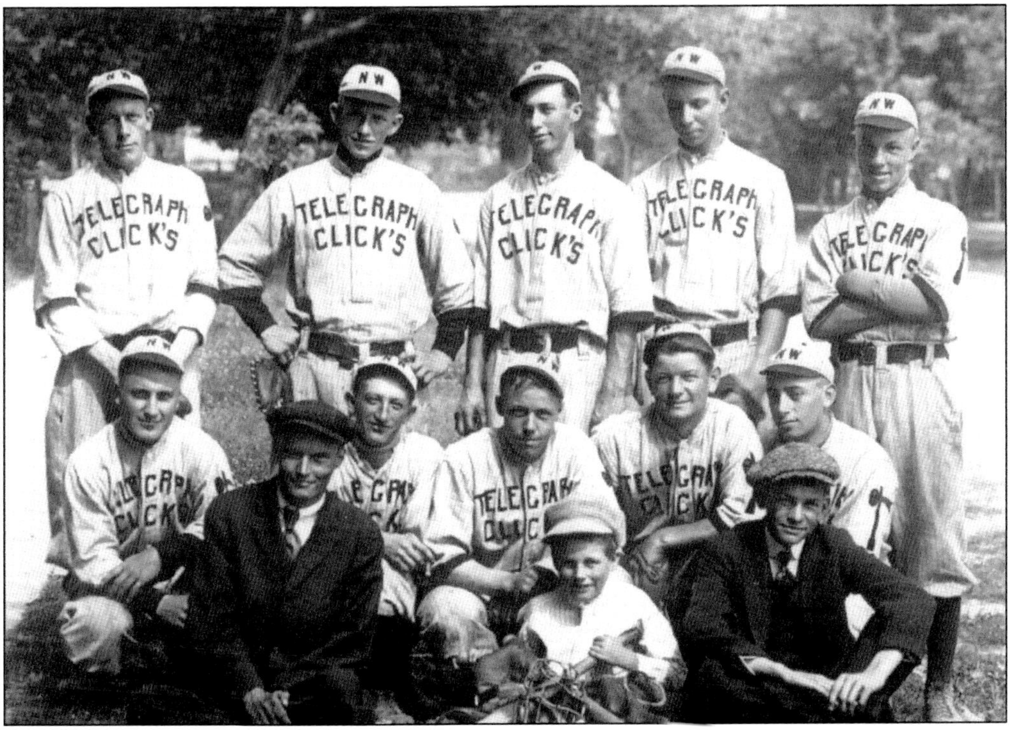

Pictured here are the "Clicks" from the Northwestern Telegraph School, 1915. (Photo courtesy of the Chippewa Valley Museum, Eau Claire, WI.)

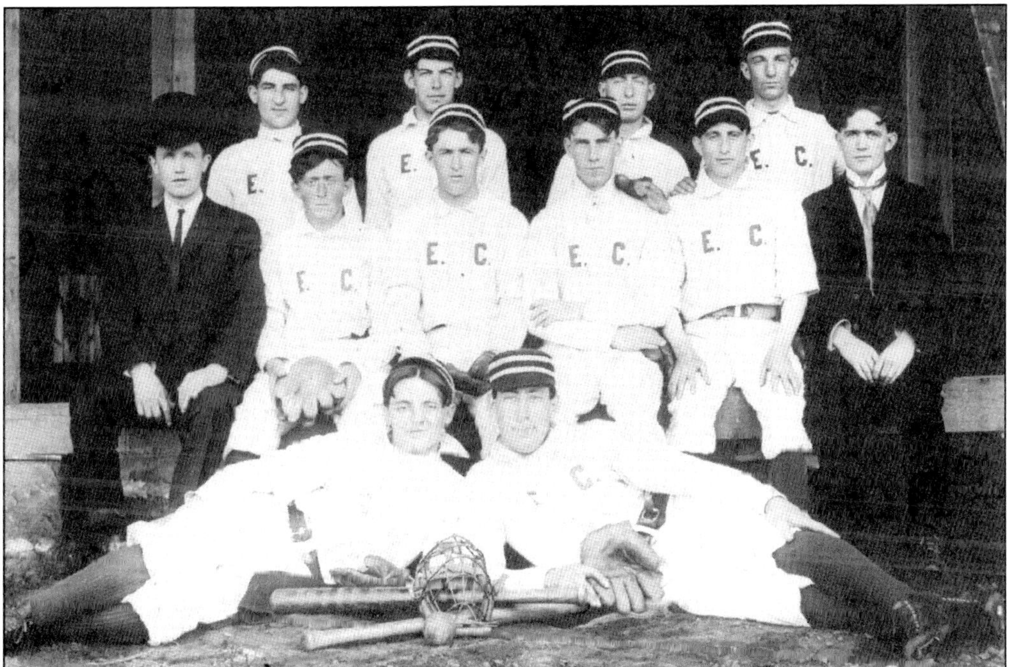

Another Eau Claire baseball team is captured without identification of names or team origin, c. 1912-1915. (Photo courtesy of the Chippewa Valley Museum, Eau Claire, WI.)

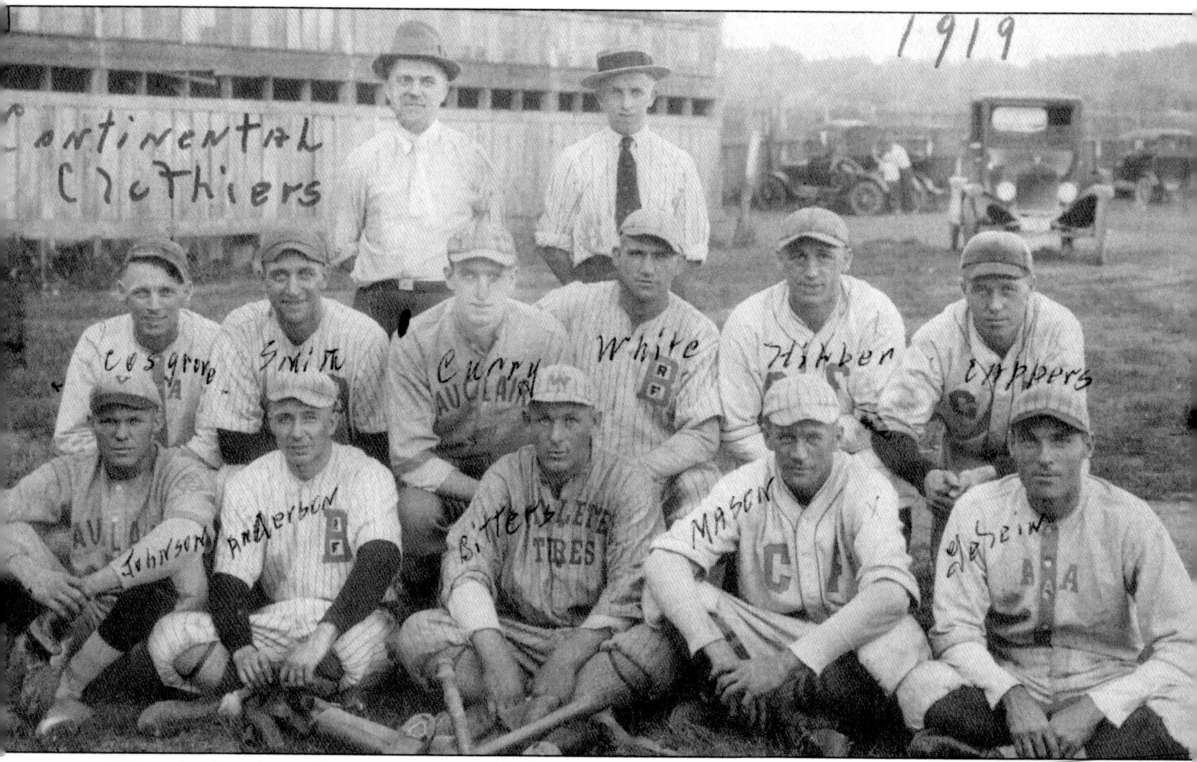

Though the players have been identified, this area team's nickname remains unknown, c. 1919. From left to right: (front row) Johnson, Eddy, Anderson, Bitters, Mason, and "Hud" Gelein; (second row) Cosgrove, Smith, Curry, Bob, (unidentified), White, Hibber, and Ehppers. The gentlemen in the far back row are unidentified. "Continental Clothiers" is written on the photo, but it appears the players are from an All-Star team of some sort. The "BRF" on a few of the uniforms likely is for Black River Falls, a town about 50 miles southeast of Eau Claire. "CF" is undoubtedly Chippewa Falls, about ten miles north of Eau Claire. Gillette Tires was an employer in Eau Claire for decades (albeit with different company names), so it would be odd that Bitters (front row, center) would have that uniform and play for another company team like Clothiers. (Photo courtesy of the Chippewa Valley Museum, Eau Claire, WI.)

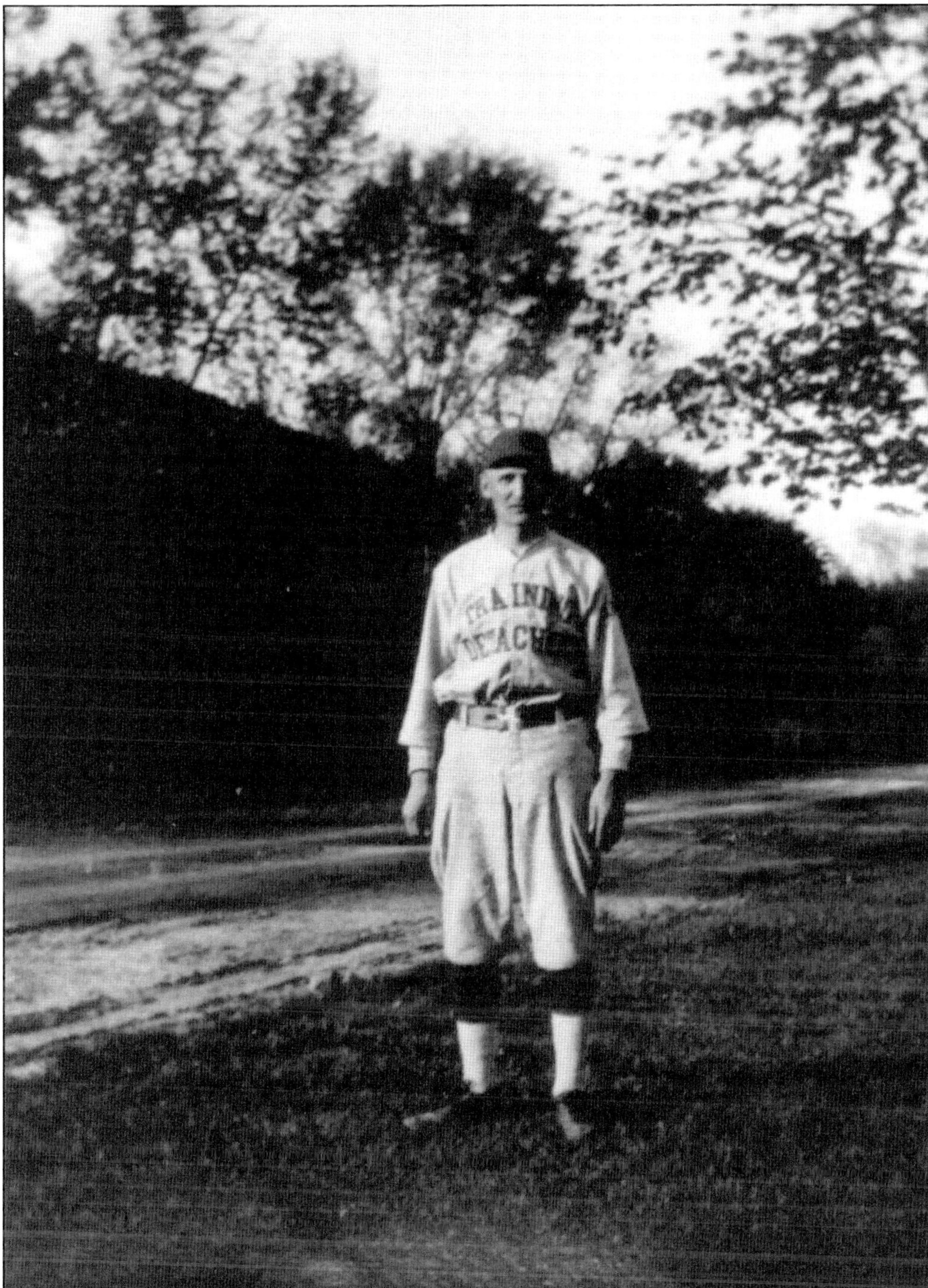

George "Dutch" Gerner, shown here in 1918 in an army baseball uniform, would go on to star as catcher for the 1922 semi-pro team in Eau Claire. After his playing career ended in 1925, he got married and moved back to Eau Claire, the town he fell in love with, in 1926. He remained there for the rest of his life, sadly passing away just days after his Golden Wedding Anniversary in 1976. (Photo courtesy of George Gerner, Jr.)

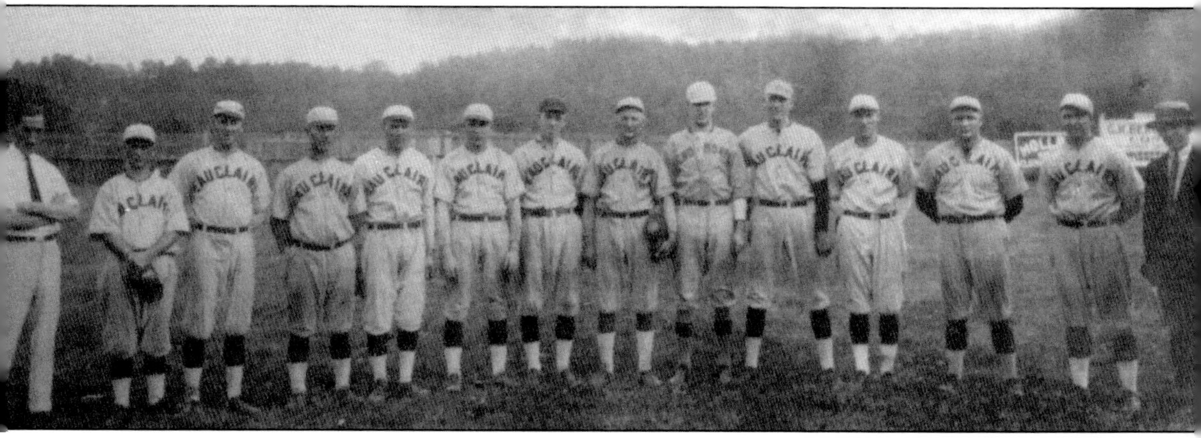

The 1922 Eau Claire semi-pro team drew extremely large crowds for the era. One game in late July had over 1,600 fans watch the home team play rival Chippewa Falls, and apparently there were even more in attendance three weeks later as every nook and cranny of the Driving Park was filled. The park was built in 1902 and the grandstand seated 500 fans. The park was torn down in 1926 to make room for residential lots. George "Dutch" Gerner is in the center with the catcher's mitt. (Photo courtesy of George Gerner, Jr.)

Two

The Golden Era

From 1933 to 1962 (with the exception of the War years of 1943-1945), the Eau Claire squads were consistently among the best in the Northern League. It truly was the "Golden Age" of baseball in Eau Claire.

Ex-Philadelphia A's ballplayer Bruno Haas was probably most responsible for the re-organization of the Northern League in 1933. He arranged for a place to play baseball in Winnipeg, Manitoba, and contacted others in the Upper Midwest to attempt to do the same. He even made arrangements with Hugo Goldsmith—the sporting goods magnate covered some of the start up costs and the league agreed to buy their uniforms and equipment from Goldsmith. Herman White was instrumental in bringing the Northern League to Eau Claire, and would later become president of the league.

Johnny Mostil was the first manager and, as it turns out, would have the longest tenure of any Eau Claire manager in his era. Playing games at Chappel Field on the north side of the city, Mostil had a hard-hitting bunch that routinely led the league in hitting and home runs. In 1937, the team moved to the brand new Carson Park, a beautiful facility built under the auspices of the WPA program. There they stayed for the remainder or their existence.

Dozens of future major leaguers got their start in Eau Claire, but probably none better known than Henry Aaron, who at age 18 made his organized baseball debut with the Bears in 1952. The future Hall of Famer and MLB home run king batted a robust .336 with nine home runs and 61 RBI in 87 games. Ask any resident of the area at the time and they will tell you they saw Aaron play that year. And every one will also say they didn't think the skinny little guy would ever be a home run hitter. The magical 1952 season didn't quite end in the storybook fashion that Hollywood would like, however. This Bear team had a phenomenal pitching staff, the second-best fielding percentage in the league, and, oh yeah, Northern League Rookie of the Year—HENRY AARON—but finished in third place and exited the playoffs in the first round.

Finishing a close second in overall popularity of Eau Claire players would probably be one Bob Uecker, the legendary voice of the Milwaukee Brewers. Despite his self-depreciating humor, Uecker was a quality player, especially in the minor leagues. Yet, during his time here, he was beginning to polish that comical side of his. Author Jerry Poling, in his book *A Summer Up North*, quotes Uecker's teammate, Doug Smith: "Uecker had everybody in the dugout on the floor laughing, and that's no kidding. He was constantly cutting himself up. It came so quickly to his mind, and he'd get the other team going, too. We all had him pegged for TV."

Popularity in Minor League Baseball in general began to wane as the 1960s rolled around. Eau Claire was one of the first victims, as dwindling attendance forced the team to disband after the 1962 season. Professional baseball has not been back since.

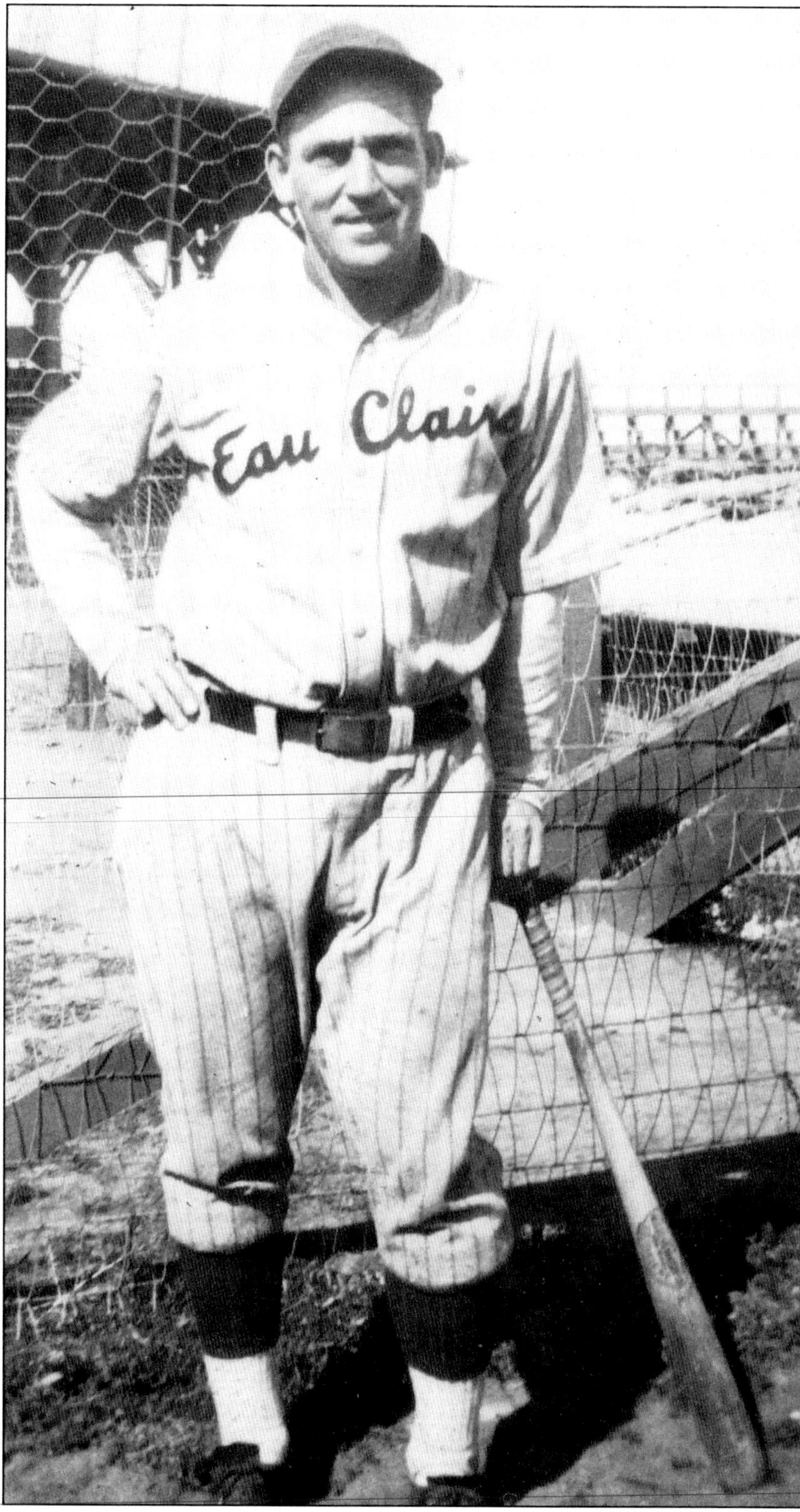

Former Chicago White Sox center fielder (and the only center fielder to catch a foul ball in a game) Johnny Mostil was chosen to be the first manager for the Eau Claire squad in the inaugural Northern League season of 1933. He would hand over the reigns to Ed Gharrity in 1938, and Mostil's five seasons as manager turned out to be the longest tenure of any Eau Claire manager during the their time in the Northern League. (Author's collection.)

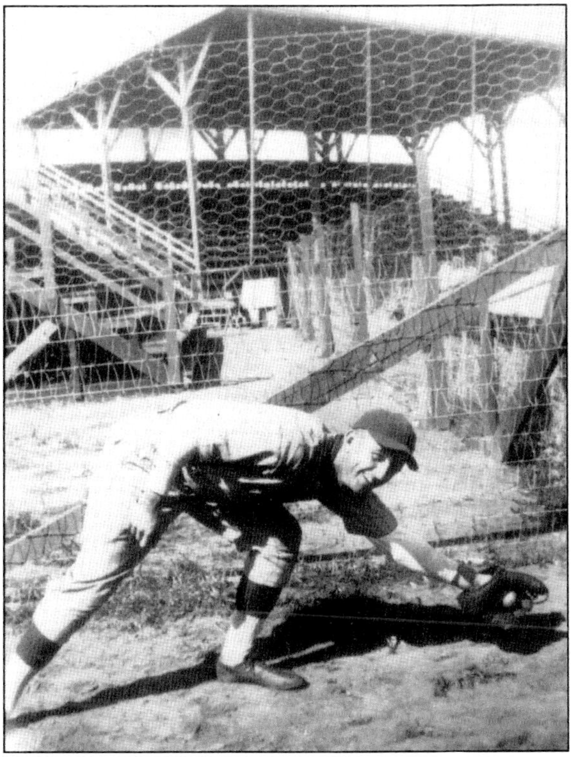

One of the original players for Eau Claire's entry into the "new" Northern League in 1933, Stan Sperry belted .318 for the team then known as the Cardinals. The fun-loving second baseman from Evansville, Wisconsin came back to Eau Claire in 1934 and hit at a .322 clip. He debuted in the majors with the Philadelphia Phillies on July 28, 1936, and later played for Connie Mack's Athletics before retiring with Louisville of the American Association in 1943. (Author's collection.)

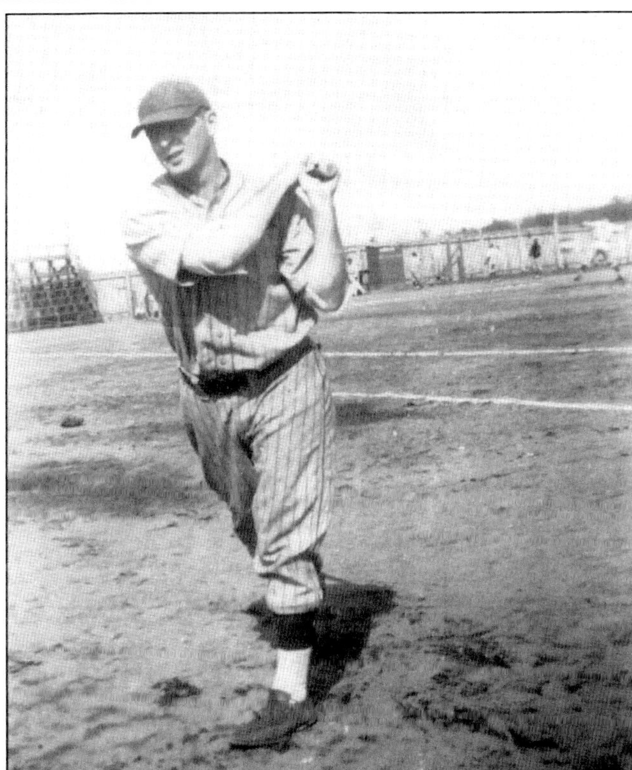

Frank Rendler played professionally for three years, 1933-1935, all under manager Johnny Mostil in Eau Claire. Rendler was the first real power threat Eau Claire would know. His 33 career home runs rank him second only to Marv Janes (42) on the all-time Eau Claire professional home run list. The center fielder was a Northern League All-Star in 1933 and 1934. (Author's collection.)

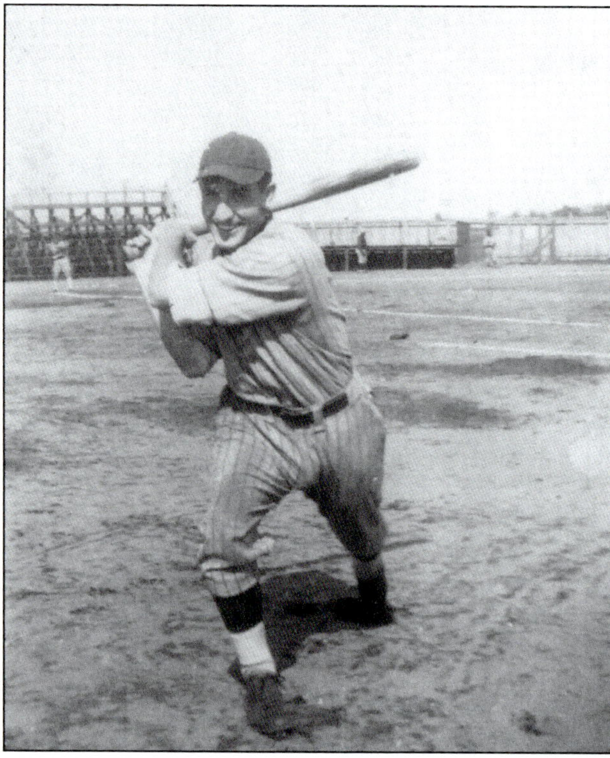

Nicknamed "Rip," as it was seemingly illegal at the time to do otherwise with baseball players with his last name, Danny Collins was another early power hitter. A first baseman, Collins slugged 29 home runs with Eau Claire from 1933 to 1935. (Author's collection.)

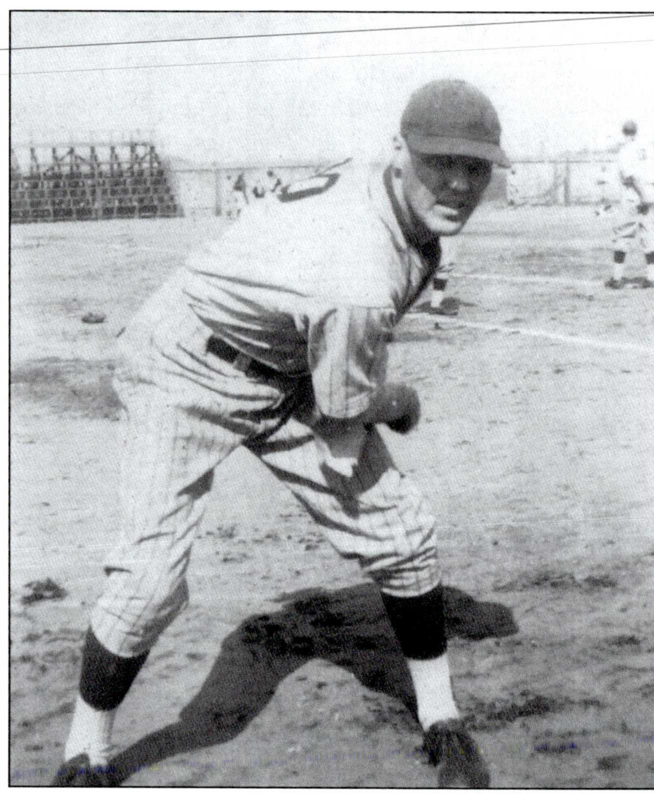

Ensio Juentenen played just two years professionally, but that was enough to land him on one All-Star team (1934). He was 11-13 in the inaugural Northern League season of 1933 and improved to 12-10 the following year. (Author's collection.)

Mike Abraham, shown here posing for the camera at Chappell Field in 1934, was another player that played only a short time professionally. Abraham handled right field duties for Johnny Mostil in 1933 and 1934. He banged out 11 homers in 1934, good enough to tie Frank Rendler for second place on the team behind Danny Collins' 12. (Author's collection.)

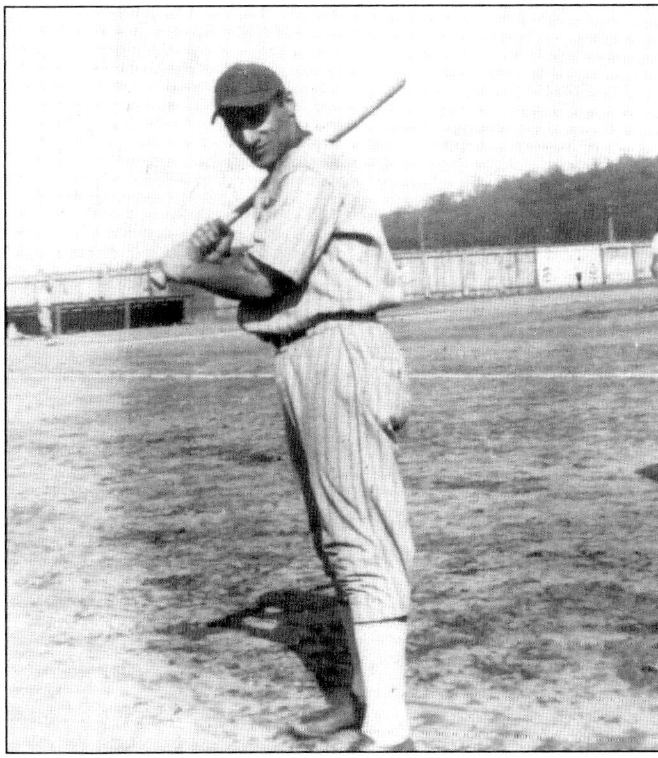

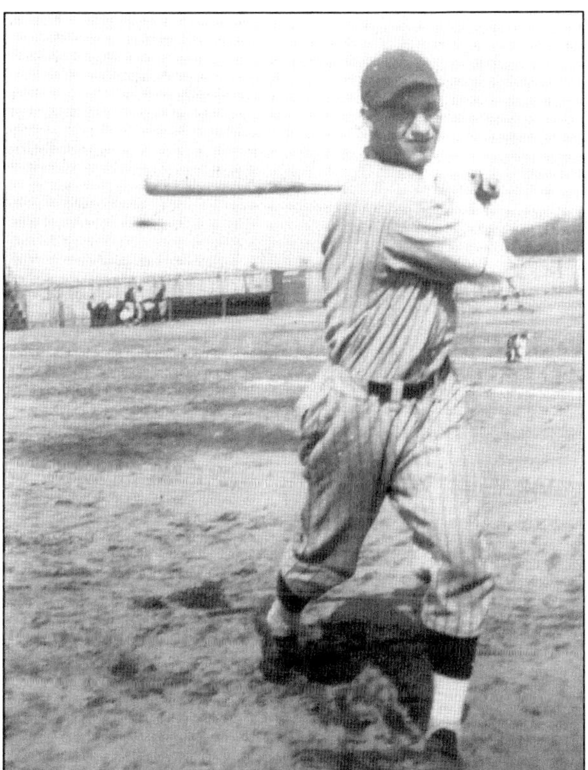

Carl Bielke's only known professional season was 1934, when he would spell Frank Rendler in center on days he wasn't pitching. Bielke went 10-11 for the Bears on the mound and contributed a nifty .373 batting average. (Author's collection.)

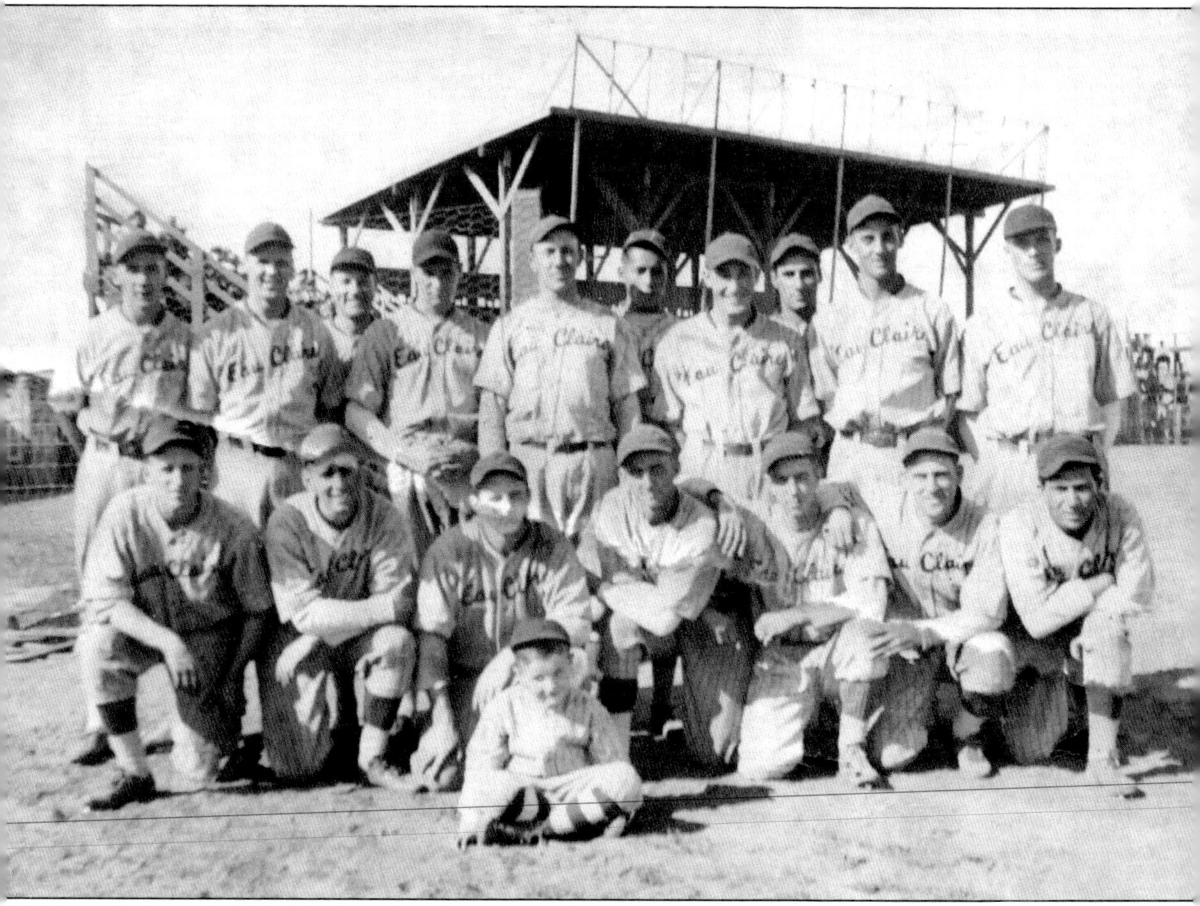

The 1934 Eau Claire Bears finished the second Northern League season with a 63-58 record under Johnny Mostil. The photo was taken at Chappel Field. (Photo courtesy of the Chippewa Valley Museum, Eau Claire, WI.)

Al Epperly (shown), along with Ted Frank and Derwin Steimling, formed a three-headed pitching monster for Johnny Mostil's 1936 Bears team. The three combined for 46 of the team's 67 wins as Eau Claire finished second in the regular season to Jamestown and their triple-crown winner Cal Lahman. (Photo Courtesy of Al Epperly.)

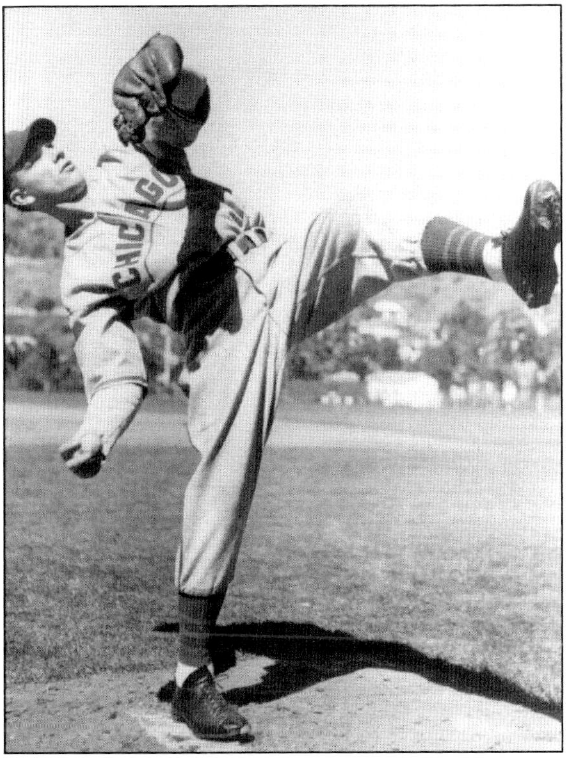

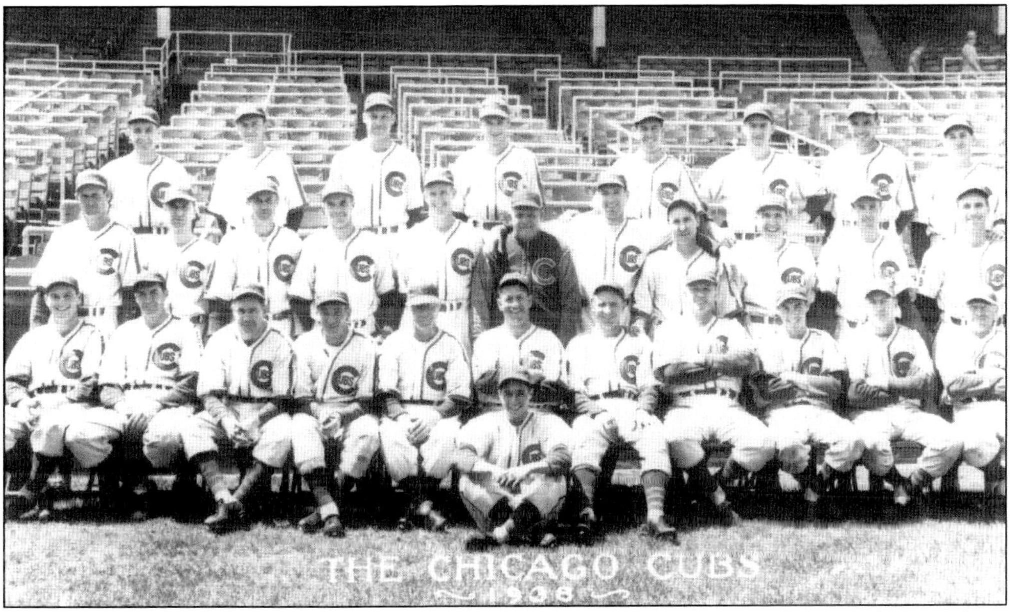

Al Epperly (pictured back row, fourth from left) had a great professional debut with Eau Claire in 1936, logging a 13-8 record. He was called up to the Chicago Cubs and made his major league debut in April of 1938. After pitching nine games, he was sent back to the minors, where he bounced around until he was called into military service in 1944. He resumed his career in 1946 in Milwaukee and finally made it back to the majors (briefly) with Brooklyn in 1950. He finished his major league career with a perfect 2-0 record. (Photo Courtesy of Al Epperly.)

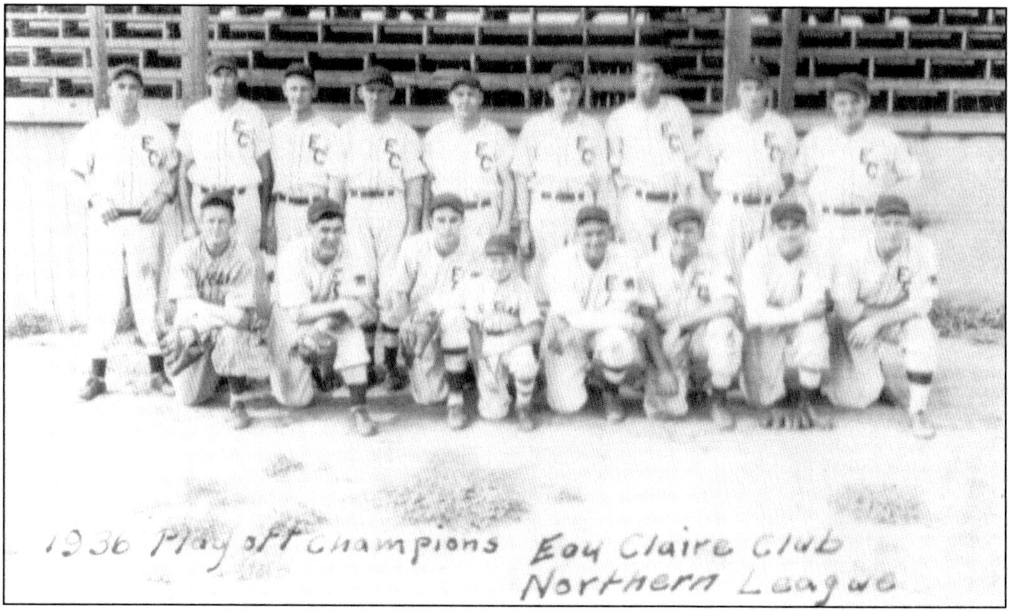

Arguably the best offensive team Eau Claire ever fielded, Johnny Mostil's 1936 squad finished the regular season in second place but won the Northern League playoffs over Winnipeg. Speaking of offense, in a game in early August, Hank Majeski went 7-for-7 with three singles, two doubles, a triple, and a homer! From left to right: (front row) Lowell Barnett, Hank Majeski, Frank Scalise, ? White (batboy), Johnny Mostil, Phil Masi, Henry Weiting, and Marv Janes; (back row) Ed Sielski, Jim Winn, Derwin Steimling, Ed Ficek, Henry Meyer, Ted Frank, Roy Hansen, Al Epperly, and Ralph Willard. (Photo Courtesy of Henry Meyer.)

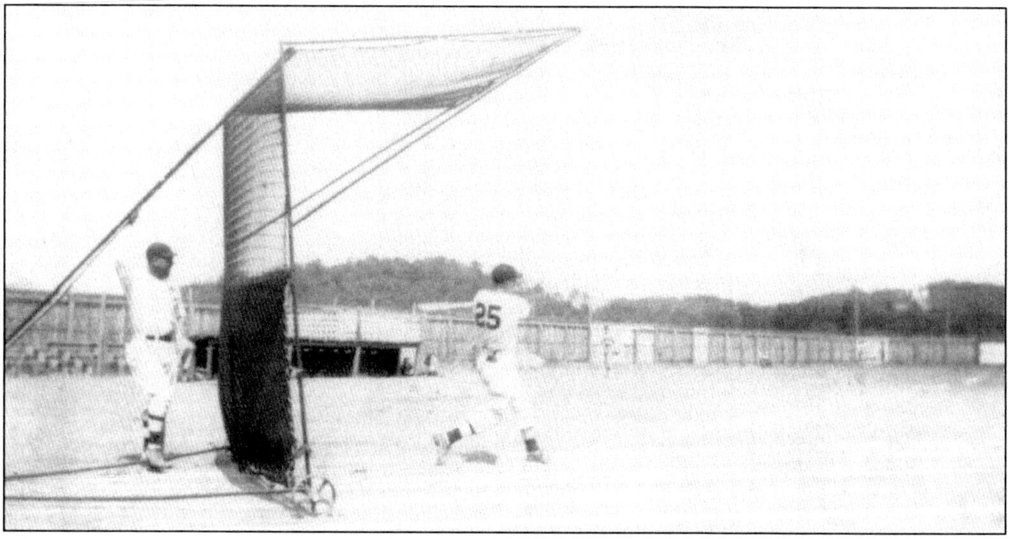

Henry Meyer set the Eau Claire single season record for RBI when he clubbed 129 to go along with 20 homers (6th highest all-time) and a .338 average in 1937. Here he is shown taking batting practice at Chappel Field. "I remember Chappel Field was like some of the high school fields," recalled Meyer. "The fences were around eight feet high, 325 feet from home plate. The field was fun to play on—if you hit it hard, it went out!" Maybe that's why three of the top six single season home run marks were set in 1936. (Photo Courtesy of Henry Meyer.)

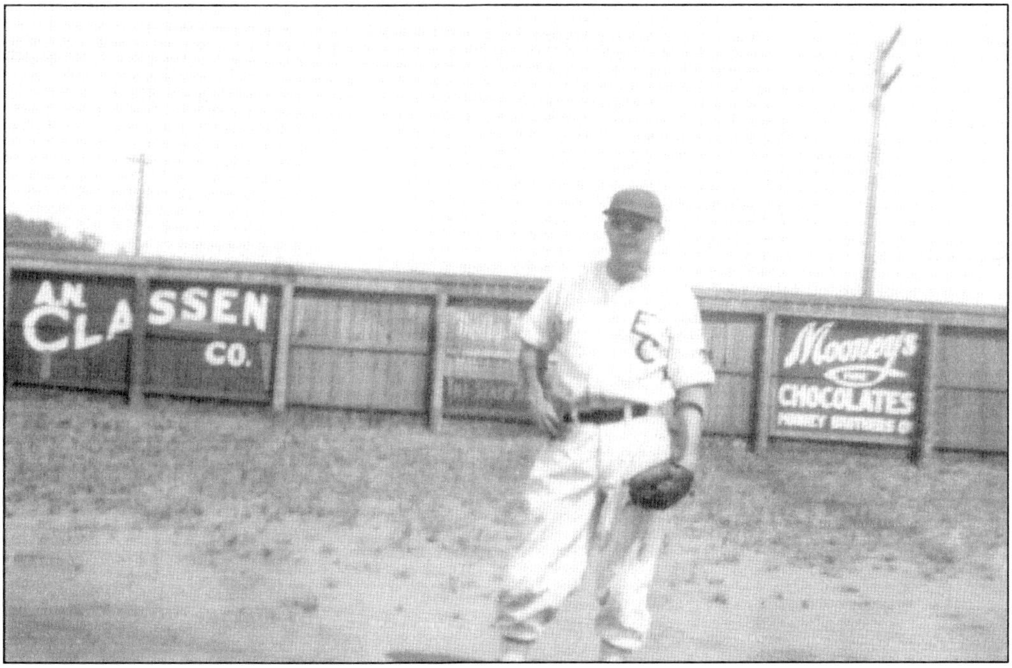

The slugging Henry "Moon" Meyer also played solid defensively, earning an outfield spot of the 1936 All-Star team. Notice the outfield "grass." An empty lot adjacent to the VFW Post is all that remains of Chappel Field. The Bears moved to Carson Park the following season. (Photo Courtesy of Henry Meyer.)

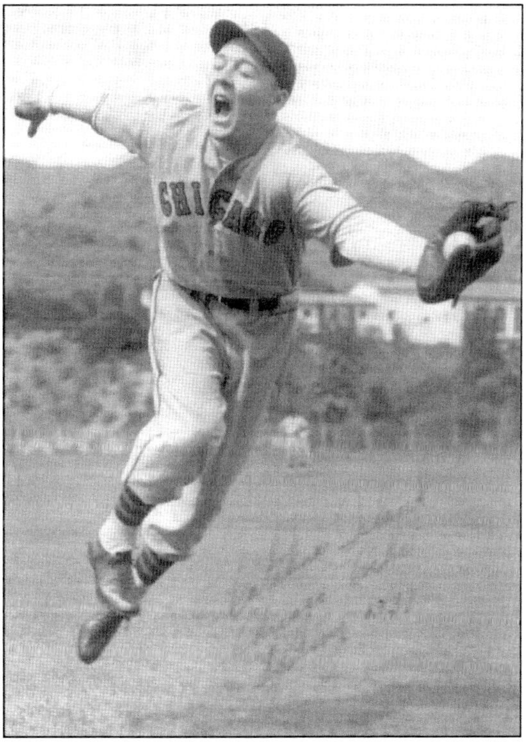

This shot of Henry Meyer features the former Eau Claire slugger making a lunging grab in spring training with the Chicago Cubs in 1937. His performance with the Bears earned him a trip to Catalina Island, California to work out with the parent club. He was assigned to Moline in the 3-I League, but would never make the majors despite solid minor league numbers. He was called to duty and did not play professionally again after 1941. (Photo Courtesy of Henry Meyer.)

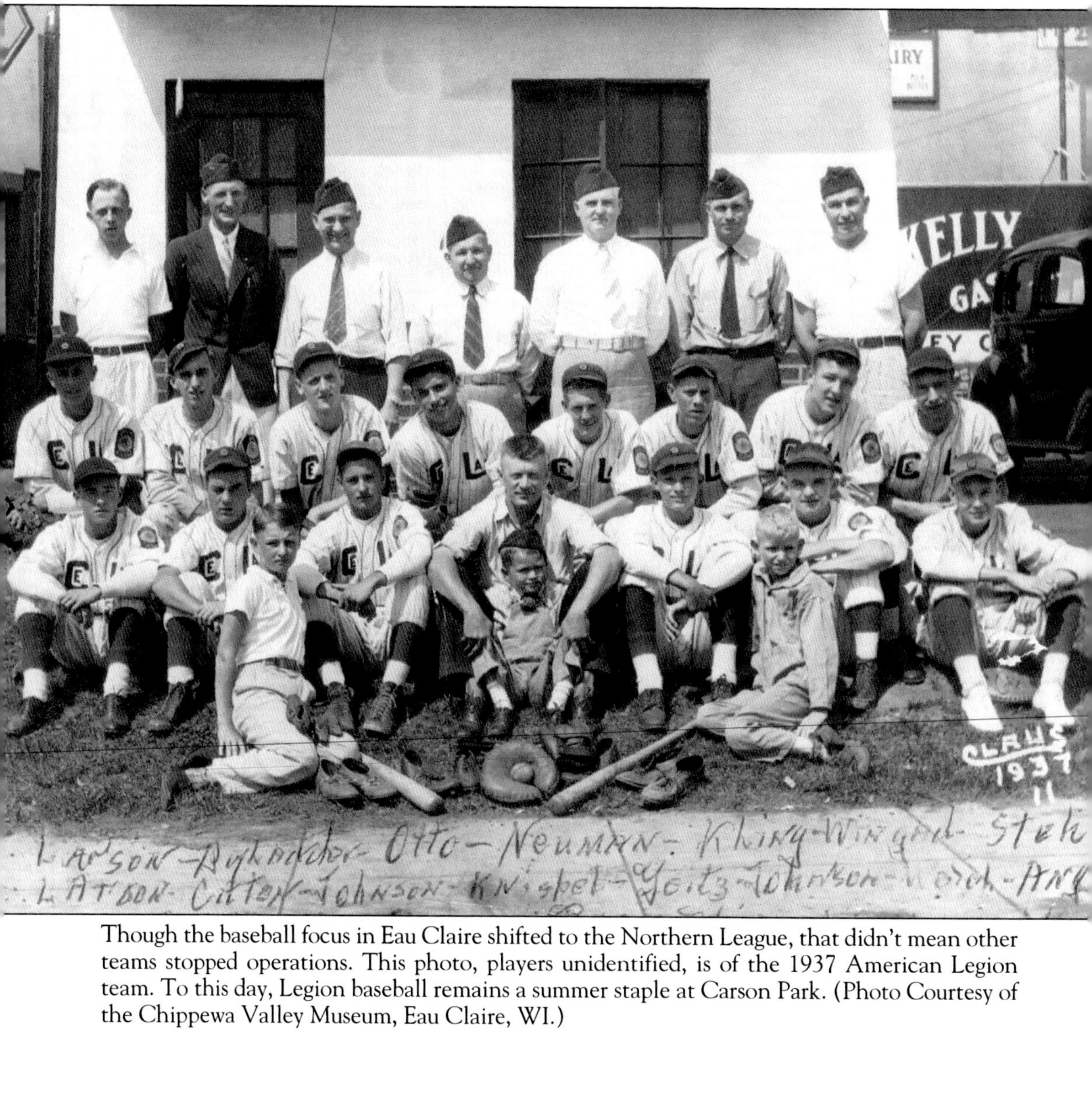

Though the baseball focus in Eau Claire shifted to the Northern League, that didn't mean other teams stopped operations. This photo, players unidentified, is of the 1937 American Legion team. To this day, Legion baseball remains a summer staple at Carson Park. (Photo Courtesy of the Chippewa Valley Museum, Eau Claire, WI.)

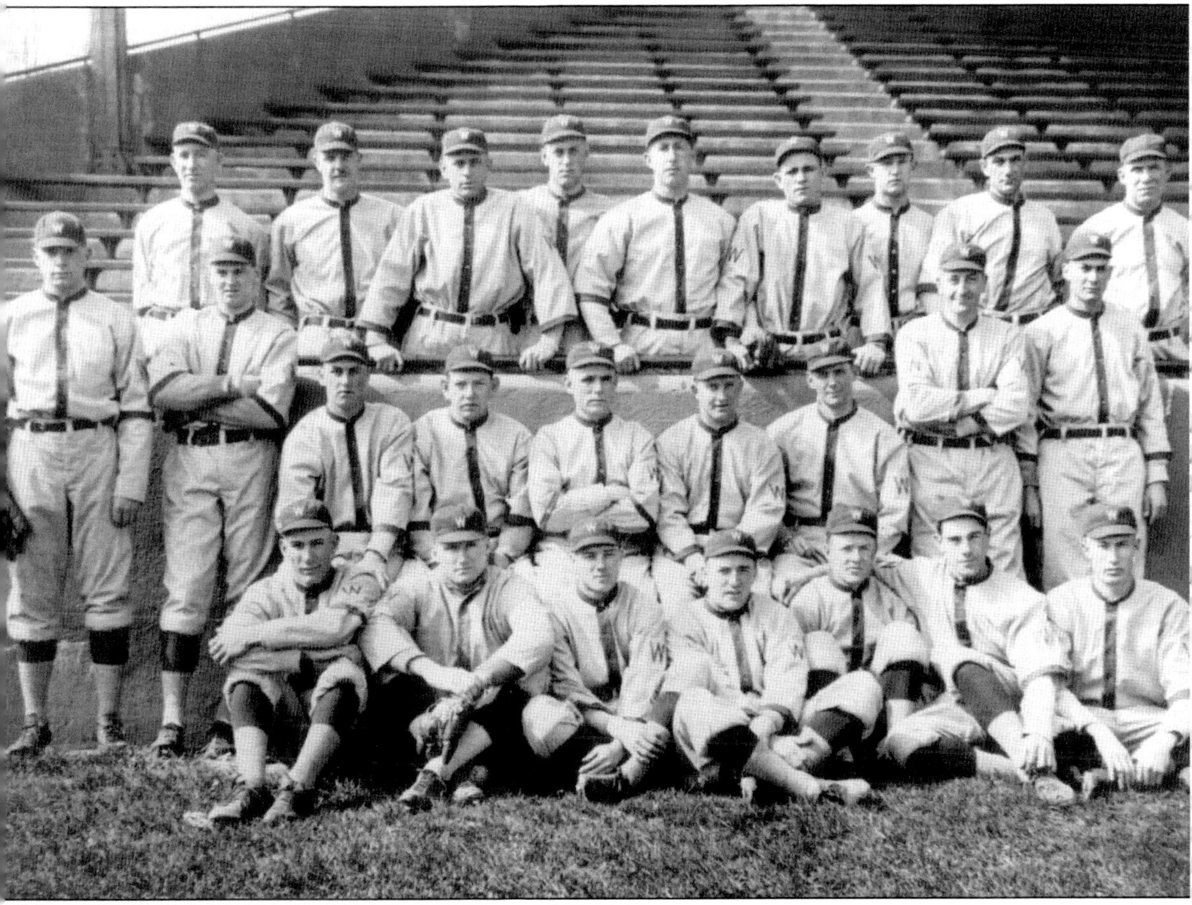

Ed "Patsy" Gharrity (shown back row, fourth from right), began his big league career in 1916 with the old Washington Senators. A fiery, hard-nosed major league catcher who challenged Ty Cobb and Babe Ruth in separate incidents, Gharrity was forced to leave the team in 1924 due to illness in the family. Because of this, Judge Kennesaw Mountain Landis banned him from baseball. He went to work for Fairbanks-Morse in Beloit, playing baseball and basketball for the company team and getting paid more than what he was earning with the Senators! At the urging of the great Walter Johnson, Landis reinstated Gharrity in 1928. After his playing career ended in 1930, he became a coach and in 1938 went to Eau Claire to become the second manager in the team's history. (Photo courtesy of William Gharrity.)

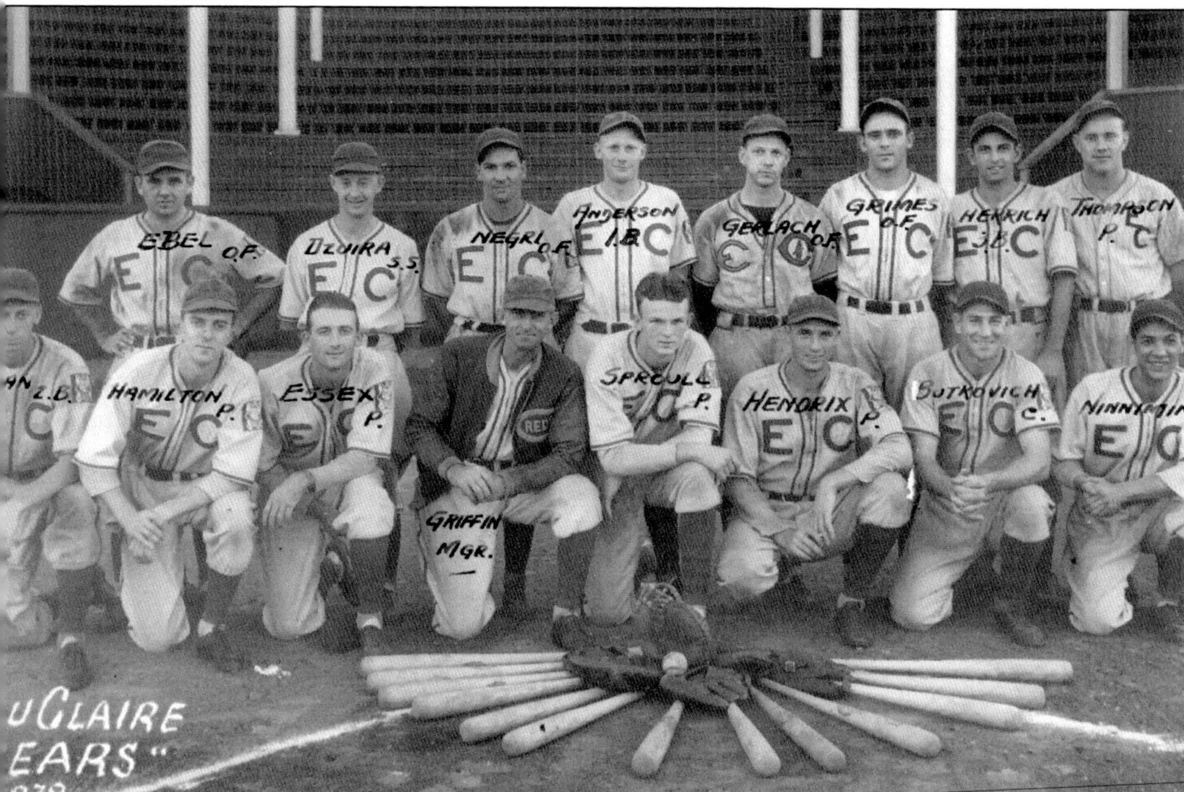

The 1939 Bears finished four games under .500, but it was good enough for fourth place in the Northern League. Forty-two-year-old Ivy Griffin, a first baseman for Connie Mack's Philadelphia A's from 1919 to 1921, led the team to a stunning upset of Duluth (four games to two) in the first round of the playoffs. Regular season champion Winnipeg then went on to beat the Bears in five games. Catcher Vince Castino (not shown) represented the team at the All-Star game. From left to right: (front row) John Nieman, Marv Hamilton, Bob Essex, Ivy Griffin, Charlie Sproull, Ralph Hendrix, Ed Butkovich, and Paul Ninnemann; (back row) Walt Ebel, John Dziura, Pete Negri, Don Anderson, Charles Gerlach, Glenn Grimes, Charles Herich, and Jerry Thompson. (Photo Courtesy of Don Anderson.)

Don Anderson (left) was in his first professional season when this photo with pitcher Bob Essex was taken in 1939. Already, though, he was establishing himself as a leader on the field and a fan favorite. Nicknamed "Whitey," Anderson played first base well and hit .298. He would be back with the Bears in 1940 and 1942. After World War II, he would become a player-manager, most notably with Carthage in the K.O.M. League. The lanky Essex was 10-13 with a 3.42 ERA in his first pro season, 1939. He also played for Eau Claire for most of 1940, going 5-11. After a brief stop in Madison, he met with great success in Green Bay, recording a combined 19-5 mark for the 1941 and 1942 seasons. (Photo Courtesy of Don Anderson.)

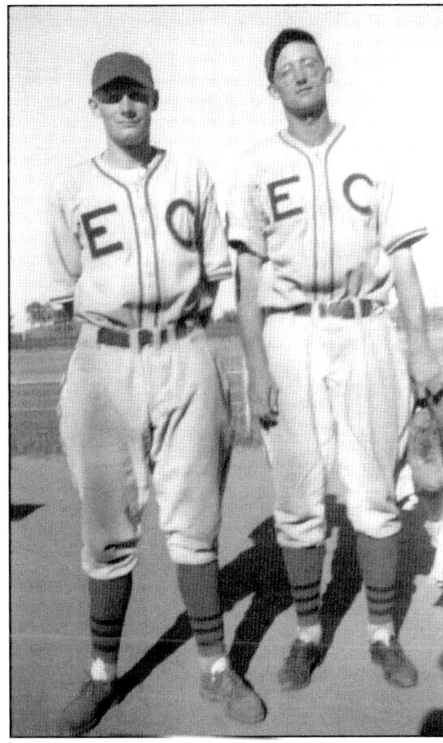

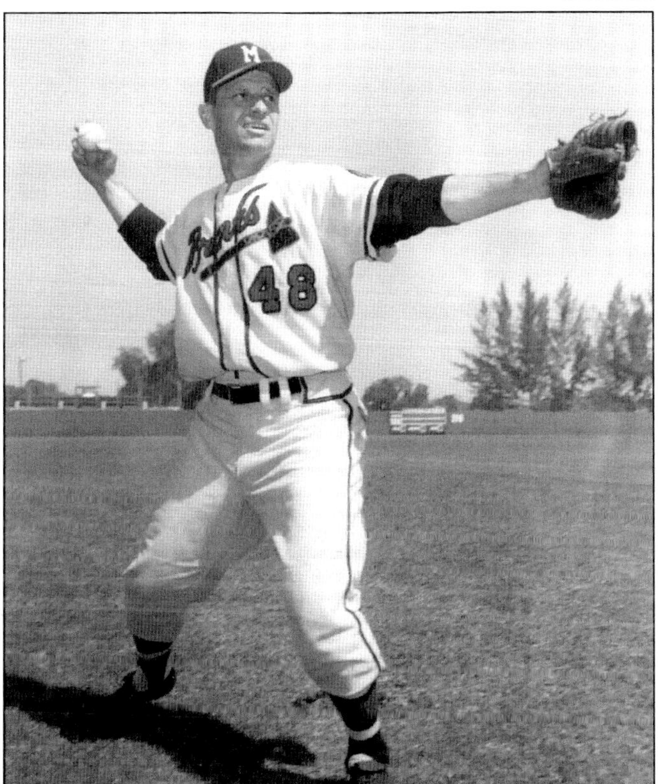

Local hero and Boyceville native Andy Pafko made his professional debut with Eau Claire late in the 1940 season. He struggled with a .209 average, but his talent was evident to more than just the local folks as he and John Lakars would be traded to Green Bay for the Wisconsin State League's reigning batting champion, Rudy Novak, before the 1941 season began. (Photo courtesy of the Chippewa Valley Museum, Eau Claire, WI.)

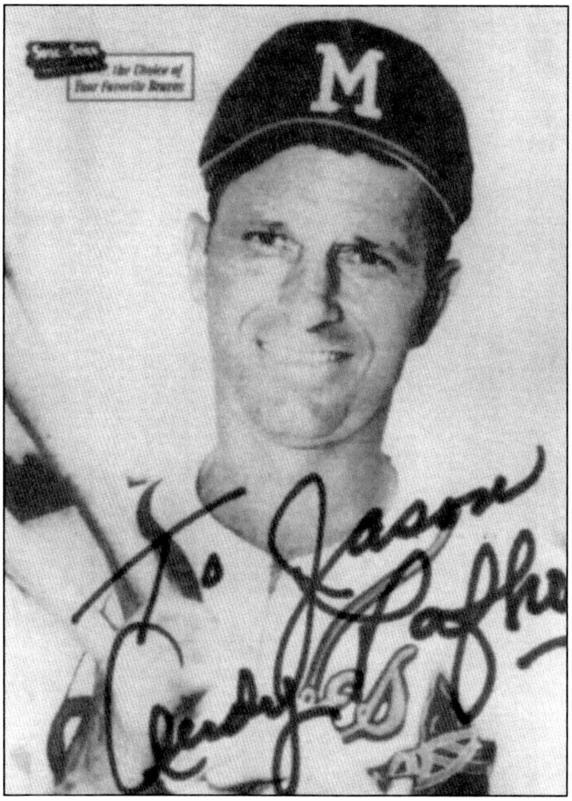

One of Andy Pafko's first road trips yielded a little embarrassment for the youngster. Teammate Don "Whitey" Anderson recalls, "On our first road trip to Duluth he went with a few of the players to a café for lunch. We all ordered pork chops, with 'gravy-a-plenty'. Andy came right off the farm, and had never eaten out. Andy was served first, so he picked up the chop with his hands, and the gravy ran all over the place before we had a chance to help him out! He really was a nice guy and had a lot of talent. And he soon learned the ropes." The effect of this event wasn't debilitating for life. "I don't remember it happening, but if Don says it did, it must be so," Pafko chuckled. (Author's collection.)

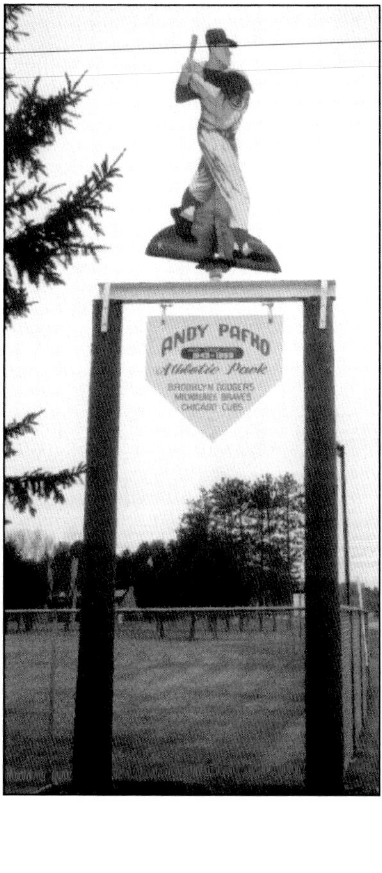

Boyceville, Wisconsin, hometown to future Eau Claire Bear and major leaguer Andy Pafko, re-named the field he grew up playing on. This photo was taken in 2003. (Author's collection.)

John Lakars, shown here in a faded photo, was involved in one of the wildest baseball games in franchise history, which took place in Duluth in 1940. His teammate, Ralph Nitz, recalled the game: "One evening, a fog came rolling in. We were leading five-three after three innings. Duluth began stalling, trying to get the umpires to call the game before four and a half innings had been played, which would have made a complete game for the records. Ivy Griffin got so mad he kicked at the bat bag, caught his foot in the strap, and knocked himself out. When play resumed, the Duluth center fielder called time and walked into the infield to 'consult' with the pitcher. On the way in, he stopped to tie his shoe. This was too much for the chief umpire. He called the game off and awarded the win on a forfeit to Eau Claire. The Duluth fans stormed our dugout, where the umpire had taken refuge. We players took off our steel-cleated shoes to use as weapons and formed a ring around the ump. We led him to our bus in the parking lot. It was kind of exciting!" (Photo courtesy of John Lakars.)

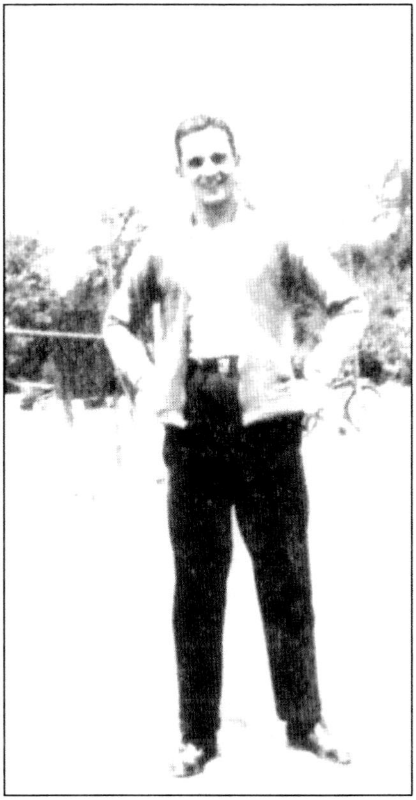

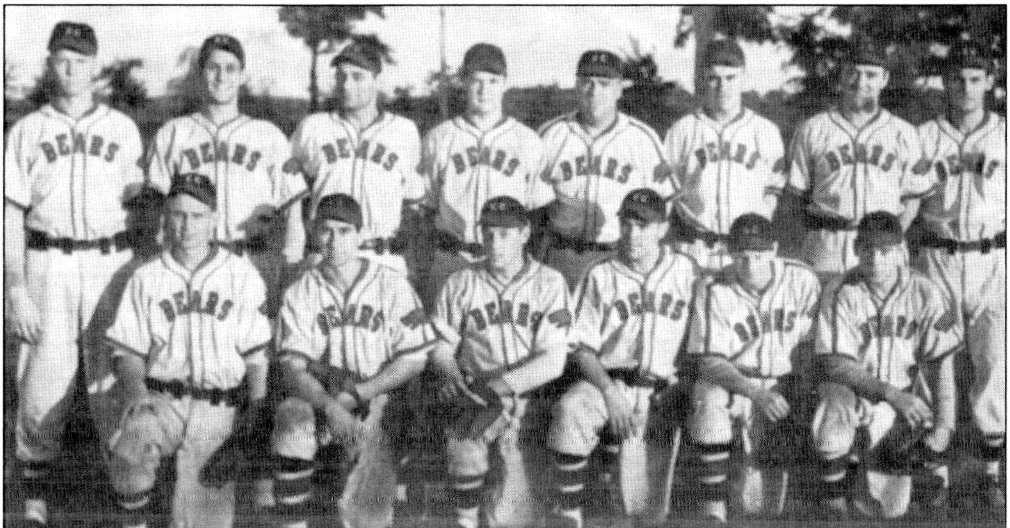

The 1941 Eau Claire Bears, shown here on a photo from a scorecard, finished the regular season in fourth place. Rosy Ryan's talented club clicked on all cylinders in the playoffs as they defeated Duluth, four games to three, in the finals. From left to right: (front row) Sheldon Bender, Dave Garcia, Don Wheeler, Ray Fontaine, Don Anderson, and Wes Westrum; (back row) Frank Nesseth, Joe LaFata, Cy Redifer, Fred Bell, Rosy Ryan, Bob Hoff, Otis Clark, and Loren Bain. (Photo Courtesy of Frank Nesseth.)

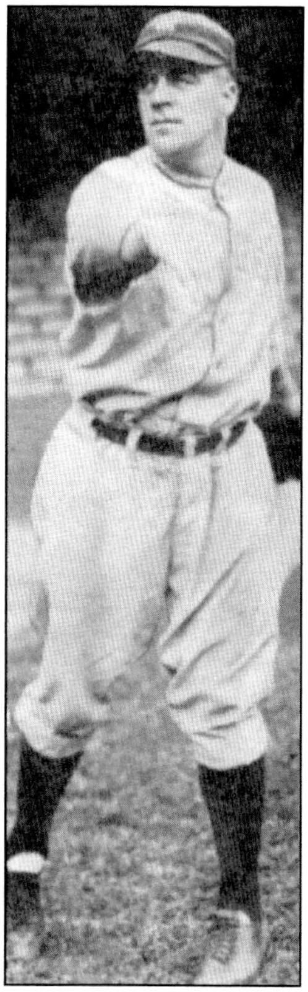

Rosy Ryan managed Eau Claire for two successful seasons—a playoff championship in 1941 and a Northern League pennant in 1942. The ten-year major league veteran was well liked by all of his players. Dave Garcia remarked, "I liked Rosy. He was very good to me and we had two pretty good ball clubs the two years I played for him there." Baseball was a family activity for the Ryans. Rosy's son was the bat boy and Rosy's wife helped out with the team, too. "Rosy Ryan's wife—if there's a heaven, she's there," proclaimed Garcia, which echoed the sentiments of teammate Warren Stemmer. (Photo courtesy of Frank Nesseth.)

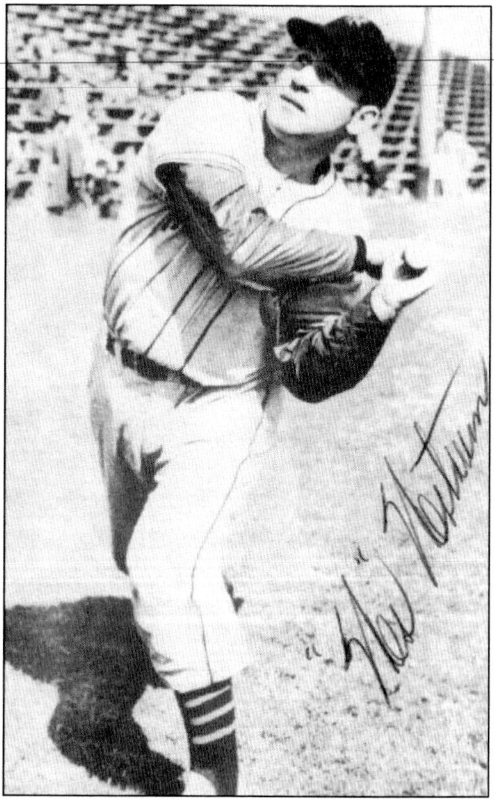

Wes Westrum was the star of Eau Claire's 1941 championship club. Named to the All-Star team that year, he hit a robust .330 with seven home runs and 70 RBI. Pitcher Otis "Otey" Clark said he had a knack for keeping pitchers focused. "When he thought you weren't pitching your very best, he would catch the next pitch in his bare hand and toss it back to you. That was a sure sign you might not be bearing down." (Author's collection.)

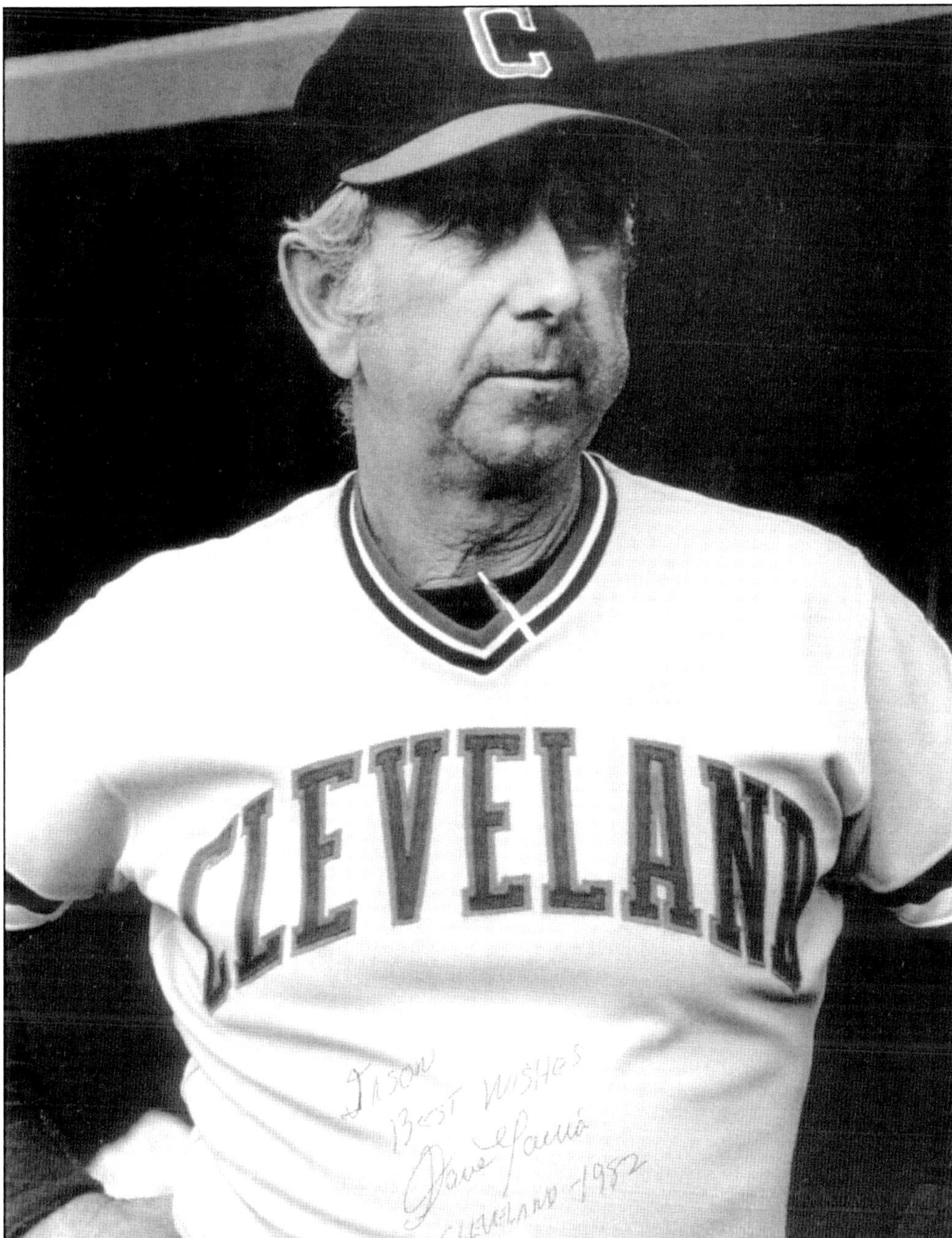

Dave Garcia began his career in professional baseball in 1939 with Lake Charles of the Evangeline League. And apart from three years of service in World War II, he pretty much hasn't stopped since. Garcia came to Eau Claire from Grand Forks in 1941 and stayed in 1942, when he hit .320 with 18 home runs and 107 RBI. He had "Major League Prospect" written all over him, but he was called to duty and wouldn't play professionally again until 1946. Garcia remained in the minors through 1957. He would later be active as a coach, manager, and in the front office for a variety of major league teams, resigning from the Colorado Rockies in 2002. "I was only 81 years old at the time," cracked Garcia. (Photo courtesy of Dave Garcia.)

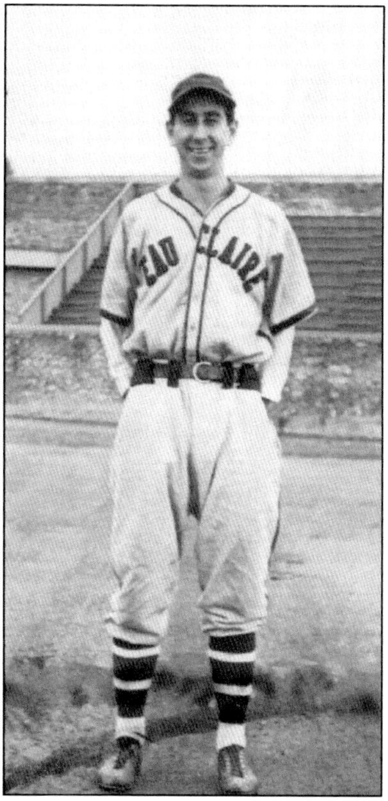

Dave Garcia was the spark in the 1941 playoffs for the Bears as well as the entire season of 1942. In 1942, the infielder hit a whopping .320 with 18 homers and 107 RBI. (Photo courtesy of Dave Garcia.)

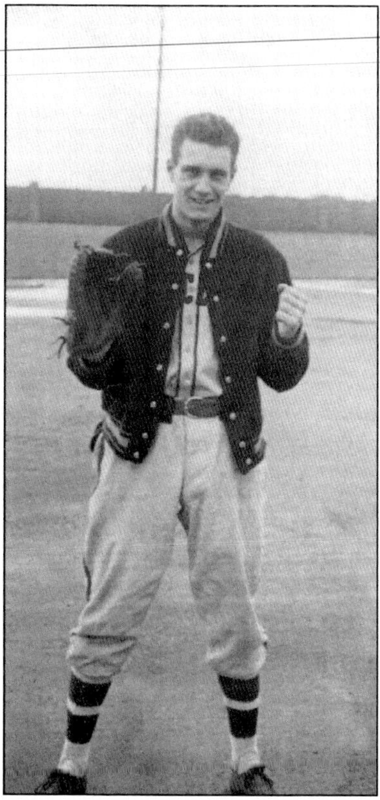

Joe LaFata was in his second professional season when this photo was taken in 1941. He handled first base primarily and hit .286 with three home runs and 45 RBI for the Bears that season. After serving in the military, he played for the Minneapolis Millers in 1945 and 1946 and made his major league debut in 1947 for the New York Giants. He finished his major league career with a .229 average in 127 games for the Giants. (Photo courtesy of Dave Garcia.)

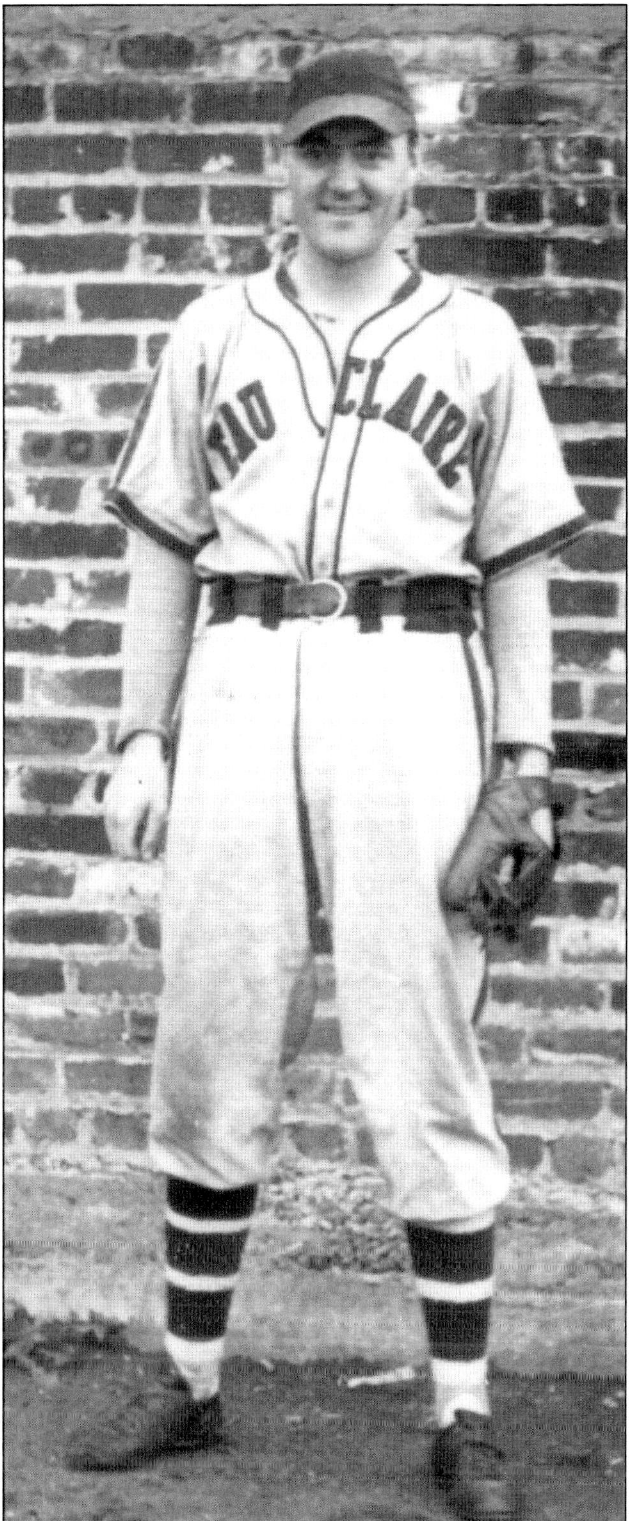

Otis "Otey" Clark pitched for Eau Claire in 1941, only a few hours drive from his hometown of Boscobel, Wisconsin. He and roommate Lauren Bain led the pitching staff that year, Clark going 14-6 and Bain 15-8. Both would eventually make the majors. Clark made an interesting observation about a difference between Eau Claire in 1941 and Boston in 1945, the year he played for the Red Sox. "We got a dollar thirty-five each day for meal money at Eau Claire, and in nineteen forty-five we got twelve fifty for meal money with the Red Sox," Clark said. "We ate just as good on a dollar thirty-five in Eau Claire as we did for that twelve fifty at Boston!" (Photo courtesy of Dave Garcia.)

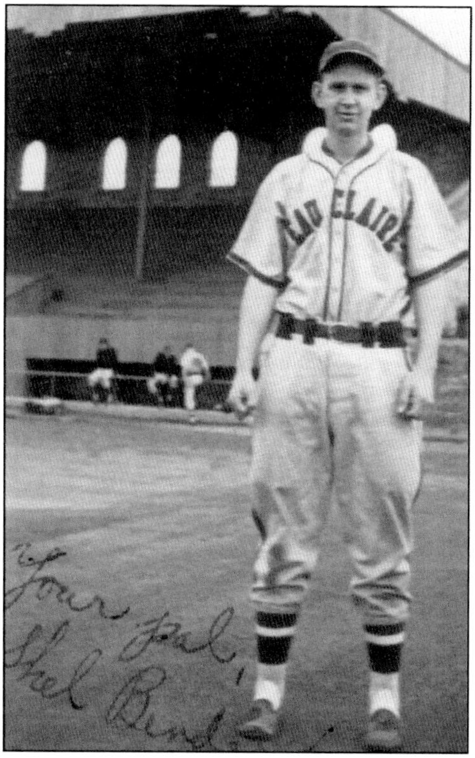

Sheldon Bender hit .269 for the 1941 Bears. After he served his military duty, "Chief" (another requisite nickname considering the last name) came back as a full-time pitcher, going 13-5 for Eau Claire rival St. Cloud in 1946. Essentially, his playing career came to an end in 1950, but Bender is still active in baseball today as an executive with the Cincinnati Reds. (Photo courtesy of Dave Garcia.)

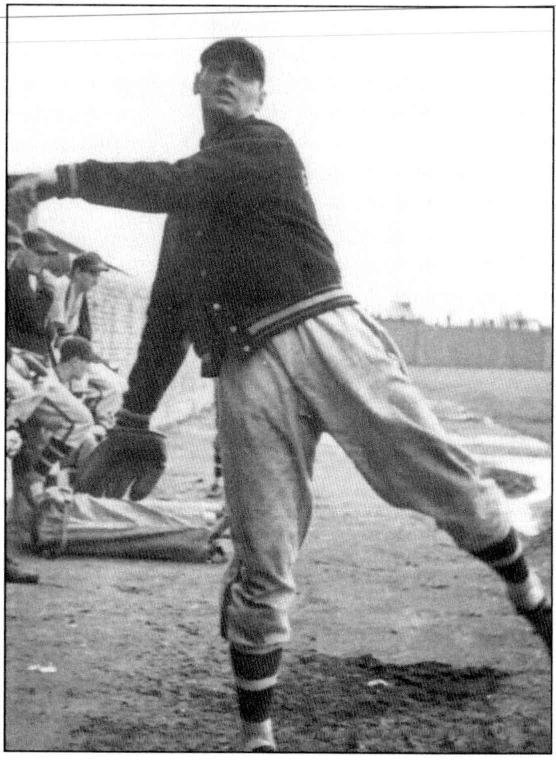

A slightly different story than most players who came through Eau Claire, Cy Redifer began his career in 1937 and played the final two seasons of his career with the Bears in 1940 and 1941. A first baseman by trade, he split time with, among others, future major leaguer Joe LaFata. Redifer held his own, though, hitting .283 in 1940 and .294 with a career high in homers (11, which also led the team) and RBI (68). (Photo Courtesy of Dave Garcia.)

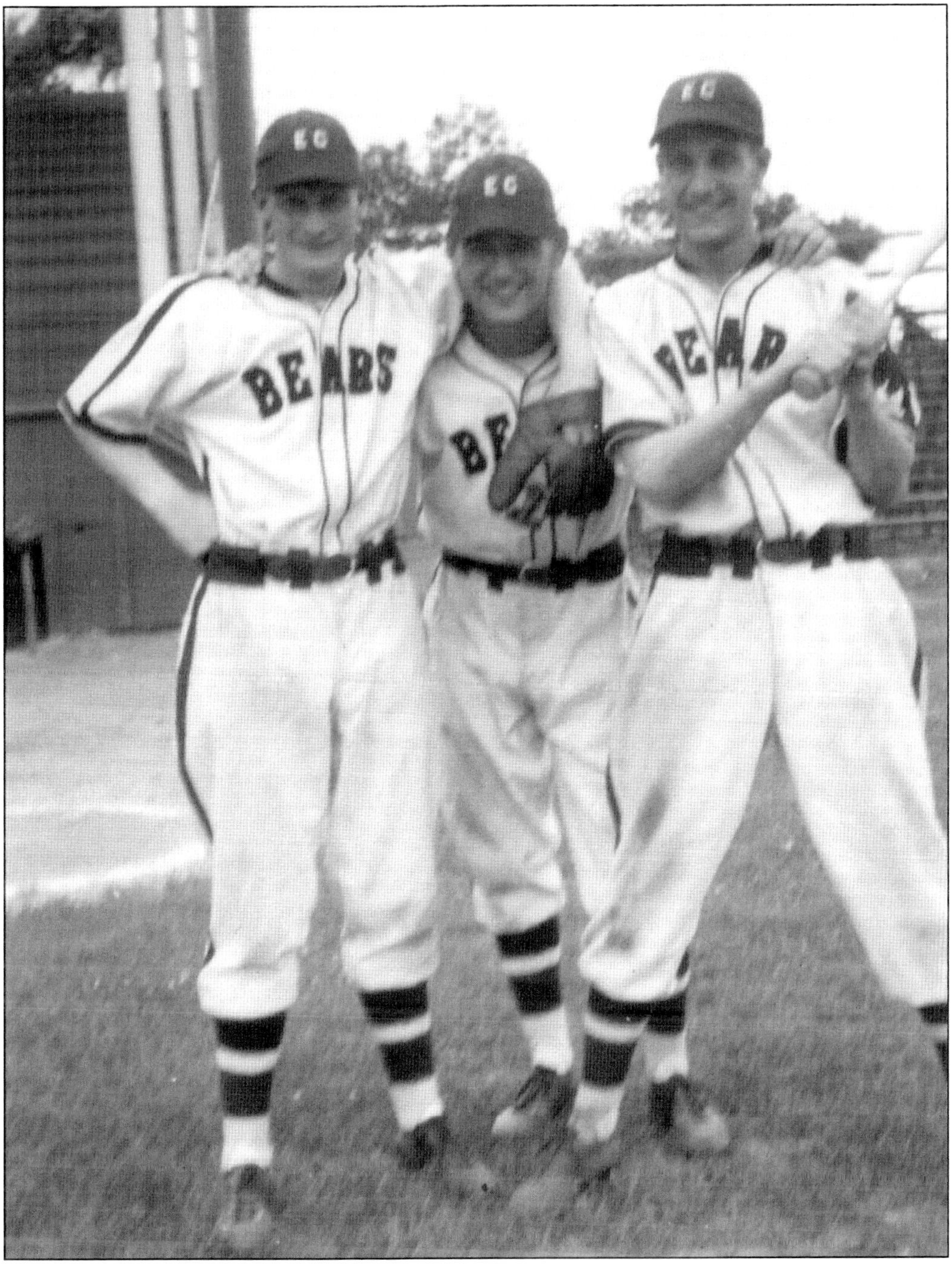

Pictured is a fearsome trio for the 1941 Eau Claire Bears. The versatile Don Anderson (left) began his career as a first baseman, then moved to third base for 1940 and finally to shortstop for 1941. Herman Florian (middle) would only play one professional season. Playing second base and right field, he hit a solid .297 with 55 RBI between Eau Claire and Winnipeg. On the right is Joe LaFata, who handled first base chores in 1941. He would hit .286 with three homers and 45 RBI for the Bears that season. Of the three, only LaFata eventually made it to the major leagues, playing in parts of 1947, 1948, and 1949 with the New York Giants. (Photo courtesy of Don Anderson.)

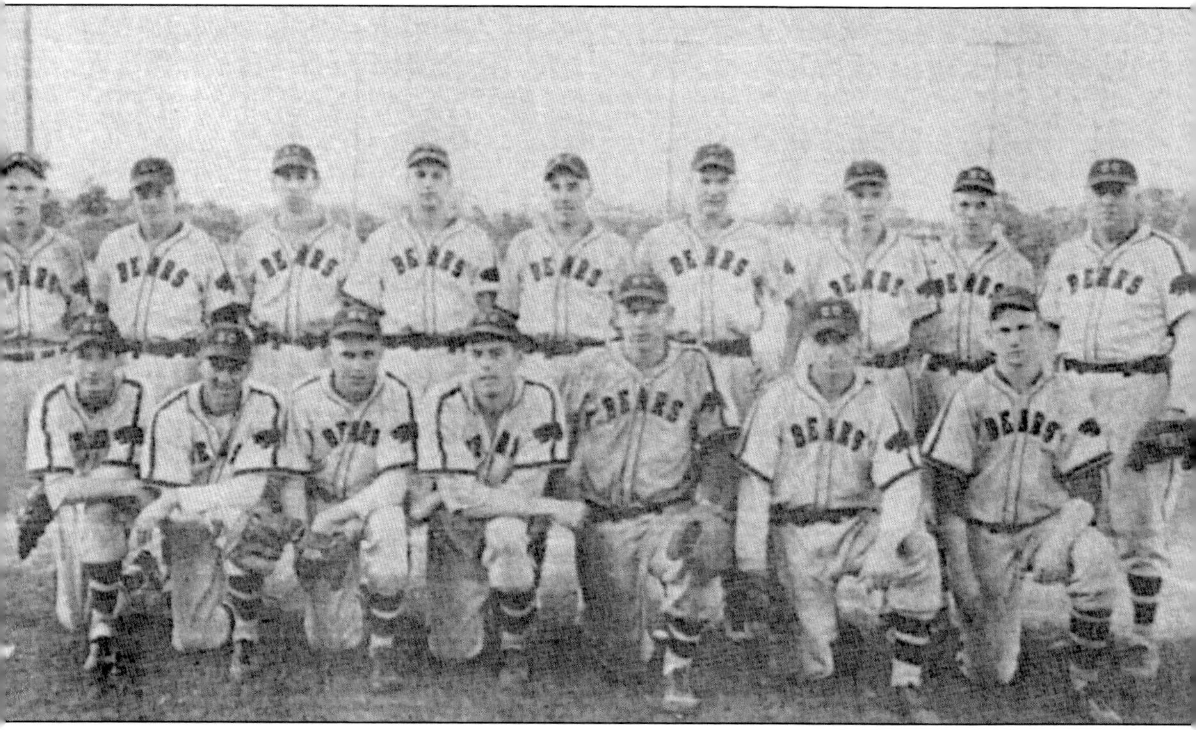

The 1942 Eau Claire Bears put together one of the finest Northern League seasons the city would ever witness. Rosy Ryan's club won the pennant with an 81-41 record, five games better than Winnipeg (managed by former Eau Claire skipper Ivy Griffin). Eau Claire's own Vic Johnson led the league in wins with 18. And could this team hit! Four regulars finished with a batting average higher than .310! Johnson would later play in the major leagues, along with teammates Don Wheeler, Red Hardy, and Clint Hartung (Dave Garcia made the majors as a coach and manager). The Bears fell to Wausau in the first round of the playoffs. (Photo Courtesy of the Chippewa Valley Museum, Eau Claire, WI.)

Don Wheeler began his career in Eau Claire in 1941, but flourished in 1942, hitting .350 with four home runs and 58 RBI for the Bears before getting called up to the Minneapolis Millers late in the season. He would make it all the way to the majors in 1949, hitting .240 for the Chicago White Sox in his only year in "The Show." (Photo Courtesy of Dave Garcia.)

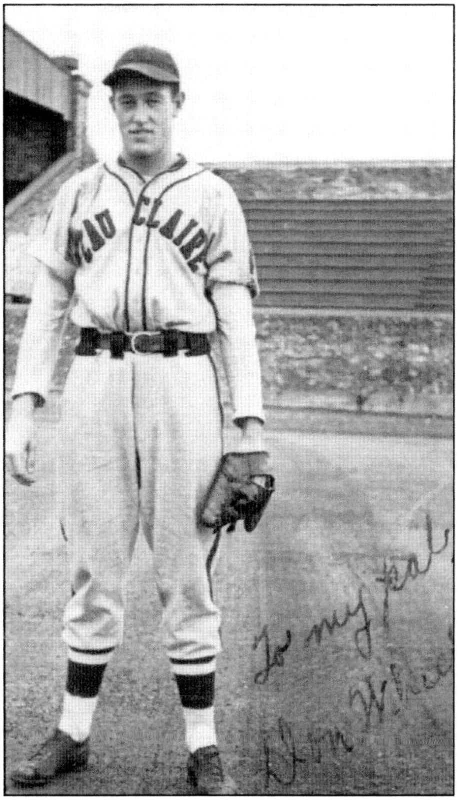

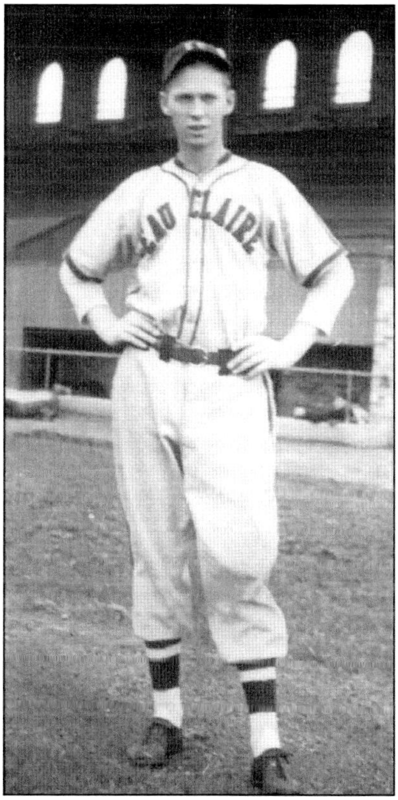

Although his record doesn't seem to indicate it to the naked eye, Frank Nesseth was a dominating pitcher for the Bears in parts of the 1941 and 1942 seasons. Teammate Dave Garcia remarked, "He was the best pitcher in the league in 1942." He went 7-5 that year for the pennant winners, with a nifty 2.72 ERA. He had shuttled between Minneapolis (American Association) and Eau Claire those two years. Nesseth was then called to military duty and would never realize his dream of playing in the majors, to the surprise of his contemporaries. (Photo Courtesy of Dave Garcia.)

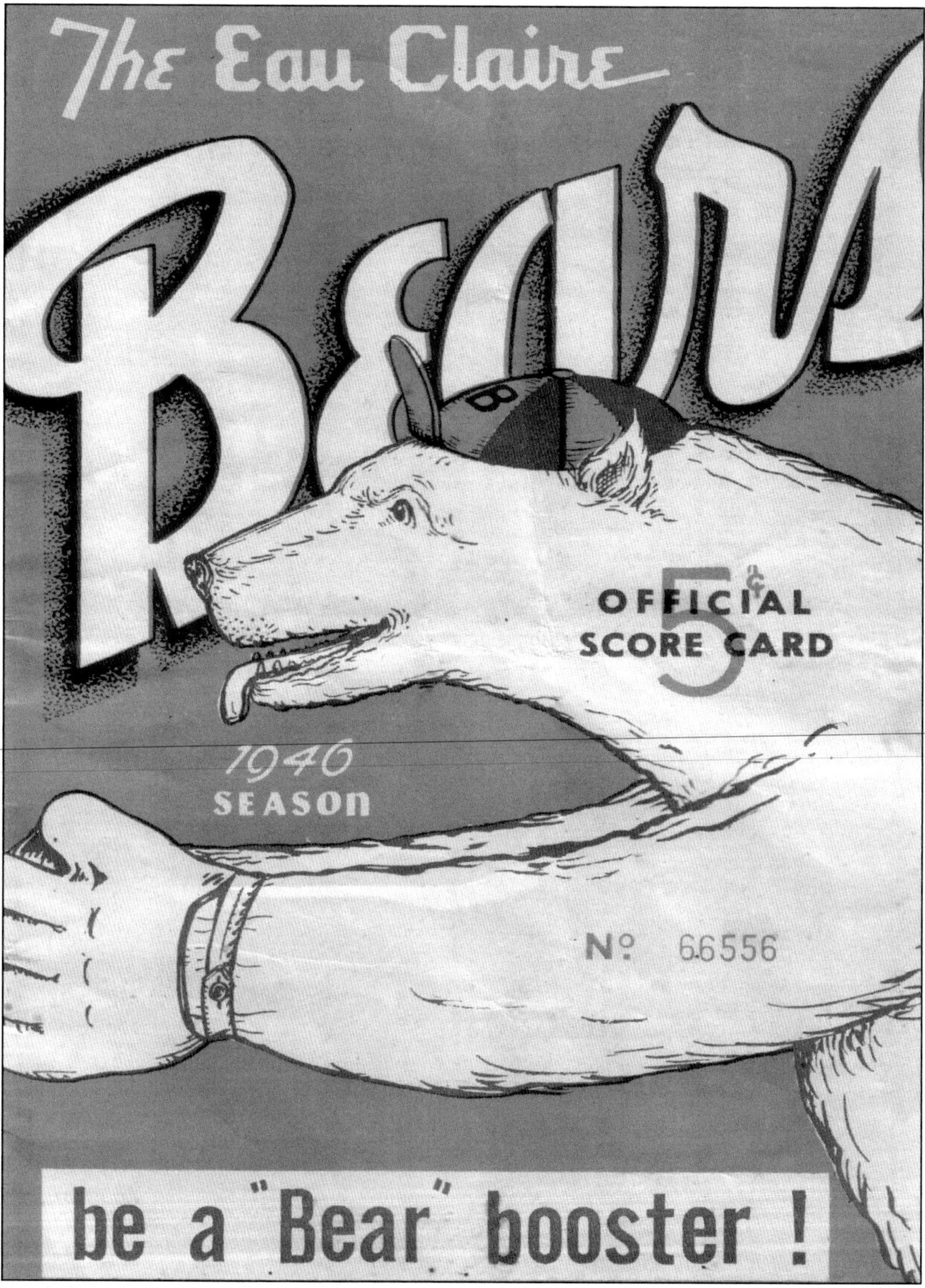

Baseball returned to the Northern League and enthusiastic Eau Claire fans in 1946 after a three-year layoff due to the War. Under manager Joe Skurski's guidance, the Bears took fourth place in the regular season, good enough to earn a playoff birth against second place Fargo-Moorehead. F-M's Bob Haas shut down the Bears on five hits as the Twins defeated Eau Claire, 6-0, in a deciding game seven. (Author's collection—1946 Eau Claire Bears program.)

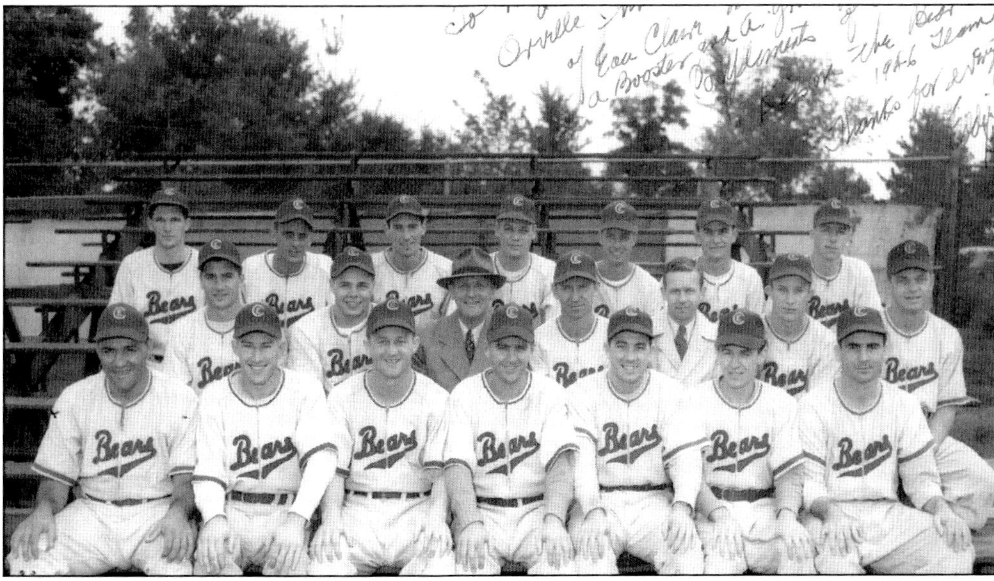

General Manager Eddie Stumpf sent this photo of the 1946 team to Eau Claire Mayor Orville Christianson. Eau Claire was ecstatic for baseball as World War II ended. Joe Skurski was the player-manager of the first professional squad in the City since 1942. Eau Claire managed a fourth place finish and a first round exit from the playoffs. From left to right: (front row) Steve Magula, Don Siegart, Jim Schymanski, Tom Swittel, Mike Oddo, Bob Harden, and Ed Jacobs; (middle row) Stan Szurma, Harold Van Hoff, Eddie Stumpf, Joe Skurski, G. Otis Linderman (club president), and Bob Eisenach; (back row) Del Burke, Andy Green, Bill "Gene" Edwards, Jim Daublender, Don Godfredson, Arnold Zolinski, and Walt Linden. (Photo courtesy of the Chippewa Valley Museum, Eau Claire, WI.)

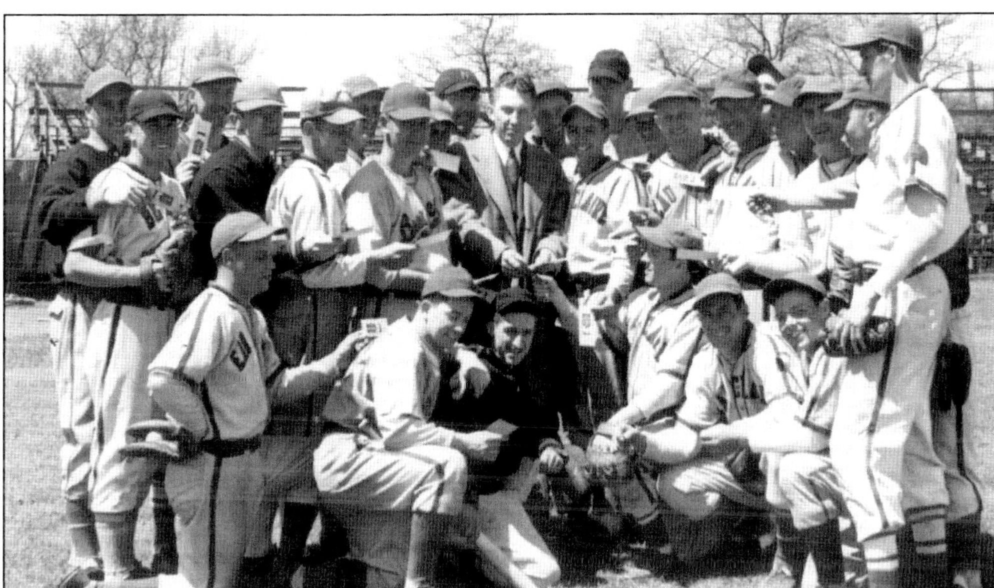

The Eau Claire squad poses with Mayor Orville Christianson (center, in suit and tie), *c.* 1946. (Photo courtesy of the Chippewa Valley Museum, Eau Claire, WI.)

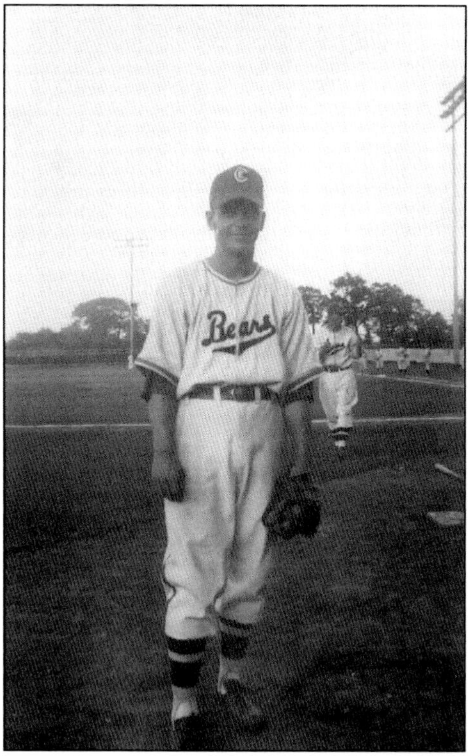

Stan Kmet made the most of his two professional seasons. The right-hander was the staff ace for the 1946 Bears, going 12-9 with a 2.76 ERA. For his career, he finished with a 24-18 record, playing for a total of four teams. (Photo courtesy of Stan Kmet.)

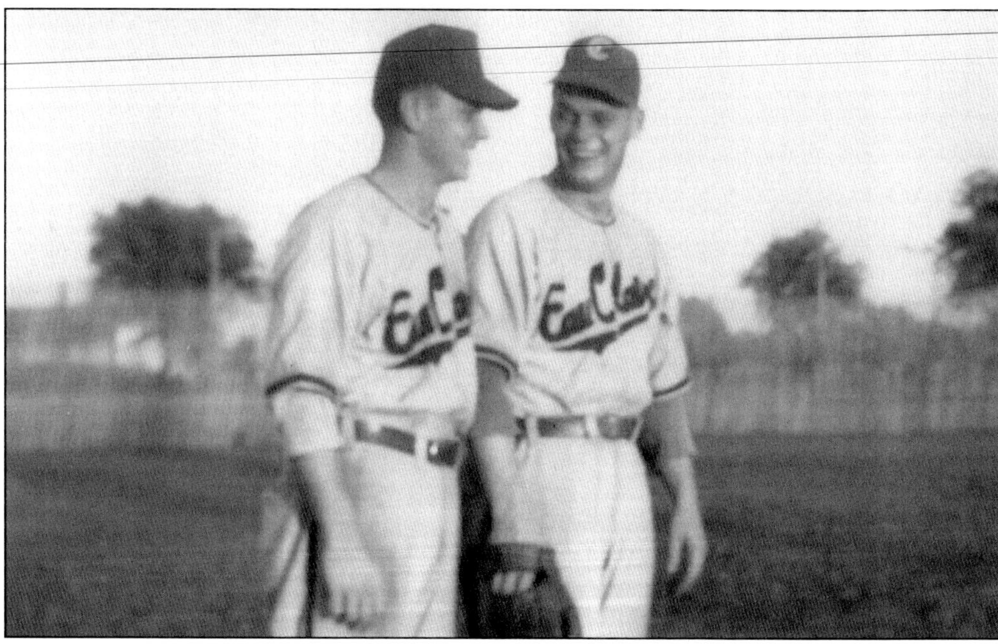

Stan Kmet (left) and Jim Daublender share a laugh. Kmet and Doublender were two of the many Wisconsonites on the 1946 Eau Claire squad. Kmet hailed from Milwaukee and Daublender from nearby Mosinee. Daublender hurled for Green Bay in 1942, going 8-5 before leaving for the War. Nineteen-forty-six was his last professional season; he recorded a 1-3 mark. (Photo courtesy of Stan Kmet.)

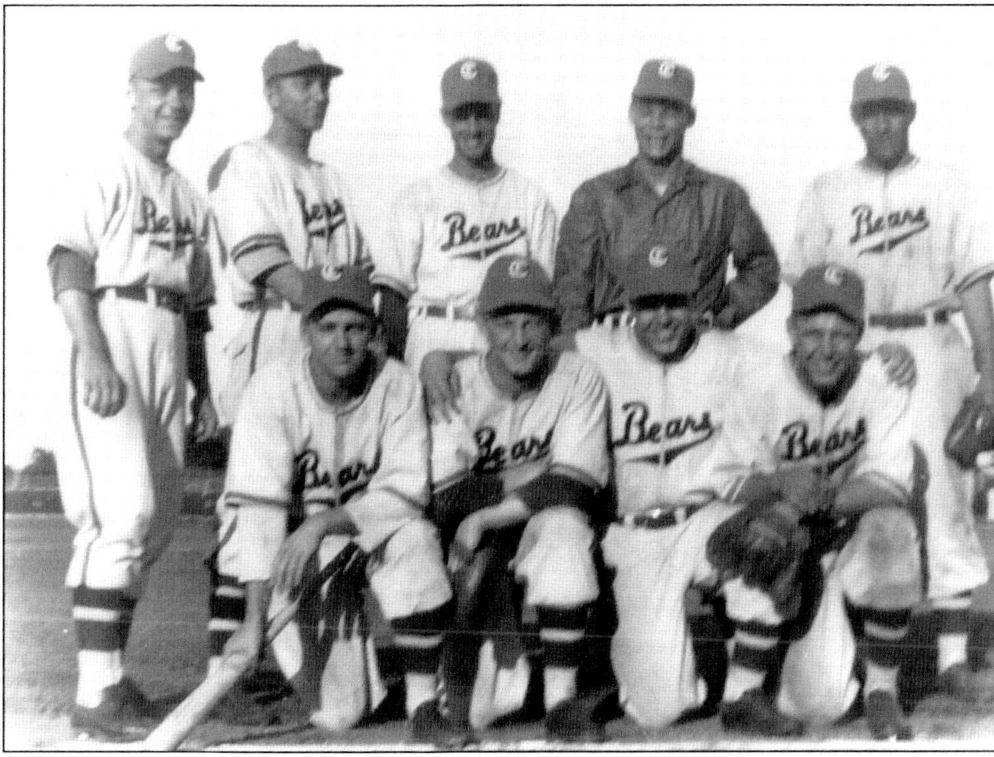

A little blurry, but nice shot of a portion of the 1946 team, from left to right: (front row) unidentified, Jim Schymanski, Harold Van Hoff, and Jim Delsing; (back row) Stan Kmet, Joe Skurski, Jim Daublender, Steve Magula, and Tom Swittel. (Photo courtesy of Stan Kmet.)

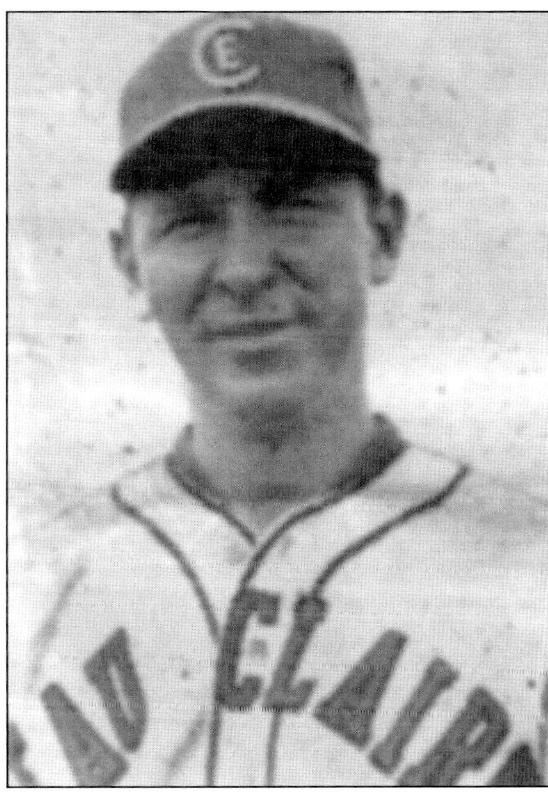

Joe Skurski was only 31 years old when he was convinced by Milwaukee Brewers farm director (and Eau Claire Bears general manager) Eddie Stumpf that he was better suited for managing than playing. As a compromise, Skurski was a player-manager with the Bears, hitting a respectable .286 with five homers and 22 RBI. He would move on to the Wisconsin State League in 1947 and crush the ball for Wausau for the next three years, driving in 251 runs in that span. (Author's collection—1946 Eau Claire Bears program.)

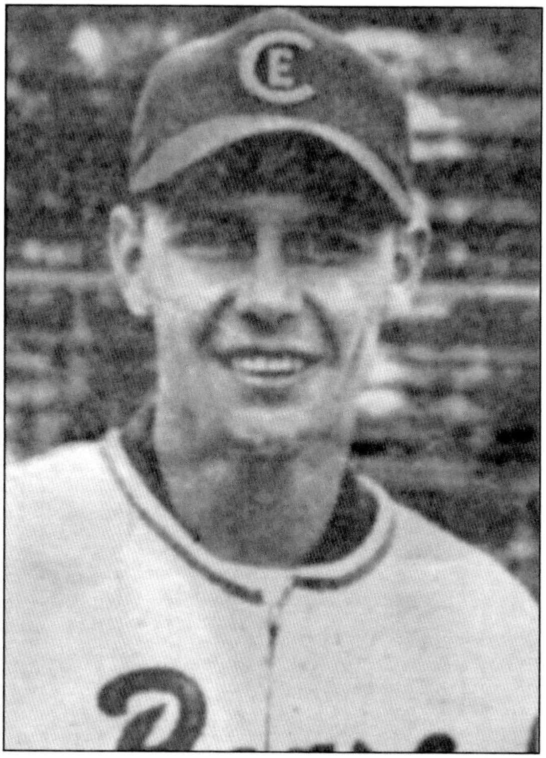

Jim Delsing broke into professional ball in 1942 with Green Bay at the tender age of 16. He missed the 1944 and 1945 seasons due to military service and resumed his baseball career with the 1946 Bears. The Rudolph, Wisconsin native played outfield that season for the first time and led the team with a blistering .377 average. Milwaukee called Delsing up at the end of July, and by season's end the Chicago White Sox had purchased his contract. (Author's collection—1946 Eau Claire Bears Program.)

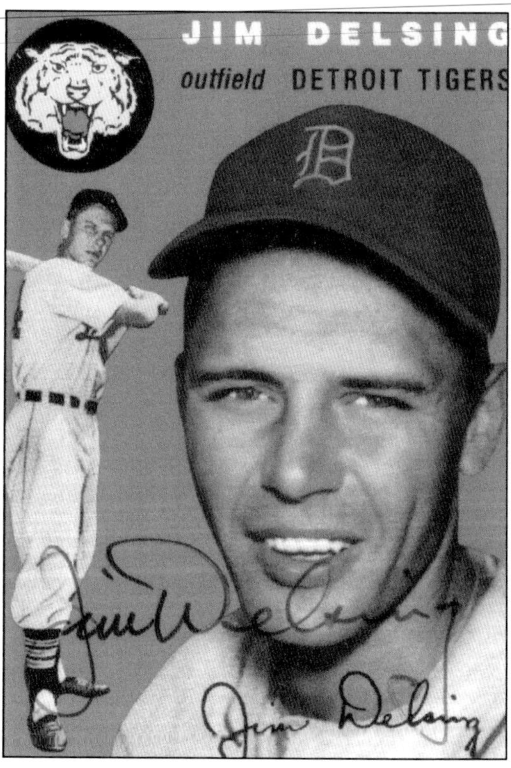

Delsing made his Major League debut in 1948 and played until 1960. The outfield instruction he received from Joe Skurski in 1946 set the stage for his 1954 season, in which he led the majors in fielding. "My only regret is I would have liked to have won the Golden Glove Award. They didn't have that award that year," Delsing said. Delsing will go down in history as the pinch runner for midget Eddie Gaedel on August 19, 1951. "Zack Taylor said 'Delsing running for Gaedel'—so there I go. He [Gaedel] pats me on the butt and goes to the dugout," Delsing recalled. (Photo Courtesy of the Topps Company, Inc.)

Hugh Wise took over the managerial reigns in 1947, and the team's strong finish the year before led to high expectations. Those expectations were not met, however, as the team limped to a fifth place finish. (Author's collection—1947 Eau Claire Bears Program.)

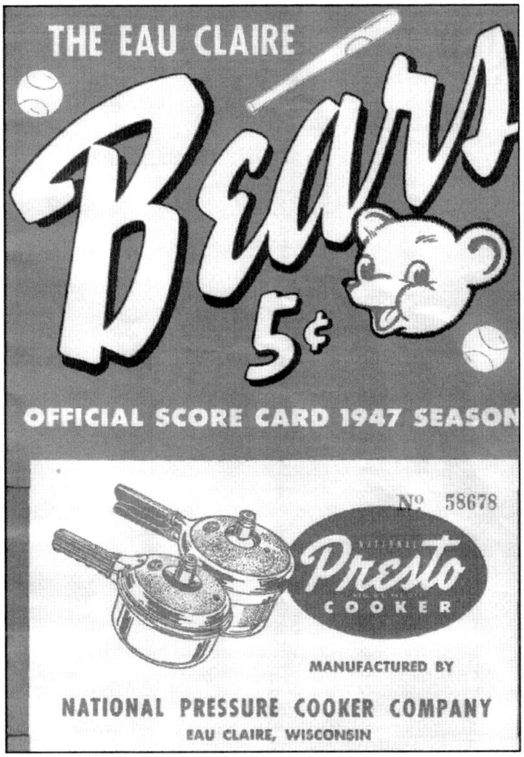

Hugh wise had a cup of coffee in the major leagues with Detroit in 1930, but would not see another at-bat in the majors despite playing in the minors until 1946. His son, Hugh Jr., would play briefly for Eau Claire in 1954. This caricature from the 1947 Bears program tells you more about him. (Author's collection—1947 Eau Claire Bears Program.)

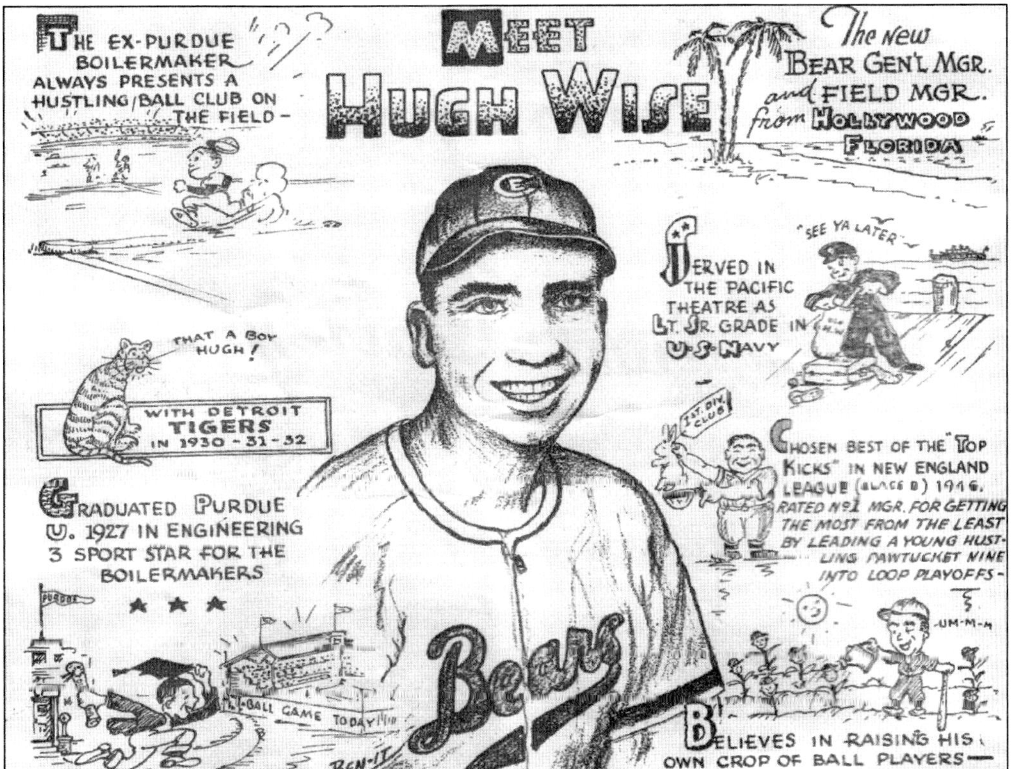

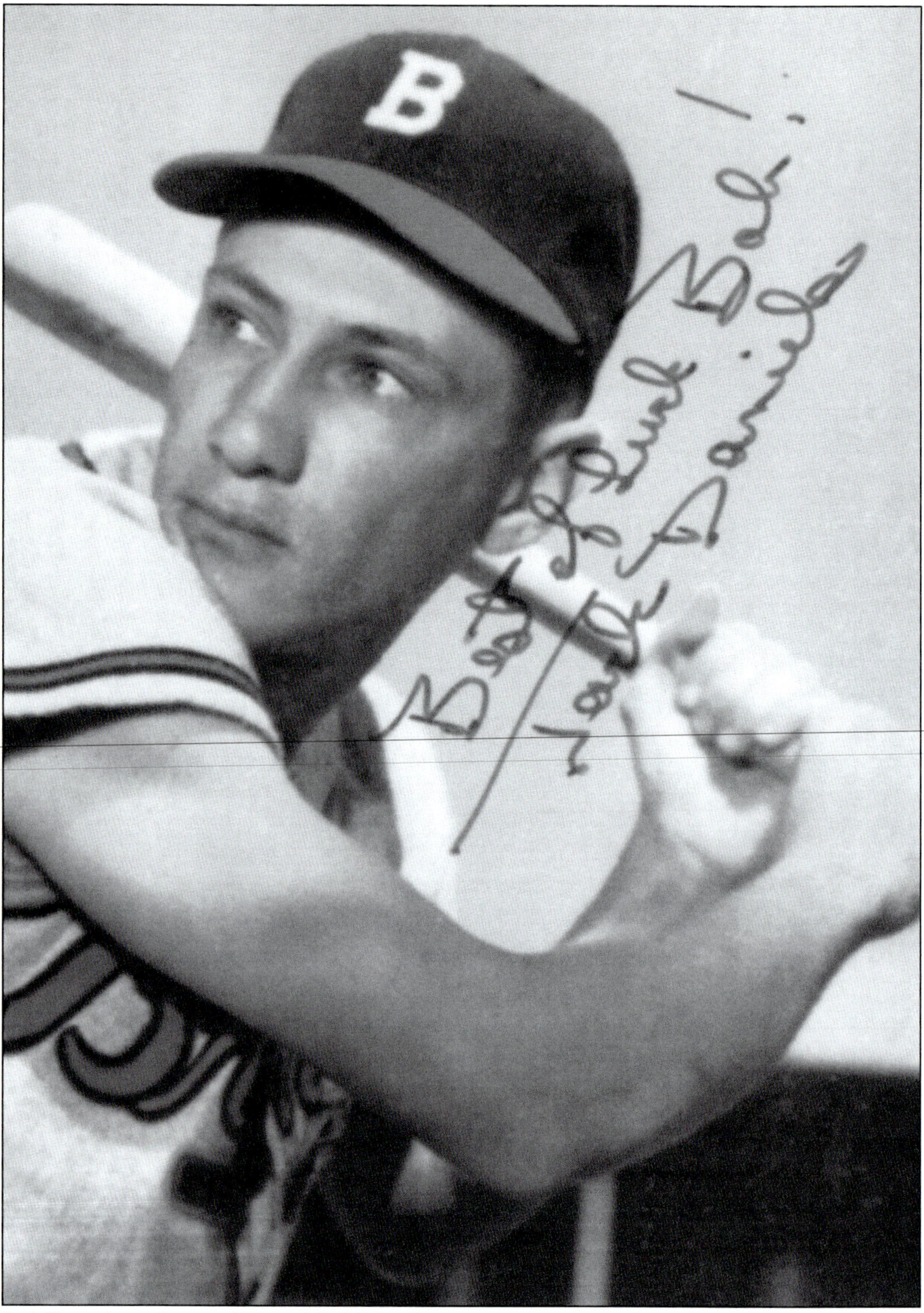

Jack Daniels, nicknamed "Sour Mash" for obvious reasons, spent eleven seasons on the diamond professionally. The outfielder's only major league season was in 1952, when he hit .187 with two home runs and 14 RBI for the Boston Braves. He hit considerably better for manager Hugh Wise's 1947 Eau Claire team (.247/6/33). (Author's collection.)

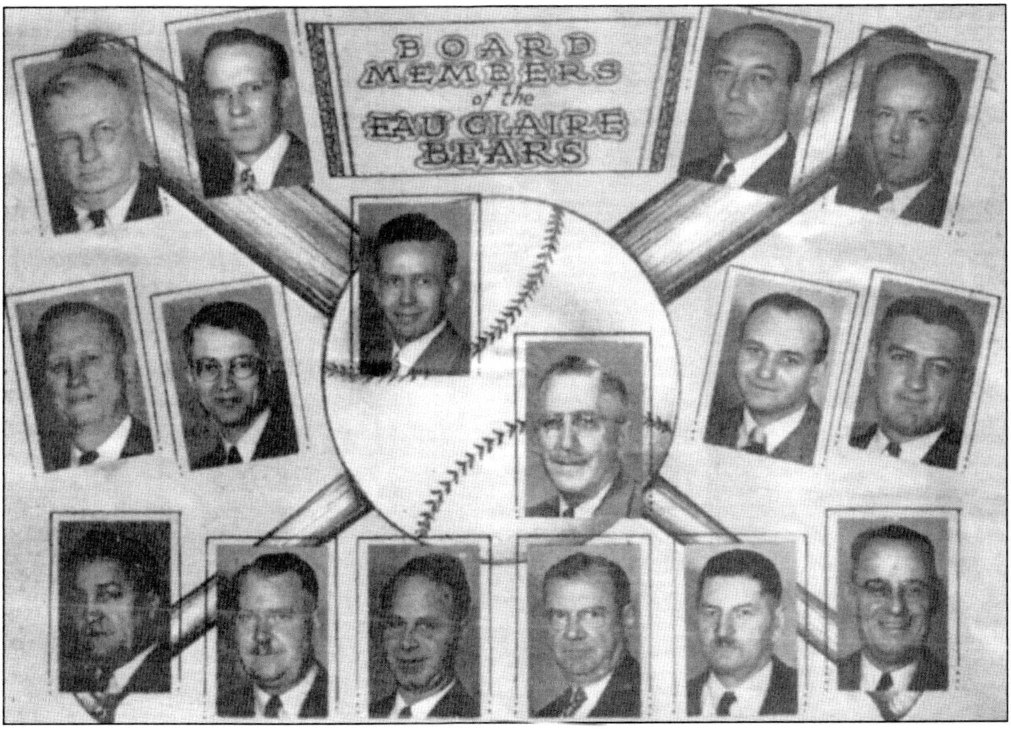

This picture from the 1947 Bears program shows some of the men who made it happen behind the scenes, many of whom kept baseball in Eau Claire for many years. From left to right: (front row) C. Paulson, T. Smeed, J. Voll, W. McIntyre, R. Edgar, and R. Morse; (middle row) H. Hutchens, J. Riley, O. Linderman, R. Scobie, C. Hansen, and P. Ulwelling; (back row) H. White, R. Bezanson, A. DeBonville, and A. Crowe. (Author's collection—1947 Eau Claire Bears Program.)

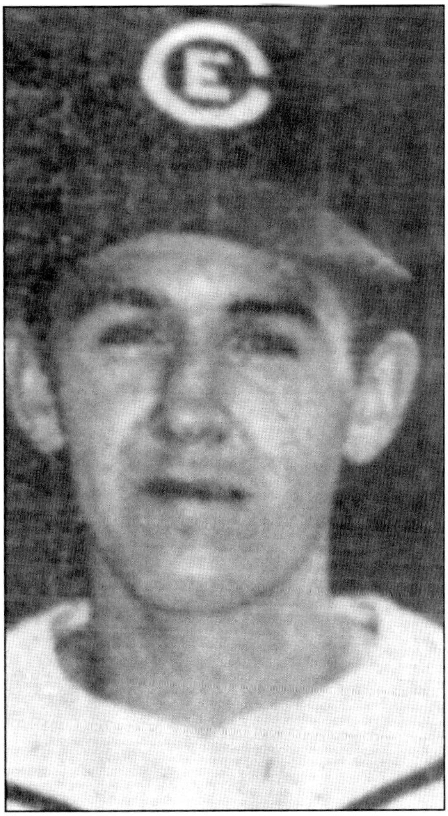

Milwaukee's own Bob Harden filled in for an injured Stan Szurma late in 1946 and played well enough to re-sign with Eau Claire in 1947. Erratic defense (.873 fielding percentage in 1946) was likely the reason he would advance no further than Eau Claire. On June 23, 1947, though, his successful hidden ball trick led to a Bear victory over Aberdeen and the ejection of Don Heffner, the exasperated Pheasants manager. (Author's collection—1947 Eau Claire Bears program.)

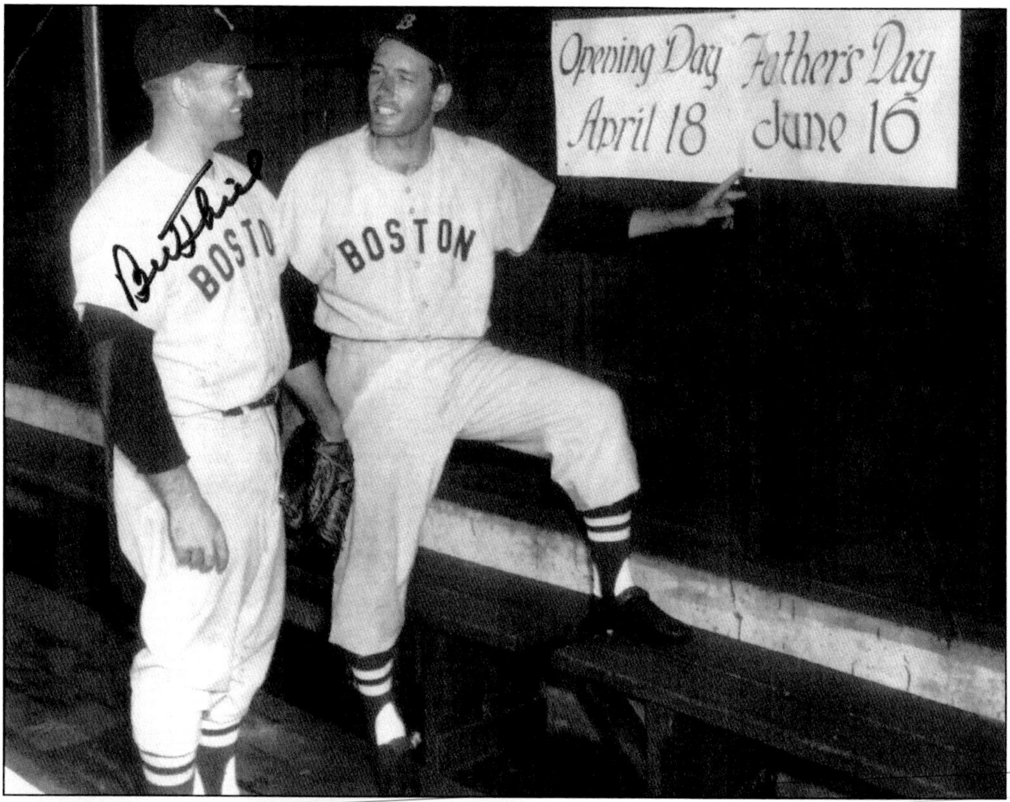

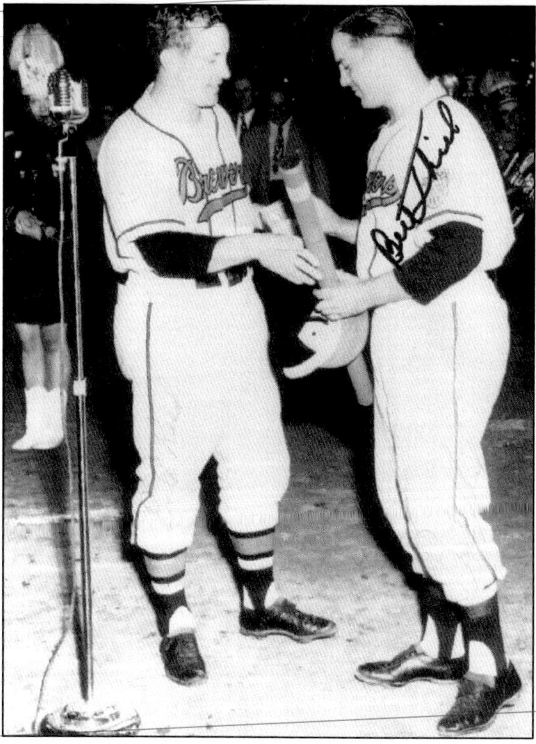

Bert Thiel began his career in Eau Claire in 1947, going 10-10 with a 3.60 ERA for manager Hugh Wise's club. Thiel explains this photo with Jimmy Piersall (right) from spring training in Sarasota, Florida a decade later: "Jim drove in the winning run in the tenth inning against the Yankees. I was the winning pitcher in relief. We both have large families. The Piersall's were expecting number five on April eighteenth and the Thiels were expecting number five on June sixteenth." (Photo courtesy of Bert Thiel.)

Eight months before he was to make his major league debut, Marion, Wisconsin native Bert Thiel was honored with his own night at Borchert Field in Milwaukee. This photo shows Bill Reed (left) presenting Thiel with a fly rod from the team. "I still use it today," Thiel said. Thiel pitched four games in relief for the Boston Braves in 1952 before being sent back to the minors, where he retired in 1961. (Photo courtesy of Bert Thiel)

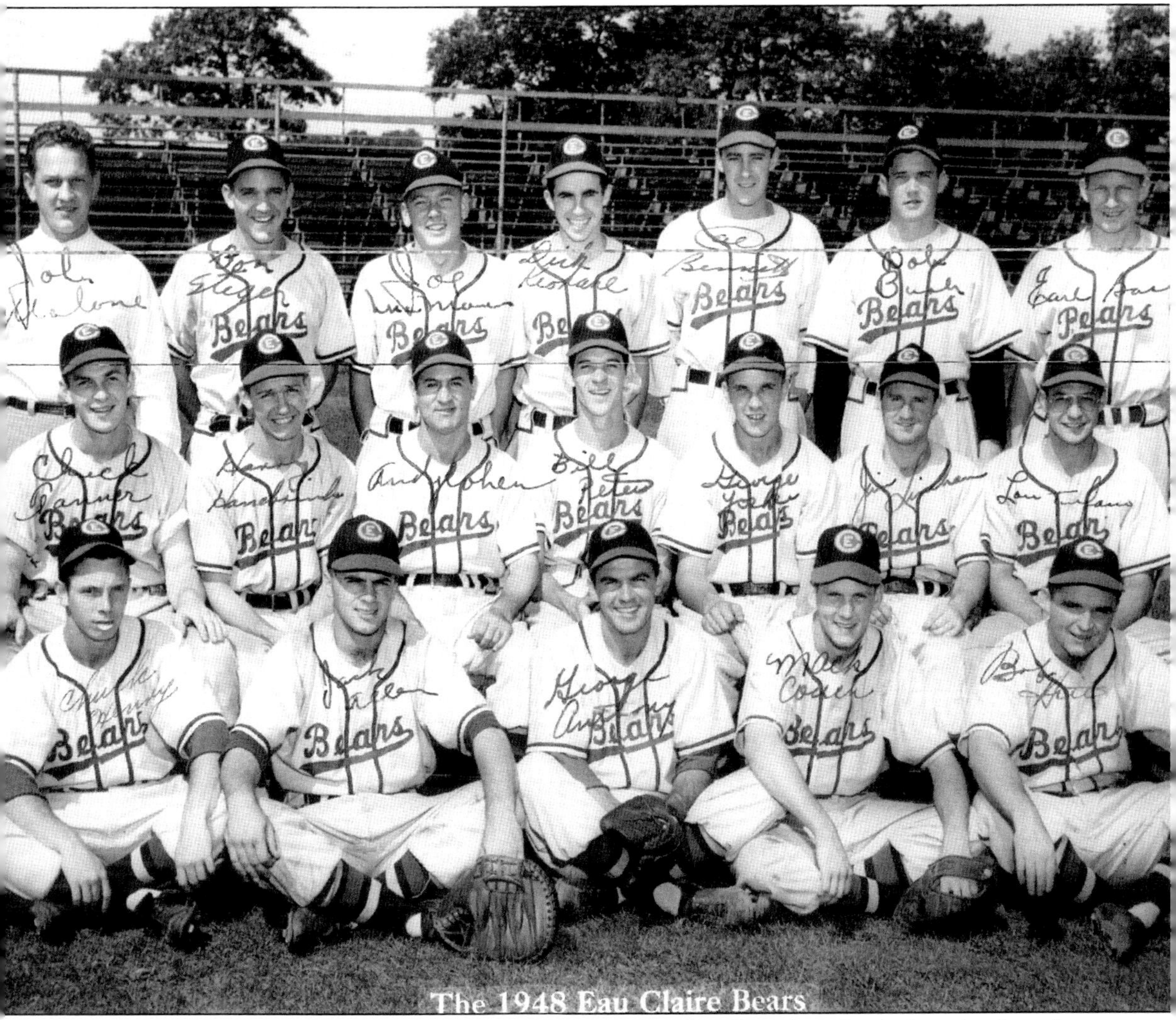

New manager Andy Cohen took the 1948 Bears to the playoffs with a third place finish and a 66-55 record. From left to right: (front row) Charles Henry, John Allen, George Anthony, Max Couch, and Bob Hitt; (middle row) Chuck Tanner, Harry Hanebrink, Andy Cohen, Clarence "Bill" Peters, George Yorke, Jim Linehan, and Lou Tufano; (back row) John Malone, Don Steger, Joe McManus, Dick Keohane, Al Bennett, Bob Bush, and Earl Bass. (Photo courtesy of the Chippewa Valley Museum, Eau Claire, WI.)

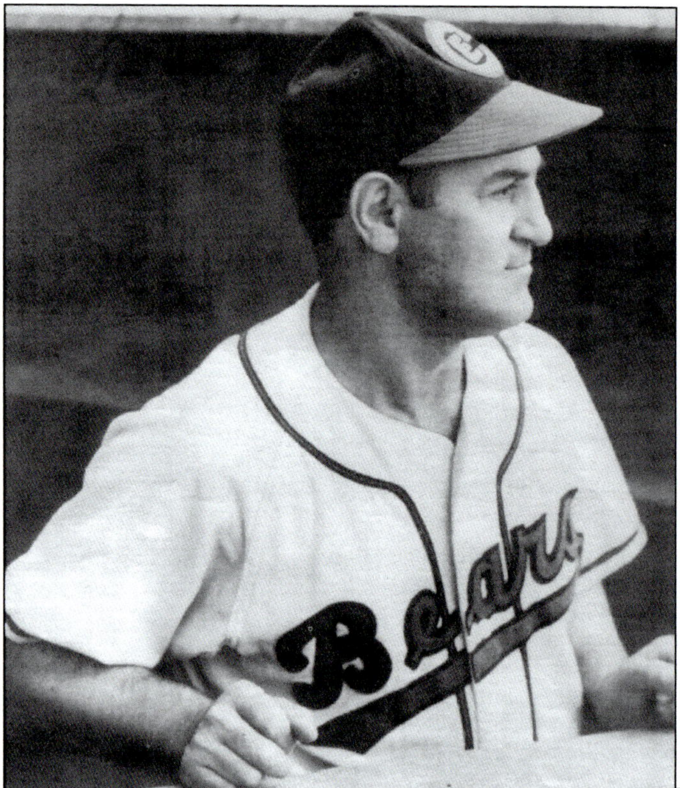

Ex-New York Giant infielder Andy Cohen prowled the Bears dugout for three seasons (1948-1950), the second longest managerial tenure for Eau Claire's professional teams. His teams went a combined 210-160 for a .568 winning percentage, and won the Northern League pennant in 1949. (Author's collection—July 9, 1950 *Eau Clarion*.)

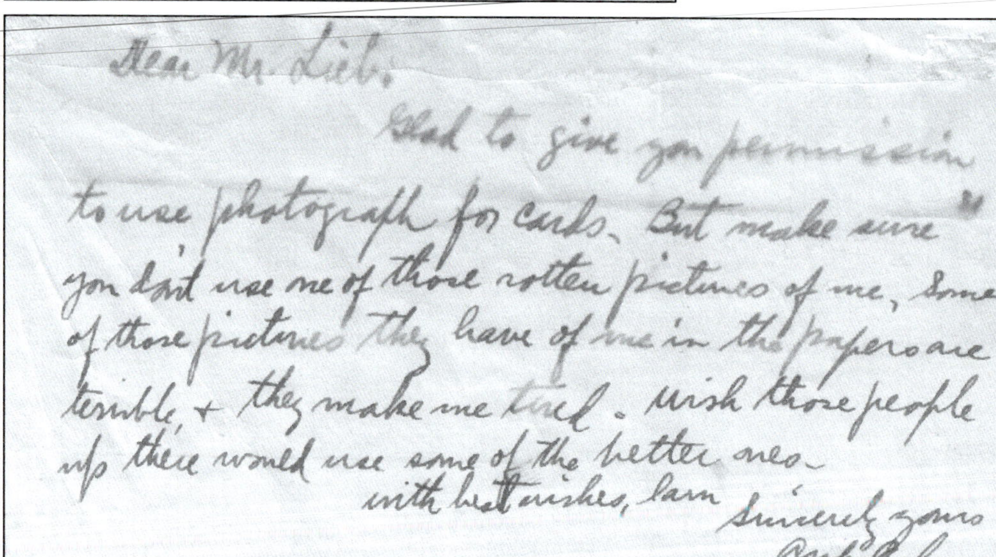

Dear Mr. Lieb.

Glad to give you permission to use photograph for cards. But make sure you don't use one of those rotten pictures of me. Some of those pictures they have of me in the papers are terrible, + they make me tired. Wish those people up there would use some of the better ones.

with best wishes, I am

Sincerely yours

Andy Cohen

This is a note to famous sports writer Fred Lieb from future Eau Claire manager Andy Cohen on the back of a 1928 contract allowing Lieb to produce baseball cards. It shows a side of a ballplayer not normally seen, especially in that era. It reads (in part): "Glad to give you permission to use photograph for cards. But make sure you don't use one of those rotten pictures of me. Some of those pictures they have of me in the papers are terrible, and they make me tired." (Author's collection.)

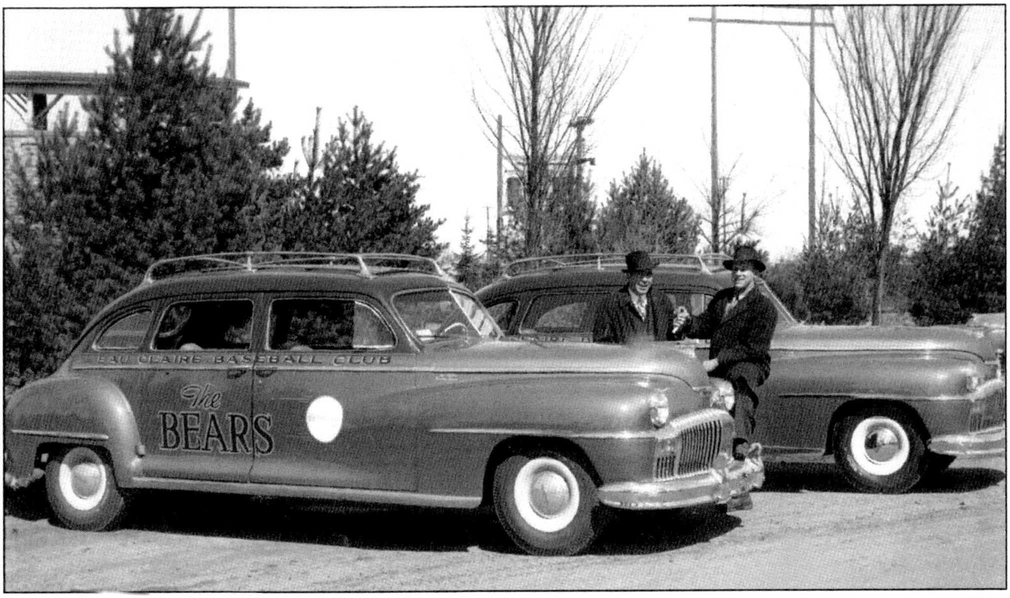

The caption given on this picture from the Chippewa Valley Museum says this is a new 1946 DeSoto sold to the Eau Claire Bears and manager Andy Cohen. However, Cohen (on the right) didn't become manager until 1948. An odometer rollback scandal revealed? Mostly hidden by the pine trees on the left of the photo is the grandstand from Carson Park. (Photo courtesy of the Chippewa Valley Museum, Eau Claire, WI.)

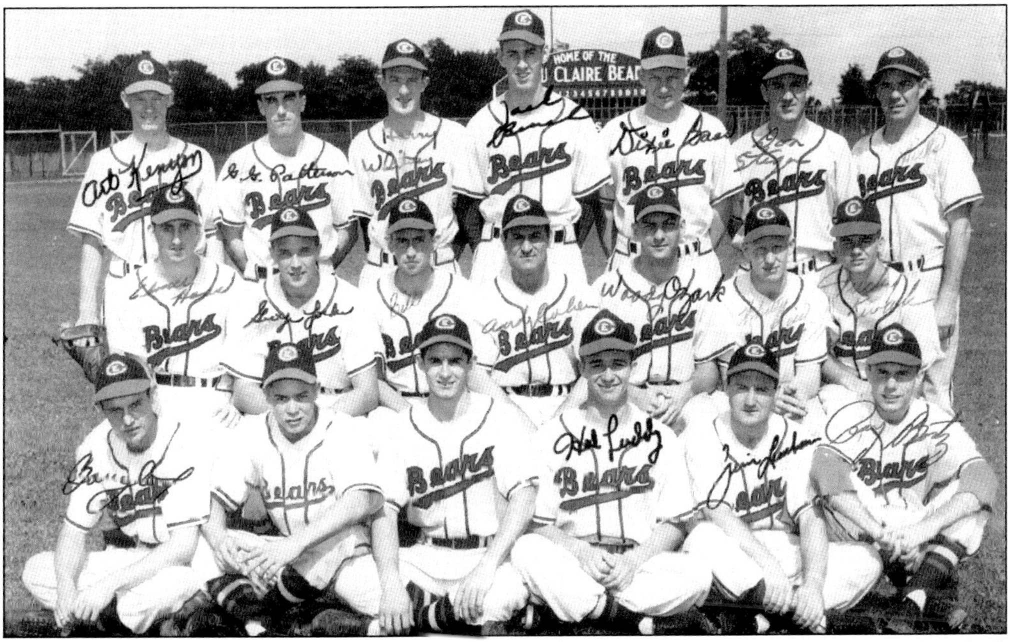

The 1949 Bears, from left to right: (front row) Barry Cox, unidentified, unidentified, Harold Luddy, Jim Linehan, and Ray Bortz; (middle row) Elmer Haas, George Yorke, Bill Sorrels, Andy Cohen, Norwood "Woody" Ozark, Bob Ries, and Karol "Ducky" Kwak, (back row) Art Kenyon, George Patterson, Harry Whitney, John Bench, Earl "Dixie" Bass, Don Steger, and Bill Hicks. (Photo courtesy of the Chippewa Valley Museum, Eau Claire, WI.)

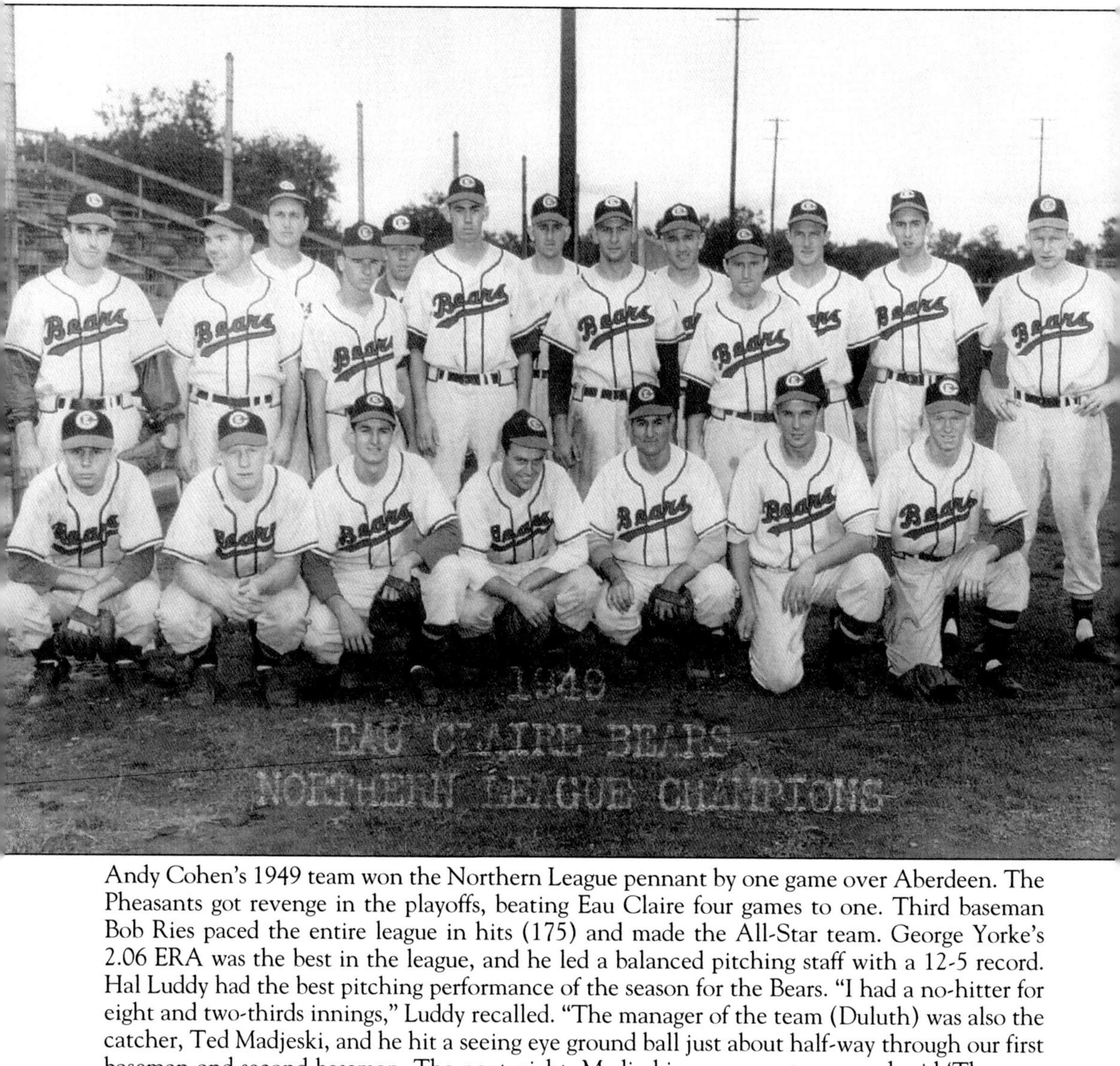

Andy Cohen's 1949 team won the Northern League pennant by one game over Aberdeen. The Pheasants got revenge in the playoffs, beating Eau Claire four games to one. Third baseman Bob Ries paced the entire league in hits (175) and made the All-Star team. George Yorke's 2.06 ERA was the best in the league, and he led a balanced pitching staff with a 12-5 record. Hal Luddy had the best pitching performance of the season for the Bears. "I had a no-hitter for eight and two-thirds innings," Luddy recalled. "The manager of the team (Duluth) was also the catcher, Ted Madjeski, and he hit a seeing eye ground ball just about half-way through our first baseman and second baseman. The next night, Madjeski came over to me and said 'That was the cheapest hit I've ever seen in my life!'" (Photo courtesy of Al Facchini.)

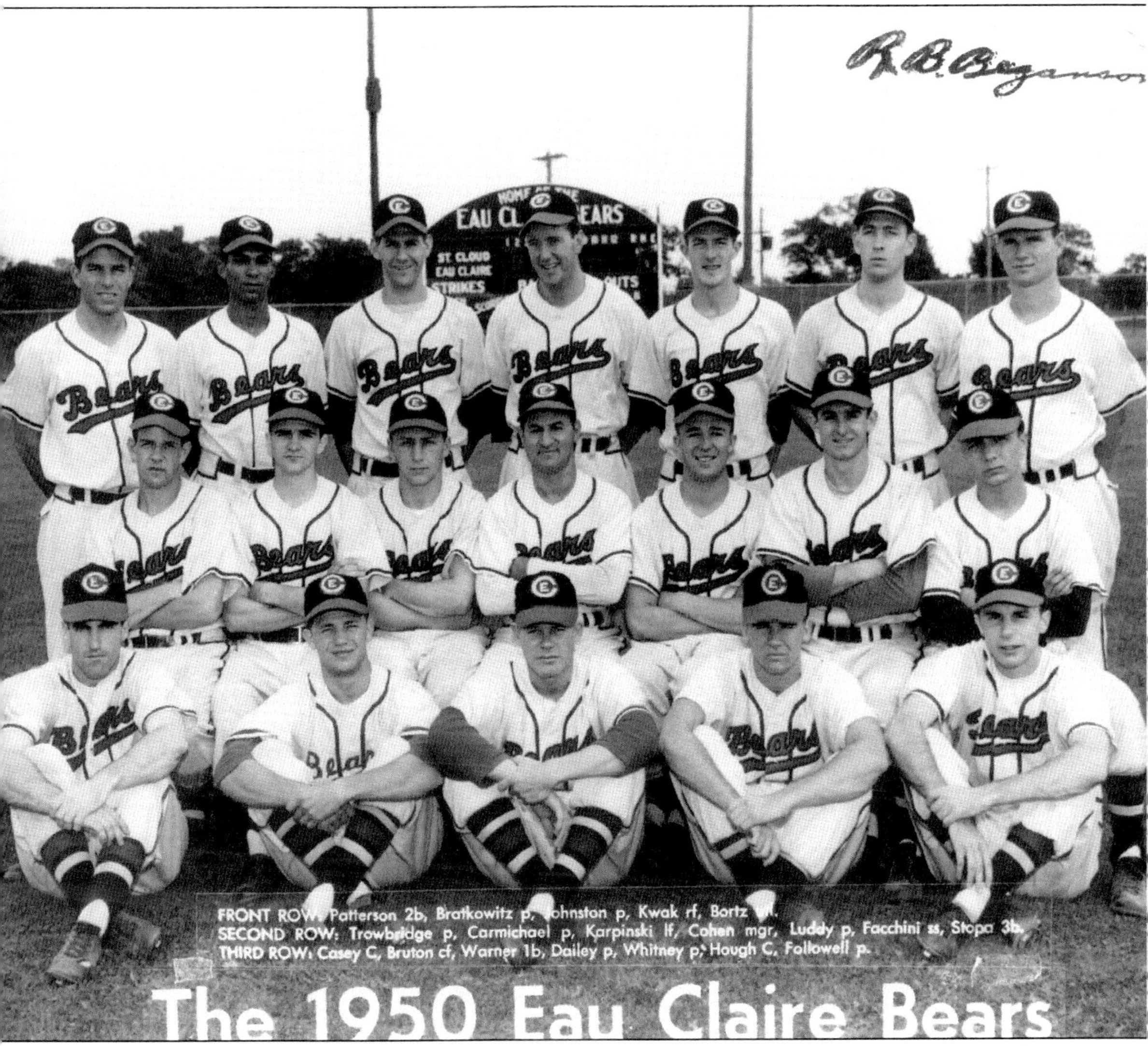

Andy Cohen led this 1950 squad to a second place finish in the regular season, going 73-53 and finishing a scant half-game behind Charlie Fox's St. Cloud Rox. Both St. Cloud and Eau Claire lost in the first round of the playoffs. Third place Sioux Falls beat fourth place Superior four games to one to claim the Northern League title. From left to right: (front row) George Patterson, Andy Bratkowitz, Paul Johnston, Karol "Ducky" Kwak, and Ray Bortz; (middle row) Bob Trowbridge, Dick Carmichael, John Karpinski, Andy Cohen, Hal Luddy, Al Facchini, and Joe Stopa; (back row) Bill Casey, Bill Bruton, Harry Warner, Gil Daily, Harry Whitney, Percy Hough, and Frank Followell. (Photo courtesy of the Chippewa Valley Museum, Eau Claire, WI.)

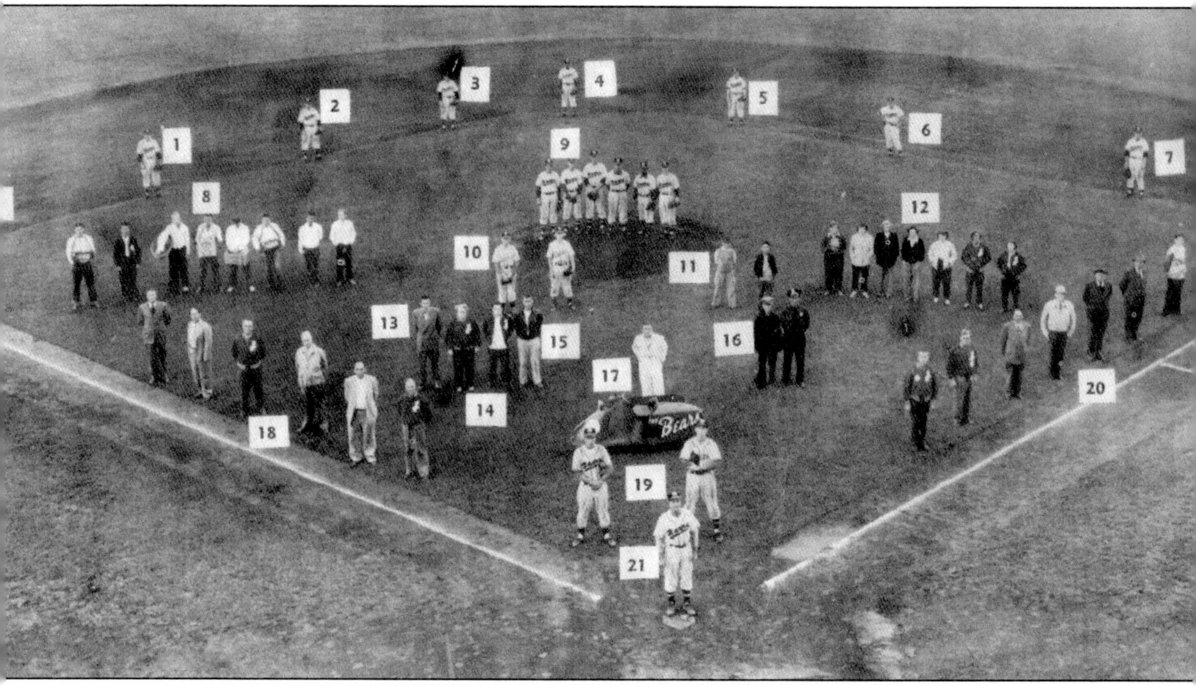

A true "team" photo, this clever photograph features the 1950 Bears, including everyone behind the scenes—even the vendors! (Author's collection—July 9, 1950 *Eau Clarion*.)

Bill Bruton (shown), along with pitcher Roy White, broke the color barrier in Eau Claire in 1950. His .288/5/58 performance, along with a league-leading 66 stolen bases, earned him a trip to the All-Star game as well as the first Rookie of the Year Award in the Northern League. The speedy outfielder progressed through the minors quickly and was an immediate fan favorite of the new Milwaukee Braves in 1953. Bruton led the league in stolen bases in each of his first three big league seasons and finished his 12-year career with a .273 lifetime average. (Photo courtesy of Al Facchini.)

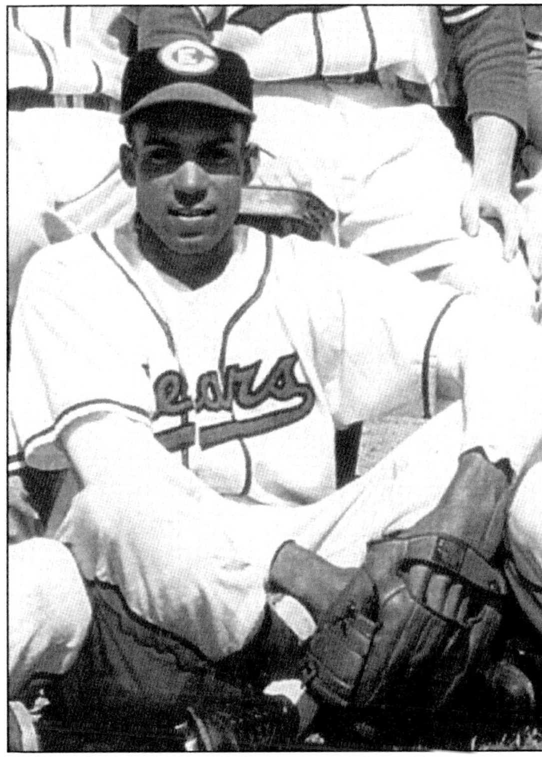

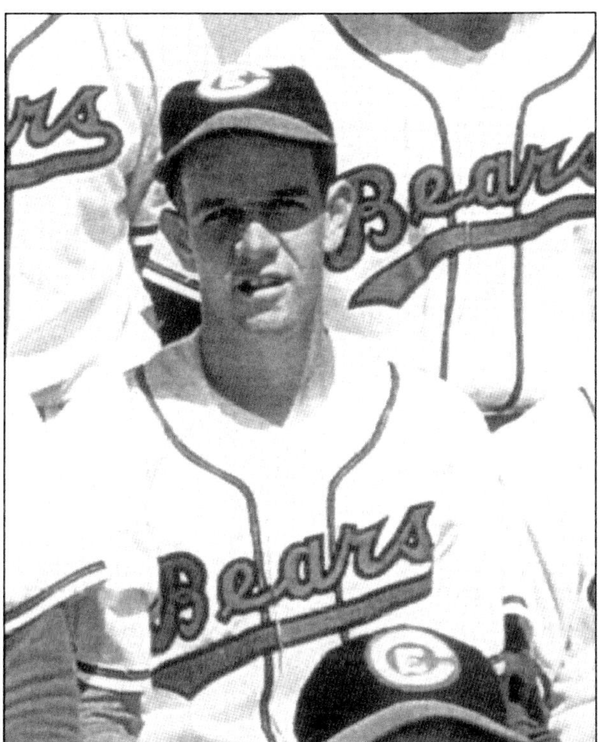

The staff ace for the Bears in 1950, Bob Trowbridge went 16-8 with a 2.97 ERA. He spent the next three years serving his country in the military, returning to pro ball with a splendid 18-8 record for Jacksonville (South Atlantic League) in 1954. He reached the Milwaukee Braves in 1956 and stayed in the majors through 1959, compiling a 13-13 career record with a 3.95 ERA, appearing mostly in relief. (Photo courtesy of Al Facchini.)

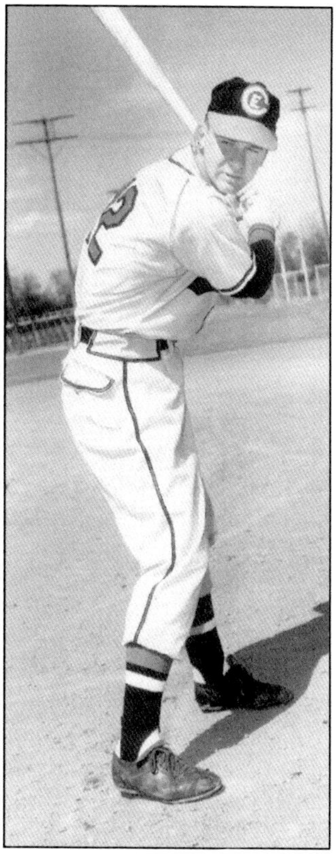

Because of his last name, Chicago native Karol Kwak had no choice but to be nicknamed "Ducky." "We would go on the road and people used to bring out those quack calls and he would just stand there and laugh," remembered teammate Hal Luddy. Kwak's play during his two seasons in Eau Claire was anything but fouled. He hit .244 with 6 homers and 67 RBI in 1949, but followed that up with a .296/19/88 performance in 1950. The talented Kwak somehow never made it out of the minors. He led the Tri-State League with a .359 average in 1953, but two years and five teams later he was out of baseball. (Photo courtesy of the *Eau Claire Leader-Telegram*.)

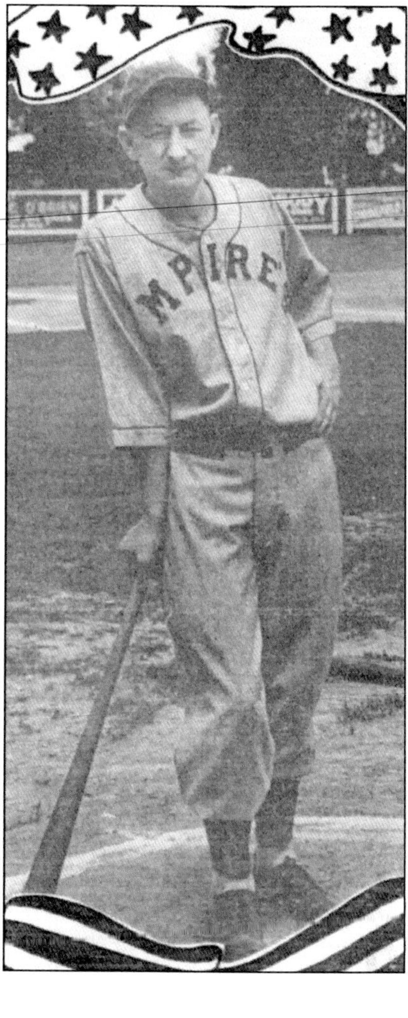

Emory "Ham" Olive was an umpire in the International League and the Northern League, and is widely regarded as the busiest and most popular umpire the "Polar Loop" ever had. After his career as a player was over, he became manager and half-owner of the "House of David" team, a barnstorming group based in Benton Harbor, Michigan. He moved to Eau Claire and began his long umpiring career—keeping active even into the 1980s by umpiring Little League games. (Photo courtesy of the Chippewa Valley Museum, Eau Claire, WI.)

Harry Warner's professional playing career began in Stroudsburg, Pennsylvania in 1946, close to his hometown of Reeders. The first baseman stayed there through 1949. That season he peaked as a player, hitting .347 with 17 homers and 125 RBI. The Braves acquired him and sent him to Eau Claire for 1950, where he "cooled down" to .285/12/90. He would play until 1962, and later became a coach for the Milwaukee Brewers. Warner still resides in Reeders in the Pocono Mountains. (Photo Courtesy of the Milwaukee Brewers.)

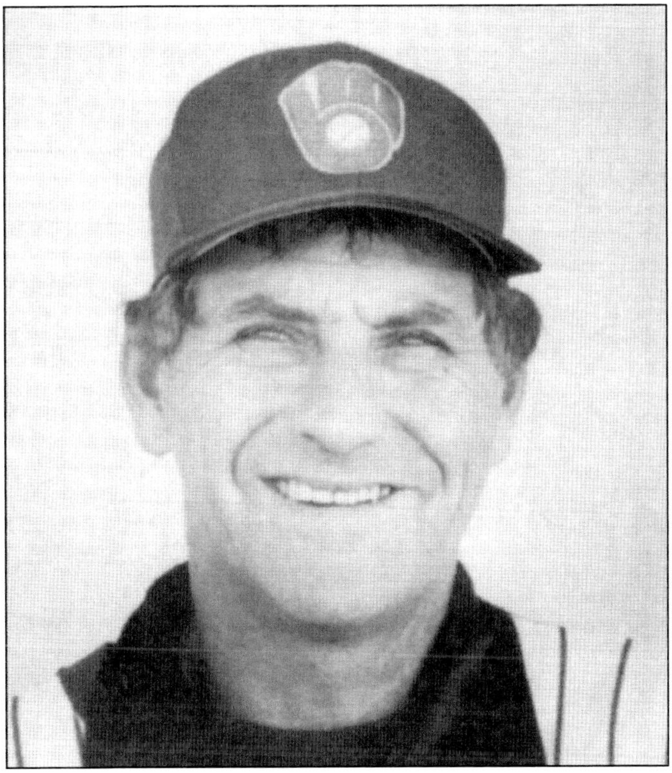

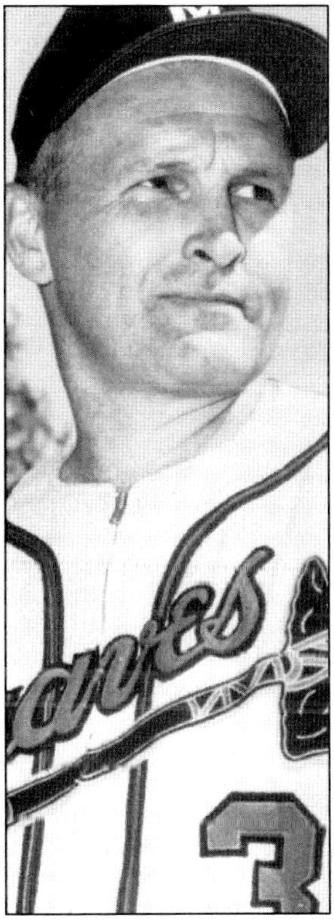

Manager Bill Adair took the reigns from Andy Cohen in 1951 and a year later led Eau Claire to the most talked about baseball season in the history of the City. The team, featuring Henry Aaron and John "Wes" Covington, was extremely talented but finished third and bowed out of the playoffs in the first round. Adair was a baseball "lifer," and his hard work was rewarded when he was briefly installed as manager of the Chicago White Sox in 1970. (Photo courtesy of *the Eau Claire Leader-Telegram*.)

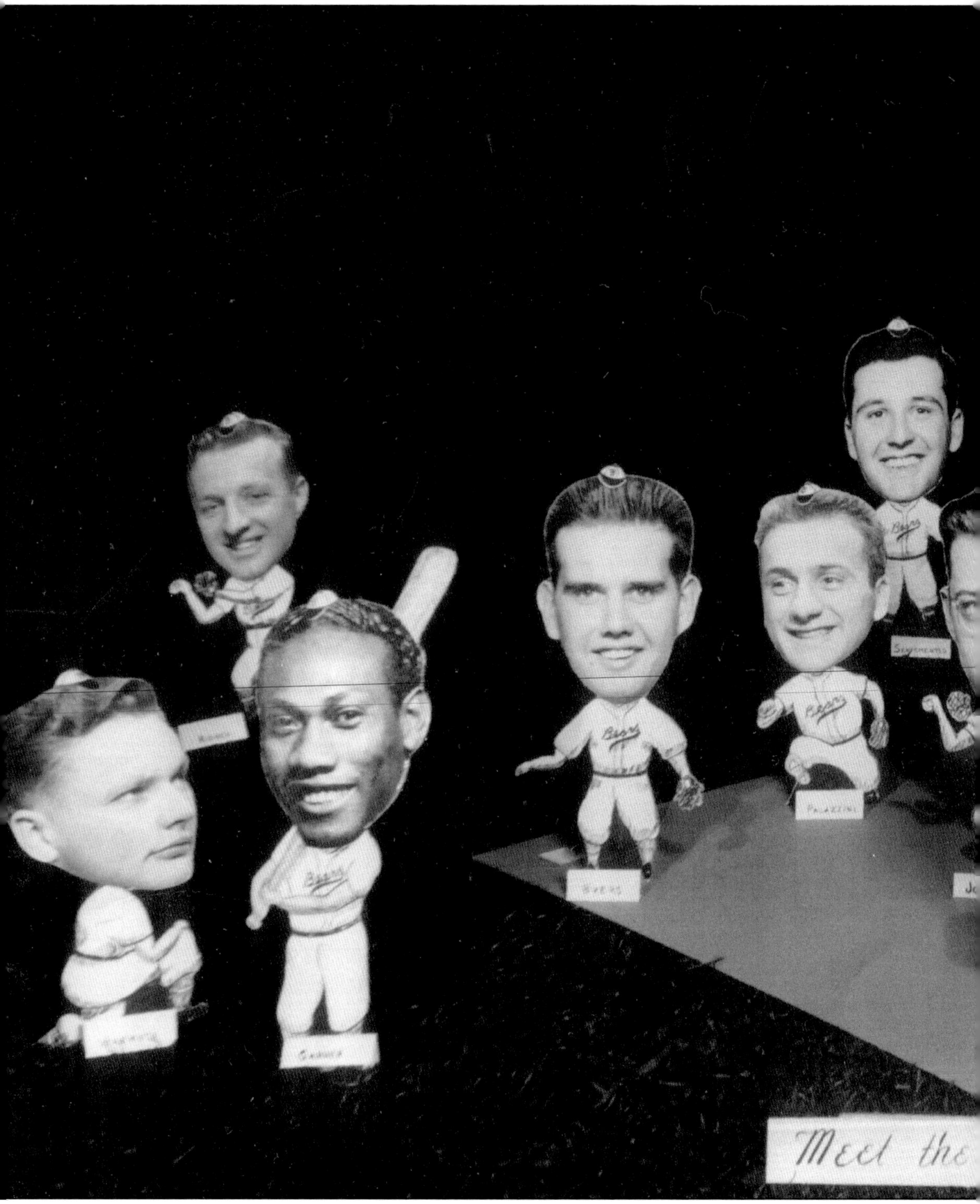

A fun composite picture from the Johnson Studio shows the 1951 Northern League Champion Bears. From left to right are Jim Warmouth, Gordon Roach, Horace Garner (Northern League Rookie of the Year), Paul Byers, Julio Palazzini, George Sentementes, Don Jordan,

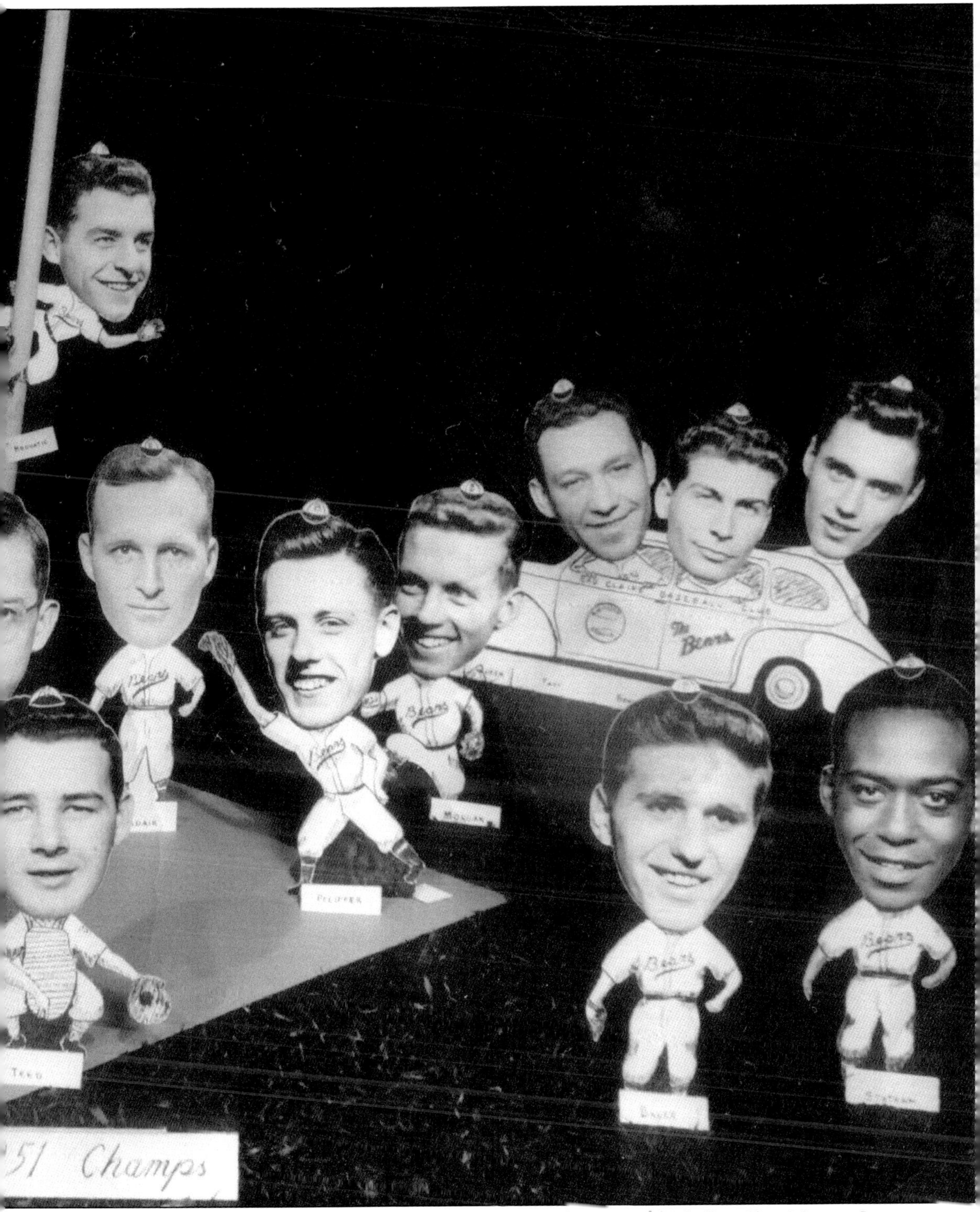

Bill Teed, Carl Hrovatic (on "flagpole"), Marion "Bill" Adair, Harold Pfeiffer, Chet Morgan Jr., Bill Queen, Bill Taft, John Brandreth, Bob Bauer, and Cliff Stratham (the last three are in the car). (Author's collection.)

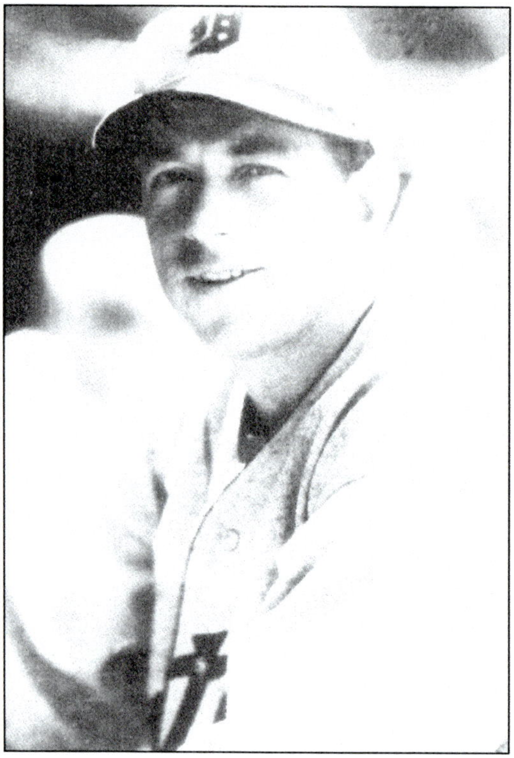

Chet Morgan St. (left) played briefly in the Detroit Tigers outfield in 1935 and 1938. His son, Chet Jr., was ready to follow in Dad's footsteps at age four! But Junior would wait until 1950 to make his professional debut, and he was in Eau Claire in 1951 and 1952. He peaked during his last two seasons, slugging 53 homers and driving in 211 for three teams in 1955 and 1956 combined. (Photo courtesy of Chet Morgan Jr.)

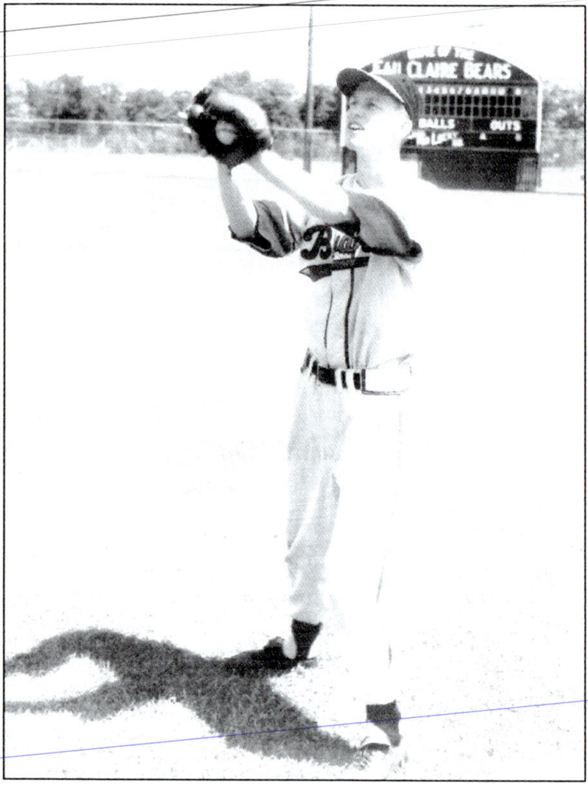

Chet Morgan Jr. is shown here patrolling right field in front of Carson Park's scoreboard in 1951. Morgan would also play for Evansville that year, but he came back to Eau Claire for the mystical 1952 season, hitting .300 with 14 homers and 63 RBI. (Photo Courtesy of Chet Morgan Jr.)

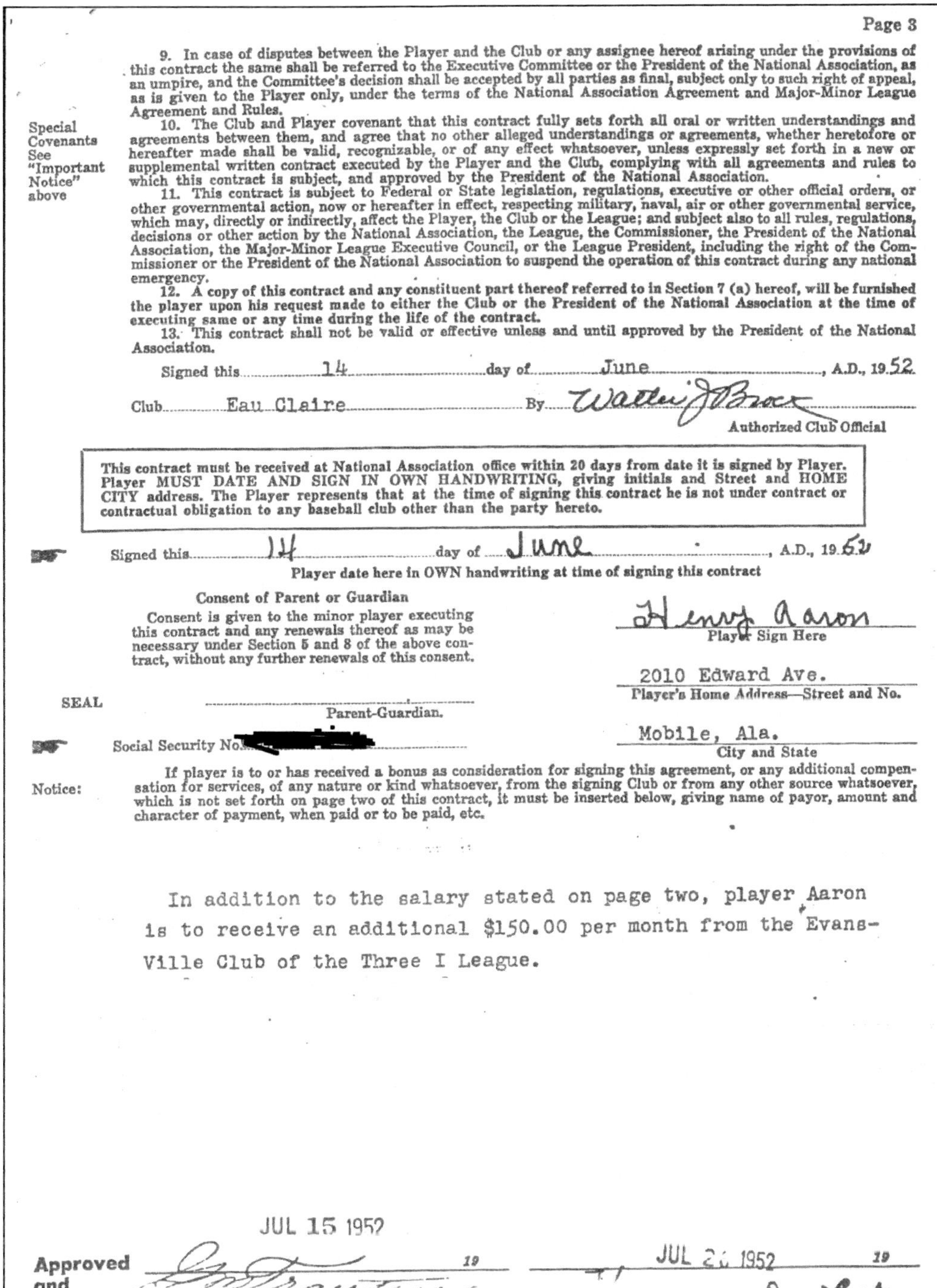

Page 3

9. In case of disputes between the Player and the Club or any assignee hereof arising under the provisions of this contract the same shall be referred to the Executive Committee or the President of the National Association, as an umpire, and the Committee's decision shall be accepted by all parties as final, subject only to such right of appeal, as is given to the Player only, under the terms of the National Association Agreement and Major-Minor League Agreement and Rules.

Special Covenants See "Important Notice" above

10. The Club and Player covenant that this contract fully sets forth all oral or written understandings and agreements between them, and agree that no other alleged understandings or agreements, whether heretofore or hereafter made shall be valid, recognizable, or of any effect whatsoever, unless expressly set forth in a new or supplemental written contract executed by the Player and the Club, complying with all agreements and rules to which this contract is subject, and approved by the President of the National Association.

11. This contract is subject to Federal or State legislation, regulations, executive or other official orders, or other governmental action, now or hereafter in effect, respecting military, naval, air or other governmental service, which may, directly or indirectly, affect the Player, the Club or the League; and subject also to all rules, regulations, decisions or other action by the National Association, the League, the Commissioner, the President of the National Association, the Major-Minor League Executive Council, or the League President, including the right of the Commissioner or the President of the National Association to suspend the operation of this contract during any national emergency.

12. A copy of this contract and any constituent part thereof referred to in Section 7 (a) hereof, will be furnished the player upon his request made to either the Club or the President of the National Association at the time of executing same or any time during the life of the contract.

13. This contract shall not be valid or effective unless and until approved by the President of the National Association.

Signed this 14 day of June, A.D., 1952

Club Eau Claire By Walter J. Brock
Authorized Club Official

This contract must be received at National Association office within 20 days from date it is signed by Player. Player MUST DATE AND SIGN IN OWN HANDWRITING, giving initials and Street and HOME CITY address. The Player represents that at the time of signing this contract he is not under contract or contractual obligation to any baseball club other than the party hereto.

Signed this 14 day of June, A.D., 1952
Player date here in OWN handwriting at time of signing this contract

Consent of Parent or Guardian

Consent is given to the minor player executing this contract and any renewals thereof as may be necessary under Section 5 and 8 of the above contract, without any further renewals of this consent.

Henry Aaron
Player Sign Here

2010 Edward Ave.
Player's Home Address—Street and No.

SEAL

Parent-Guardian.

Mobile, Ala.
City and State

Social Security No. [redacted]

Notice: If player is to or has received a bonus as consideration for signing this agreement, or any additional compensation for services, of any nature or kind whatsoever, from the signing Club or from any other source whatsoever, which is not set forth on page two of this contract, it must be inserted below, giving name of payor, amount and character of payment, when paid or to be paid, etc.

In addition to the salary stated on page two, player Aaron is to receive an additional $150.00 per month from the Evansville Club of the Three I League.

JUL 15 1952

Approved and 19 JUL 2? 1952 19

Henry Aaron's first professional contract was signed June 14, 1952. Eau Claire would pay Aaron $200 per month while Evansville (3-I League, also a Braves affiliate) would also chip in $150 a month. The shortstop would debut the following night, hitting RBI singles in his first two at bats in a 4-3 loss to St. Cloud. (Photo courtesy of the Chippewa Valley Museum, Eau Claire, WI.)

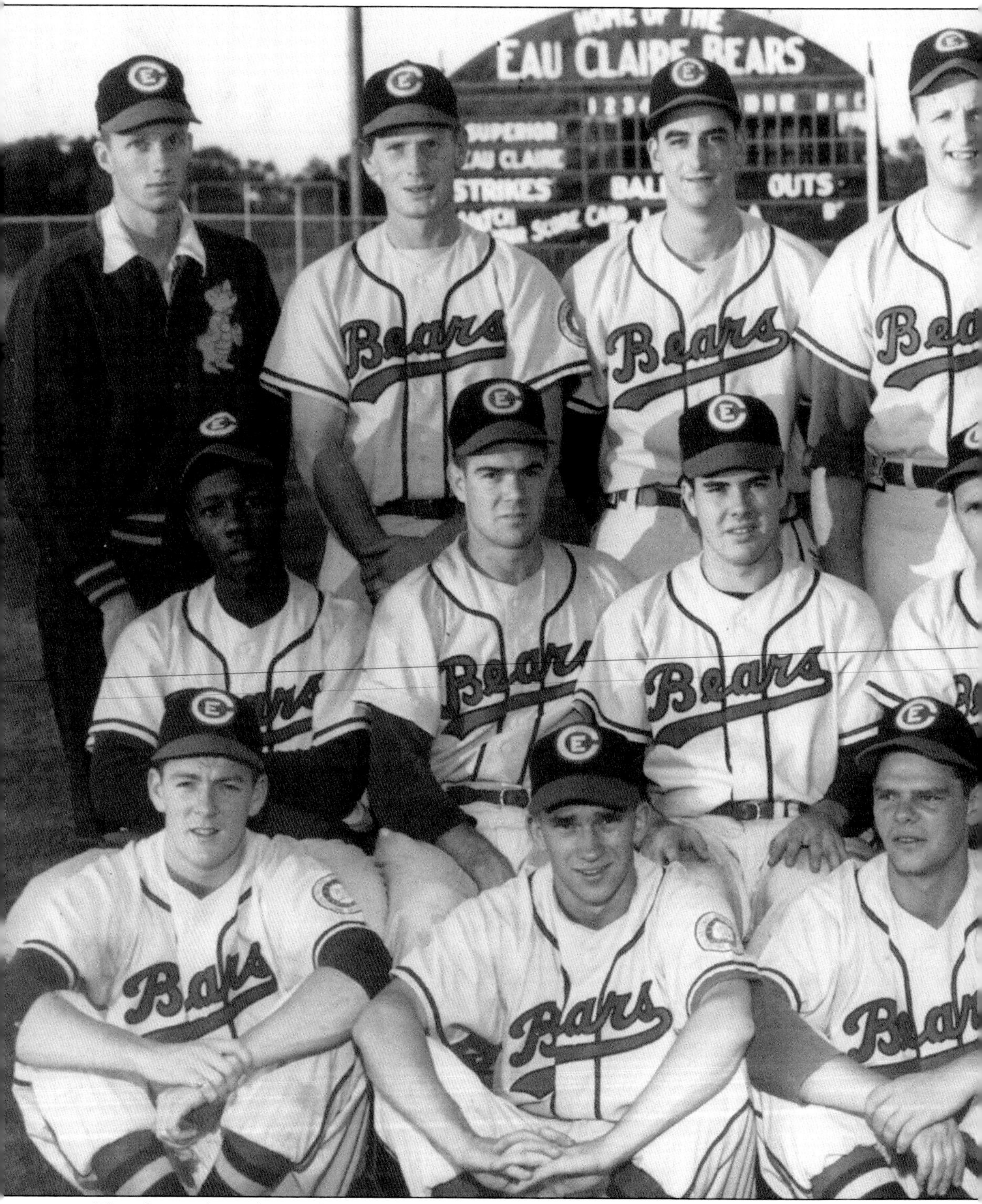

This photo is legendary in the Eau Claire area. The '52 Bears are the most talked about team in the city's history—period. From left to right: (front row) Bill Conroy, Johnny Goryl, Bobby Brown, Don Jordan, and Joe Subbiondo; (middle row) Henry Aaron, Don Auten, Charley Doehler,

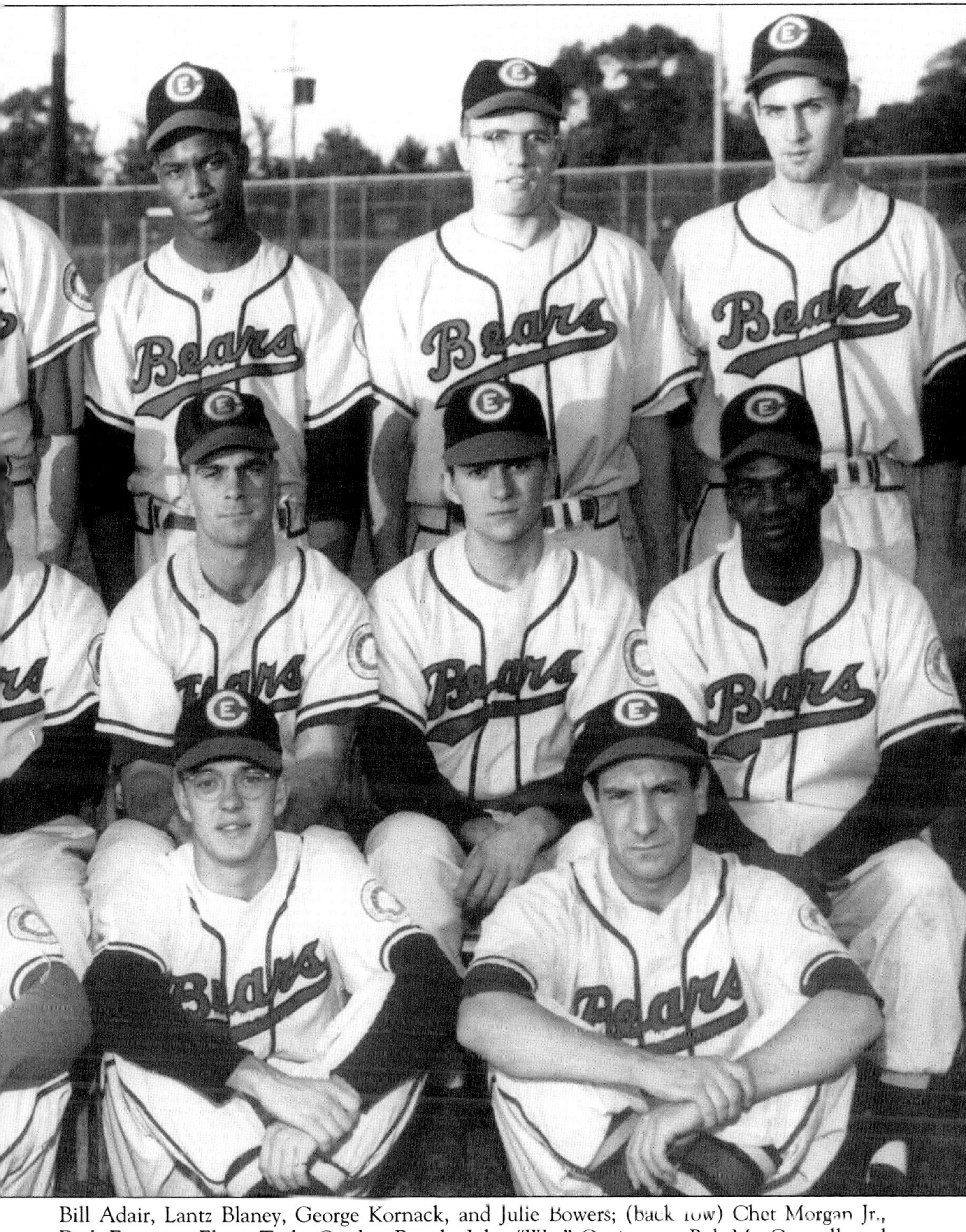

Bill Adair, Lantz Blaney, George Kornack, and Julie Bowers; (back row) Chet Morgan Jr., Dick Engquist, Elmer Toth, Gordon Roach, John "Wes" Covington, Bob MacConnell, and Ken Reitmeier. (Photo Courtesy of the Chippewa Valley Museum, Eau Claire, WI.)

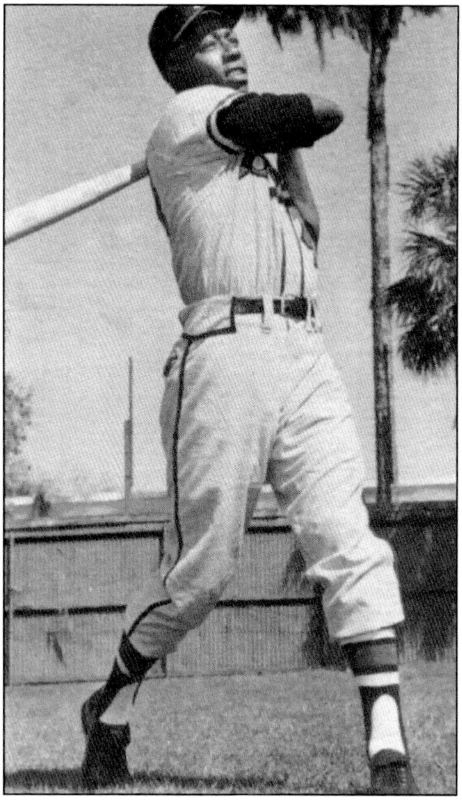

The baseball world didn't know exactly what was about to hit it, but those in Eau Claire may have had a clue. The June 11, 1952 *Eau Claire Leader* reads: "The Bears may put a new shortstop into action Friday, a Negro named Aaron, who was signed by the Boston Braves while hitting at a sensational clip for the Indianapolis Clowns." Aaron would win the Northern League Rookie of the Year honors despite playing only 87 games for Eau Claire in 1952. (Author's collection—1961 Milwaukee Braves Yearbook.)

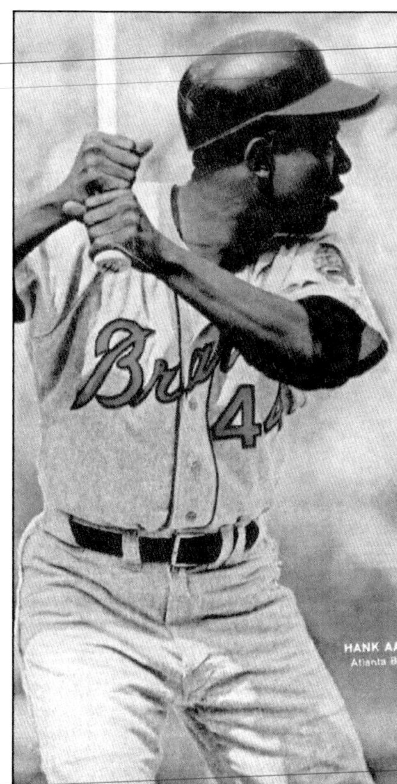

1952 Bears teammate Chuck Doehler describes Henry Aaron's legendary wrists: "We played this game 'Bend the Beer Cans', which were made of steel back then. I could bend six in a row, but I needed both hands and used my thumbs to bend them along the seam. Hank could do six one-handed, with his pinky on one end and thumb on the other, and using his index finger to push in the seam! His wrists were like a vise!" (Author's collection. Quote from *Seton Hall Alumni Magazine*, Fall, 1992.)

Upon arrival in Eau Claire, Henry Aaron was a bit nervous. "A scared-to-death, 17-year-old came to our house, and he was just shaking," said Joyce Buzzell, whose husband Clell was responsible for finding housing for players. Clell had stopped off at home after picking up Aaron from the airport. "If you can imagine the most gangly, gawky, shyest kid you can think of—that was Henry Aaron. I think he thought we were going to bite him!" (Photo courtesy of the Chippewa Valley Museum, Eau Claire, WI.)

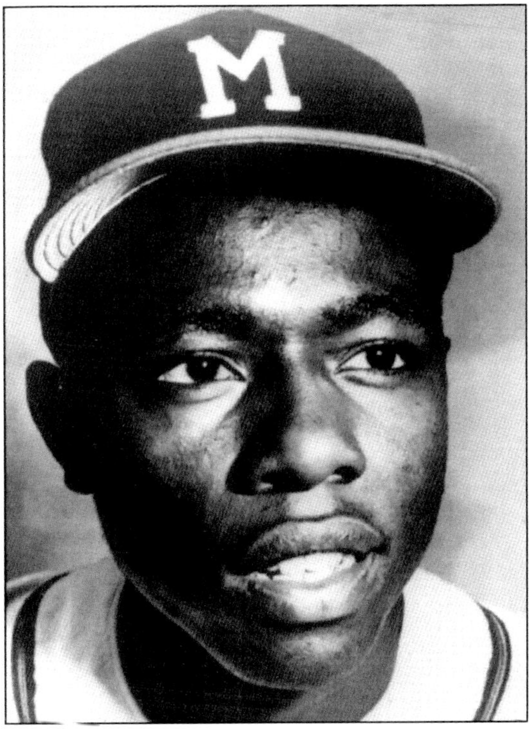

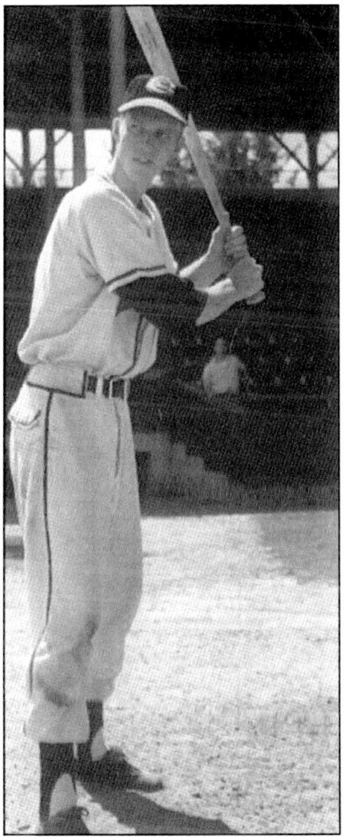

On June 14, 1952, Chet Morgan ripped a second inning double off of St. Cloud Rox pitcher Art Rosser. He would come around to score on a single by newcomer Henry Aaron, who was making his first professional plate appearance. Morgan doubled in his next at-bat in the fifth, and Aaron drove him in again with another single! (Photo courtesy of Chet Morgan Jr.)

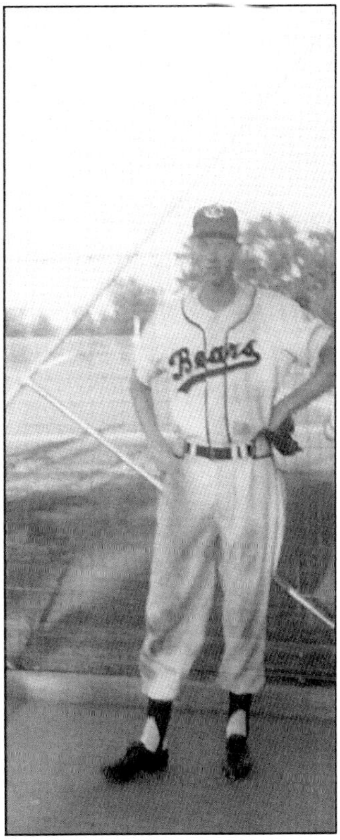

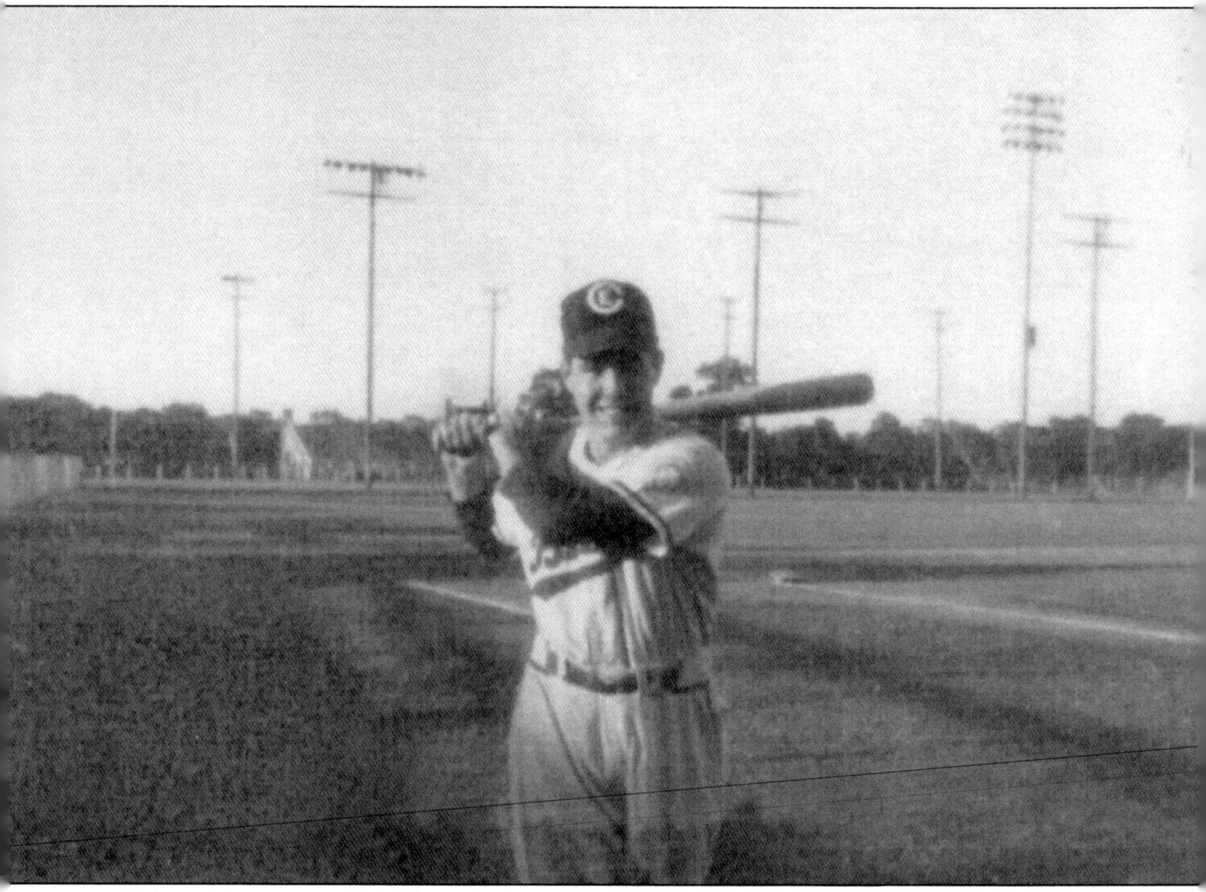

Although his time in Eau Claire, and in organized baseball, was brief, Charles Doehler has one of the city's most amazing baseball connections, and very few people know about it. Doehler, in addition to playing, was the secretary of his Babe Ruth League in Newark, New Jersey in 1948. When the legendary Ruth died that year, young Charley was given the task of placing a baseball in the casket of the slugger. However, the buses carrying the players were late in arriving to Yankee Stadium. The Babe's wake was over. And to make matters worse, Doehler had become separated from the rest of his teammates. Somehow, Charley made his way into the stadium and ran to where he thought the Babe was. He found Mrs. Ruth next to the casket, which was now closed. A security guard had stopped Charley, who felt like he had let his teammates down. Mrs. Ruth saw the crying boy was distressed and motioned for him to join her. Doehler told Mrs. Ruth the whole story, and Mrs. Ruth asked the security guard to find Charley's teammates. When the team arrived, the casket was opened and Charley gave the ball, inscribed "Safe at Home," to the fallen hero. Four years later, after Eau Claire's Wes Covington went down with an injury, the newly signed Doehler checked into the YMCA. He shook hands with his new roommate. "My name is Charley Doehler but my friends call me 'Chuck'." "Pleased to meet you, Chuck," replied his roommate. "My name is Henry Aaron, but my friends call me 'Hank'." (Photo Courtesy of Charles Doehler. Quotes from an unpublished article titled "Charley's Farewell to the Babe, by former Seton Hall professor Thomas A. Duff.)

Johnny Goryl was a quiet star on the 1952 team that featured the likes of Aaron and Covington. He hit .294 with 8 home runs and 25 RBI after coming to the Bears from Evansville in the 3-I League. He went back to Evansville in 1953 and part of 1954 before returning to Eau Claire to club 9 homers and 90 RBI to go with a .314 average for Charlie Root's Braves. 2001 marked 50 years of professional baseball for Goryl, who to this day is active in the Cleveland Indians organization. (Photo Courtesy of the Cleveland Indians.)

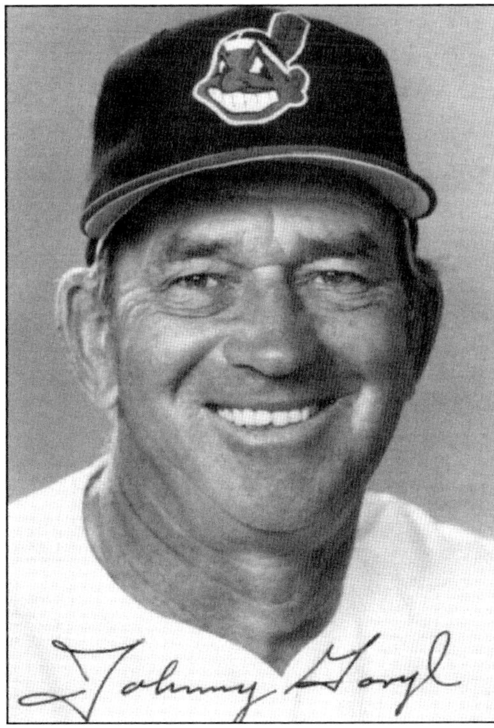

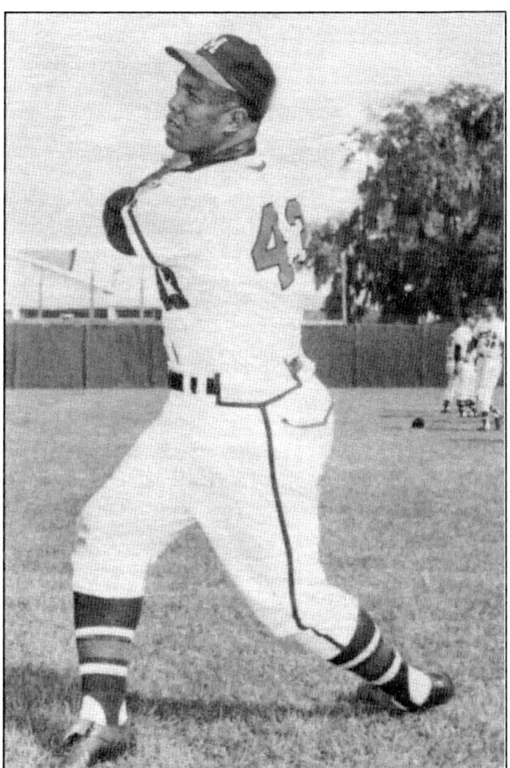

While Henry Aaron's 1952 season was the stuff of local legend, Wes Covington's performance that same year often goes overlooked. His .330 average, 24 homers (the third highest season total in Eau Claire professional history), and 99 RBI (fifth highest season total) only earned him fifth place in the Rookie of the Year honors. (Author's collection—1961 Milwaukee Braves Yearbook.)

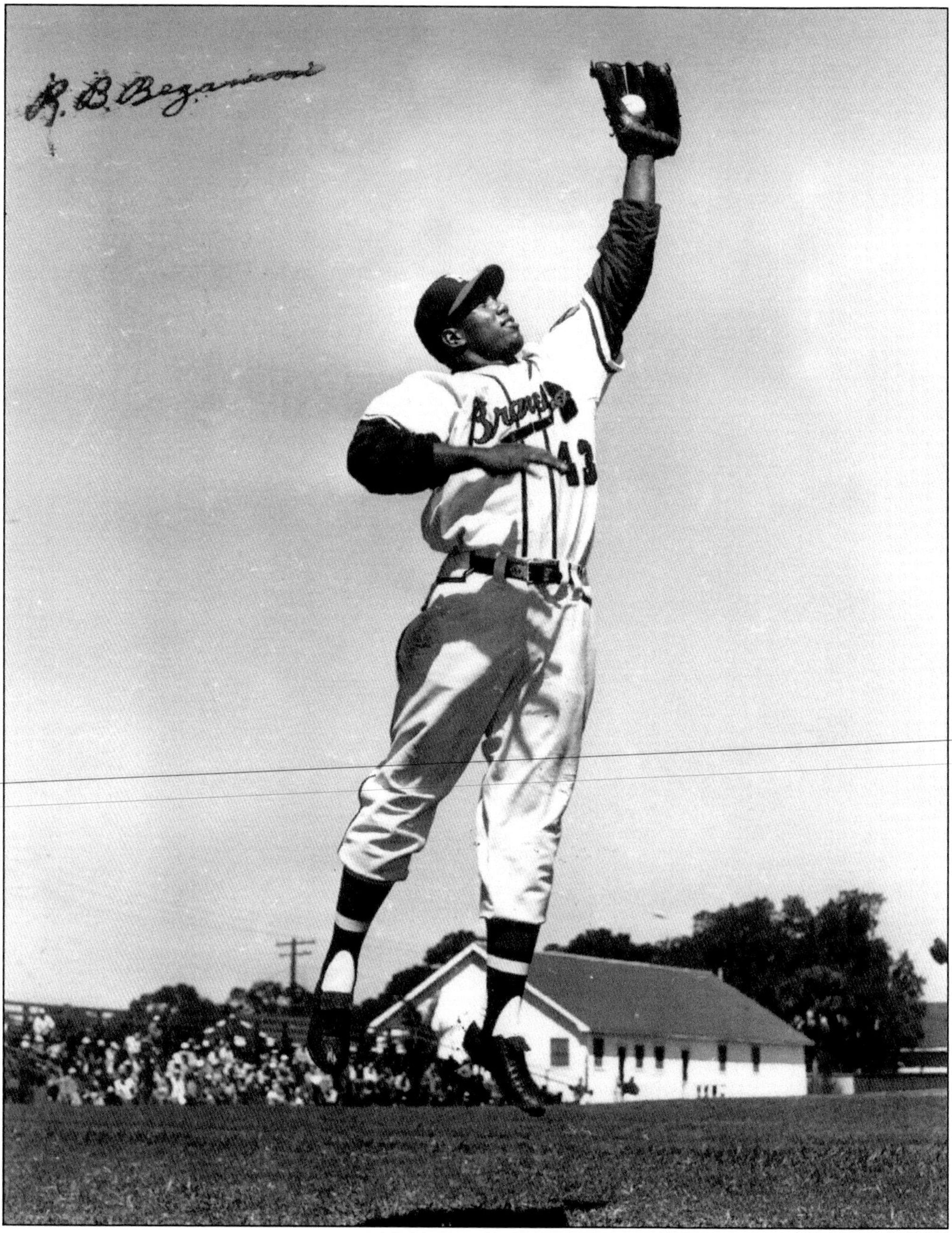

Wes Covington makes a grab in spring training, *c.* 1955. Known as "John" or "Flash" Covington during his 1952 season in Eau Claire, he could have easily grabbed the Northern League Rookie of the Year honors with his performance that season. However, he was injured for a few weeks during the pennant run, which may have also hurt his chances for the award. (Photo courtesy of the Chippewa Valley Museum, Eau Claire, WI.)

Bobby Brown spent two successful seasons pitching for Eau Claire. He went 10-5 with a 3.20 ERA for the 1951 champion Bears and followed that up with 14-10 / 3.29 performance in 1952. His best outing of 1952 is a difficult choice. With the Bears clawing for the top of the Northern League in late July, he took the ball in the first game of a double-header against St. Cloud and shut down the Rox on four hits. Manager Bill Adair asked him how he felt after the game. He felt good enough to take the hill again in game two. And he wasn't lying: he fired a three-hit shutout. A career minor leaguer, he finished a remarkable 77-39 in six professional seasons, and never had an ERA over 3.89. (Photo courtesy of Al Facchini.)

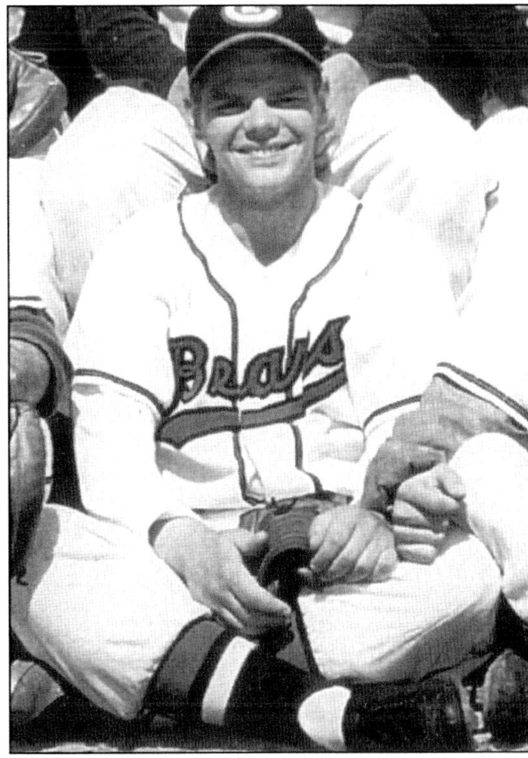

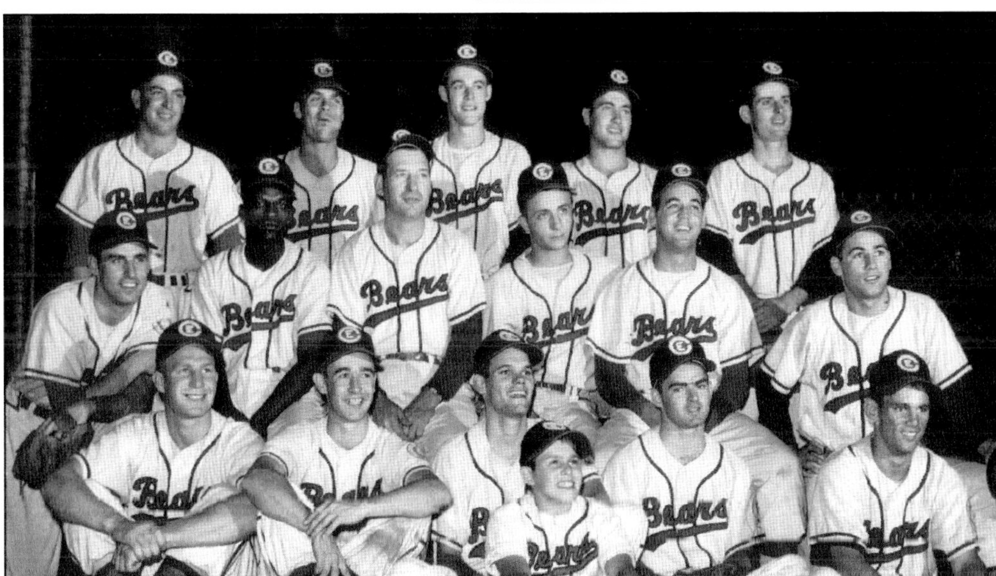

The last season the Eau Claire squad was known as the Bears, 1953, was a disappointment for fans spoiled by the previous year's excitement. The team finished a dismal 49-77 under first-year manager Rex Carr. From left to right: (front row) Ray Harbaugh, Wes Sell, Jack Lutz, Butch McLaughlin, and Virgil Tieken; (middle row) Charlie Wrinn, Julie Bowers, Rex Carr, Joe Stopa, Mike DelPiano, and Bill McKeon; (back row) Bill Colby, Lantz Blaney, George Edwards, Sam Long, and Don Straub. (Photo courtesy of Virgil Tieken.)

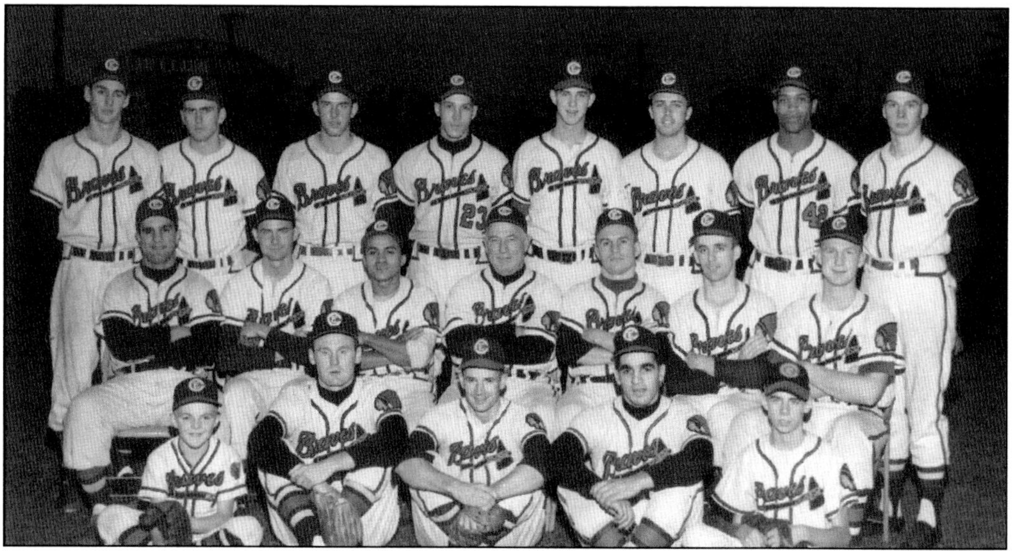

In 1954, in response to the Boston franchise moving to Milwaukee, Eau Claire changed their team name to "Braves." The team finished in fourth place under manager Charlie Root, a nice improvement from the dismal 1953 season. From left to right: (front row) S. Erickson (bat boy), Bill DuBrava, Charles Graham, Frank Benevides, and B. Nelson (bat boy); (middle row) Frank Calo, Jack Schlarb, Bill Figueroa, Charlie Root, Jim Mertlik, Ray Lague, and Ray Harbaugh; (back row) Georges Maranda, Gene Schiller, Al Zebrowski, Bill Wright, Vic Rehm, Bill Robertson, Rufus "Tippy" Johnson, and Don Edinger. (Photo courtesy of the Chippewa Valley Museum, Eau Claire, WI.)

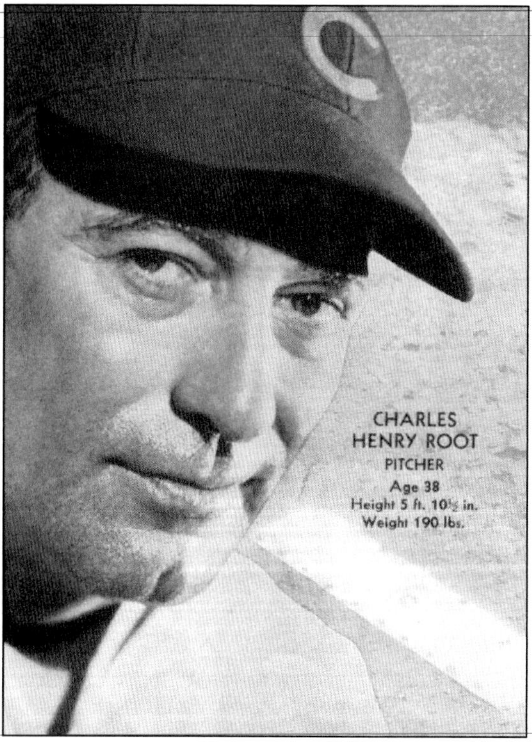

Famous for being the pitcher for Babe Ruth's "Called Shot" in the 1932 World Series, Charlie Root had heard enough by the time he was managing Eau Claire in 1954. Frank Benevides, who played for Root that season in Eau Claire: "We just knew we couldn't bring it up around him." (Author's collection—a 1937 Chicago Cubs autograph book.)

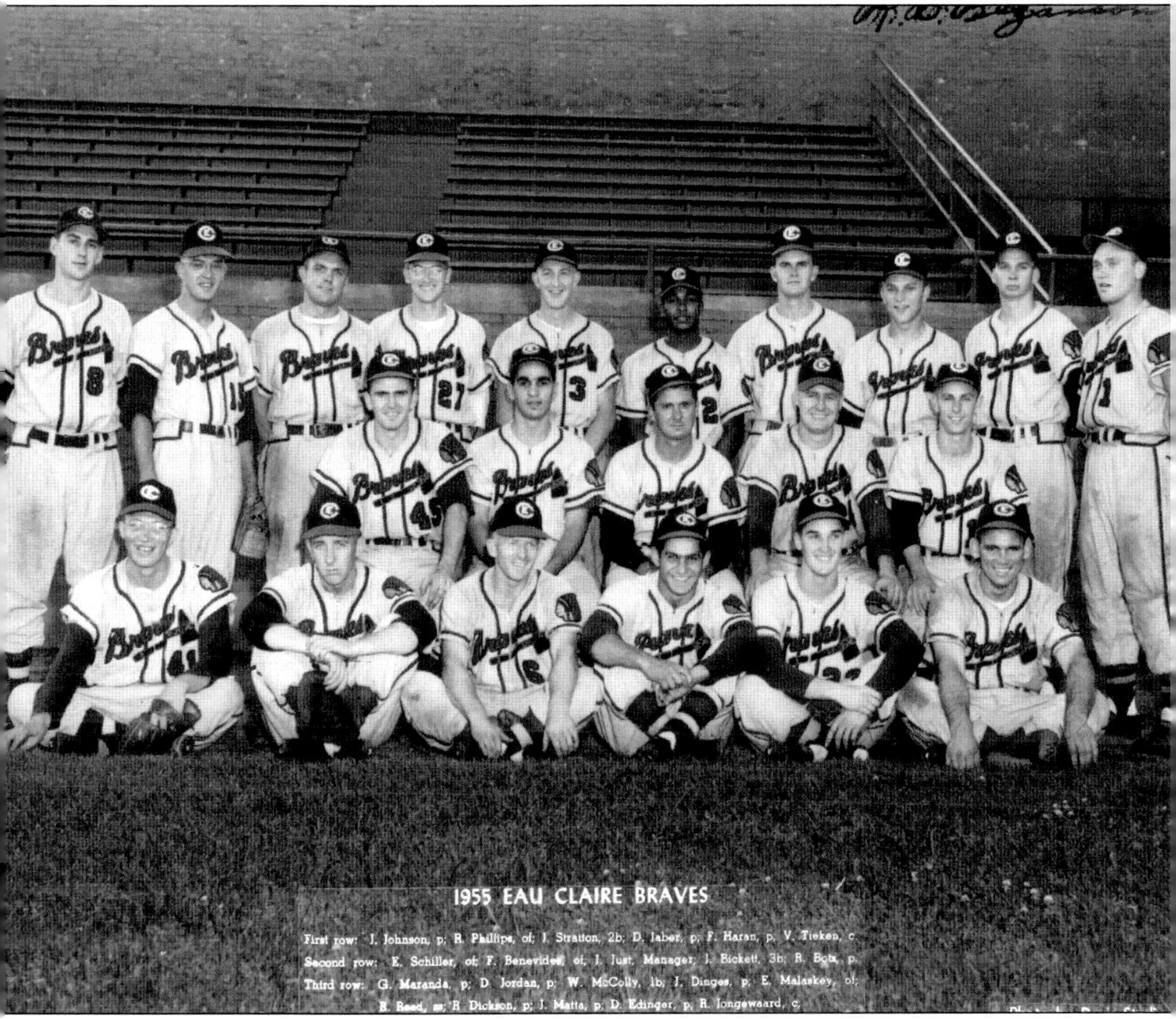

Under Joe Just, the 1955 Braves charged to an 81-43 record and the regular season pennant. Truly a team effort, Eau Claire had no major superstars that year but played one of the best seasons in the city's history. John Stratton, Dick Phillips, and Roger Jongewaard all made the All-Star squad that year, while Lee Maye, Bob Botz, and Georges Maranda would all reach the major leagues. From left to right: (front row) ? Johnson, Dick Phillips, John Stratton, Don Jaber, Frank Horan, and Virgil Tieken; (middle row) Gene Schiller, Frank Benevides, Joe Just, Jack Bickett, and Bob Botz; (back row) Georges Maranda, Don Jordan, Bill McColly, Jim Dinges, Ed Molaskey, Ray Reed, Richard Dickson, John Matta, Don Edinger, and Roger Jongewaard. (Photo Courtesy of the Chippewa Valley Museum, Eau Claire, WI.)

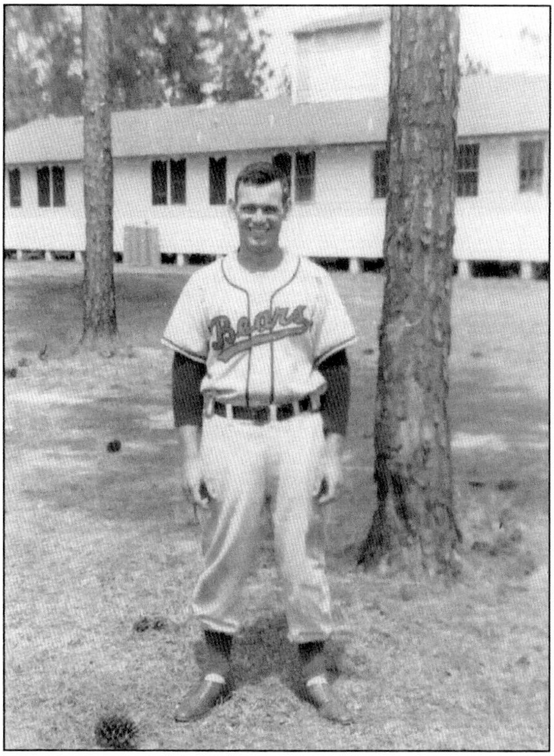

Virgil "Deacon" Tieken played from 1953 to 1957, and he spent at least some time in Eau Claire for four of those five years. Tieken is shown here in spring training in 1955. (Photo Courtesy of Virgil Tieken.)

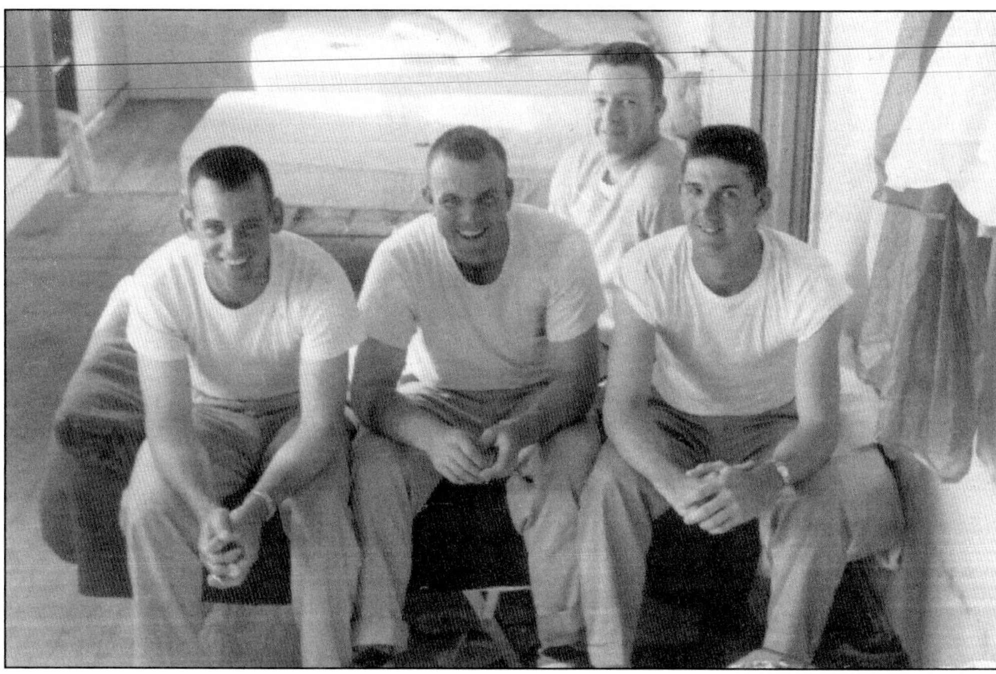

Pictured, from left to right, are Virgil Tieken, Bill McColly, Bill Rittman, and Mike Walsh. This was taken in a bunkhouse (known as "the teepee") for players at spring training in 1955 in Waycross, Georgia. Tieken and McColly would be assigned to Eau Claire that season. Walsh had hit .286 in a brief stop in Eau Claire in 1954. (Photo courtesy of Virgil Tieken.)

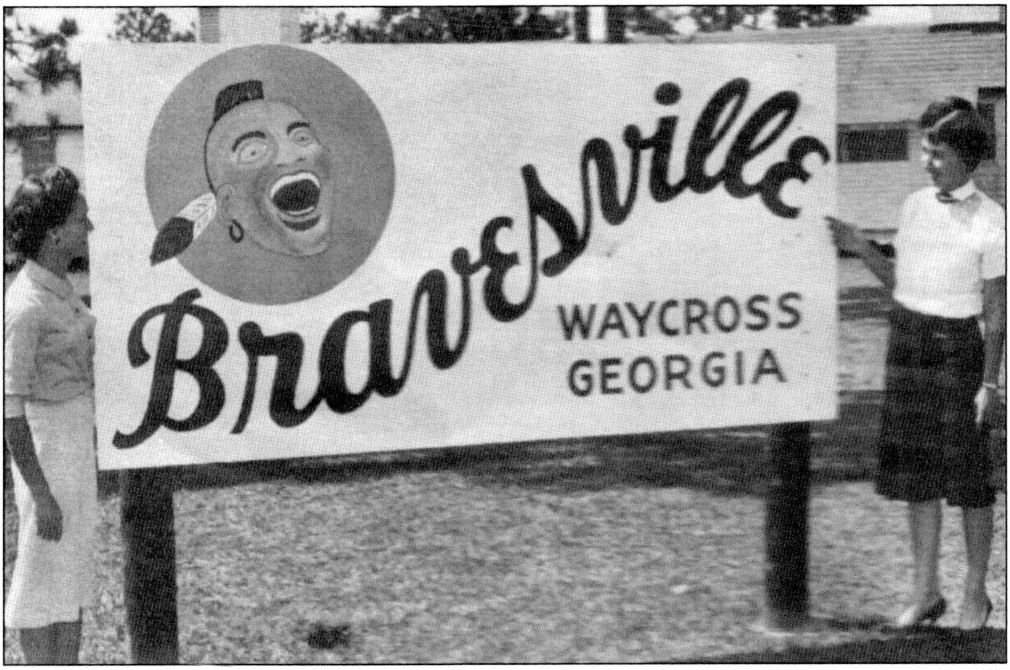

Despite the amount of money he and many teammates signed for, Bob Botz still nervously joined his teammates at spring training in Waycross, Georgia weekly to look at a bulletin board. Botz describes the scene: "Oh, am I on the Greyhound Squad today? No? Good! I didn't get cut!" Waycross was the long time home of Braves training camp. (Author's collection—*1961 Milwaukee Braves Yearbook*.)

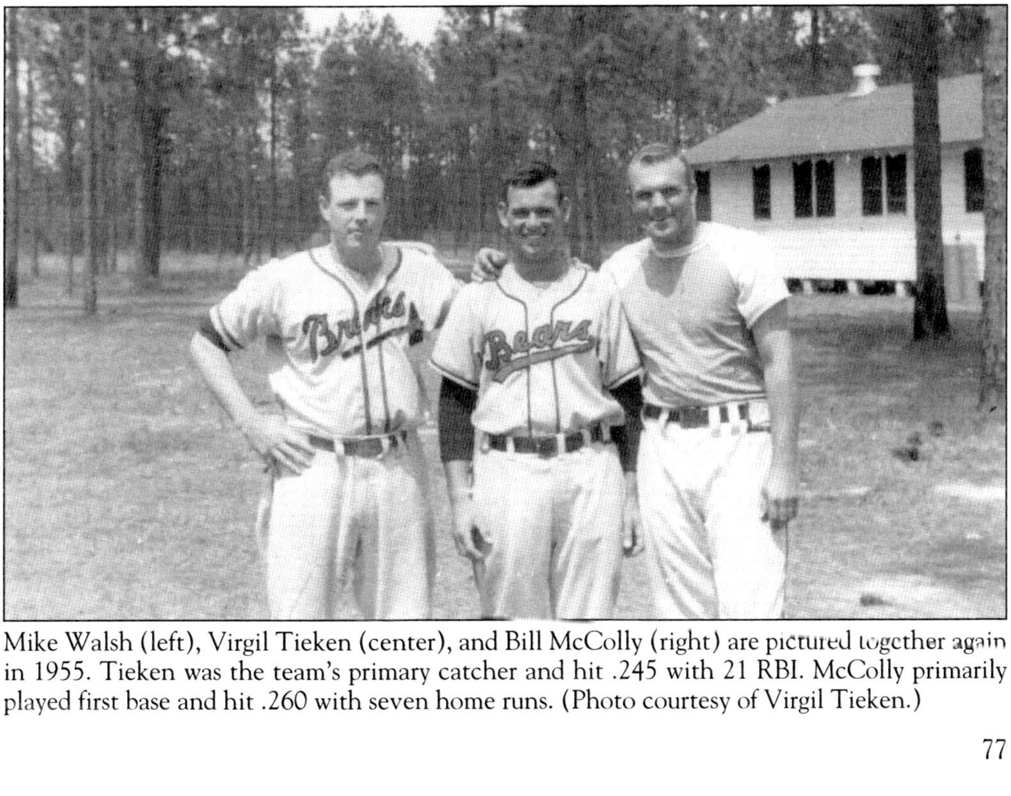

Mike Walsh (left), Virgil Tieken (center), and Bill McColly (right) are pictured together again in 1955. Tieken was the team's primary catcher and hit .245 with 21 RBI. McColly primarily played first base and hit .260 with seven home runs. (Photo courtesy of Virgil Tieken.)

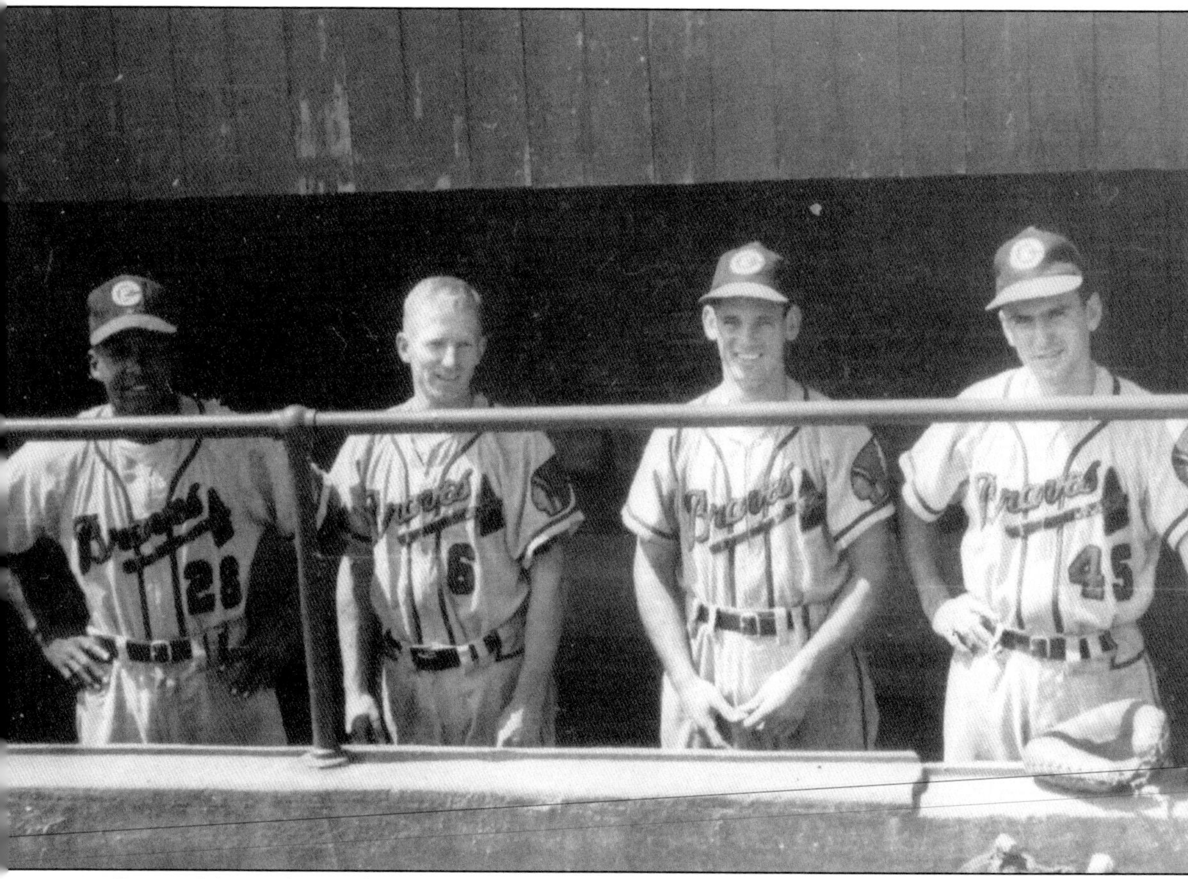

Pictured during the regular season of 1955 in Superior, Wisconsin, from left to right are Ray Reed, Johnny Stratton, Virgil Tieken, and Gene Schiller. Reed played sparingly in 1955 but would lead the 1956 team with a .337 average. California native Stratton started at second base for most of the season and led the team in homers with 16, more than double his nearest teammate. Schiller hit over .300 in 1954 and 1955 for Eau Claire. (Photo courtesy of Virgil Tieken.)

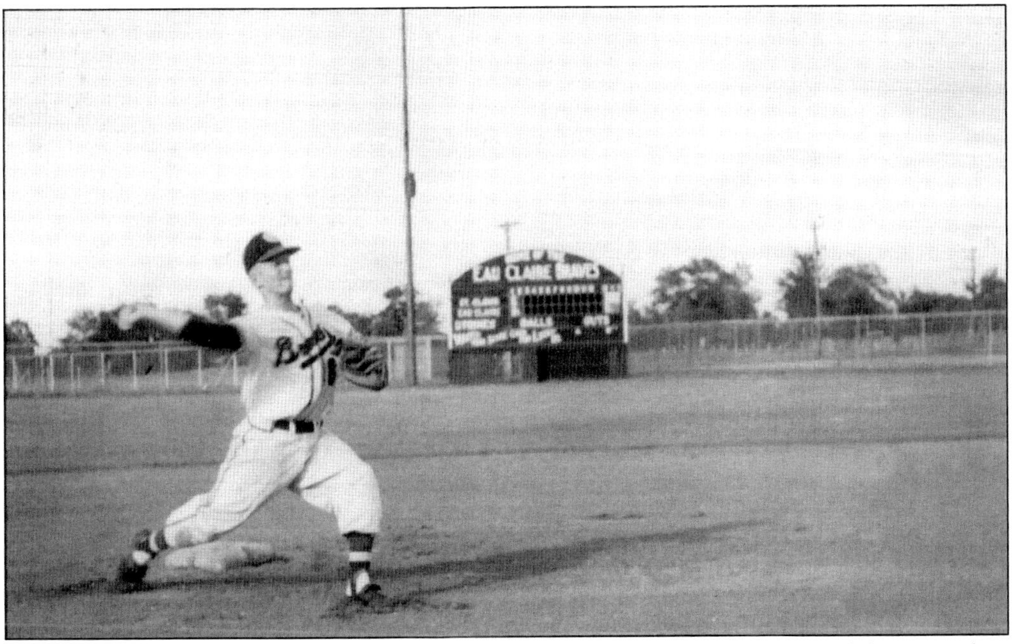

Johnny Stratton is shown here "turning two" before a game at Carson Park. Along with his potent bat, Stratton could also be counted on for his consistent defense. (Photo courtesy of Virgil Tieken.)

Eau Claire was one of four minor league stops for Lee Maye in the 1955 season. He hit .211/0/2 in very limited action for the Eau Claire Braves. He made his Major League debut in 1959 with Milwaukee and played in the majors until 1971. Maye was also an accomplished singer. His band, Arthur Lee Maye and the Crowns, cut several albums over the years. (Author's collection—*1961 Milwaukee Braves Yearbook.*)

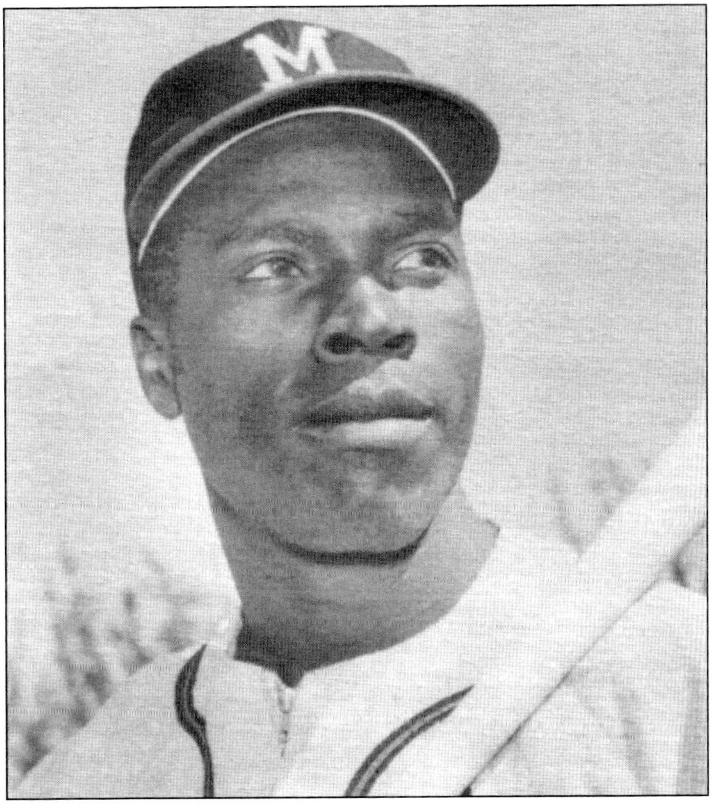

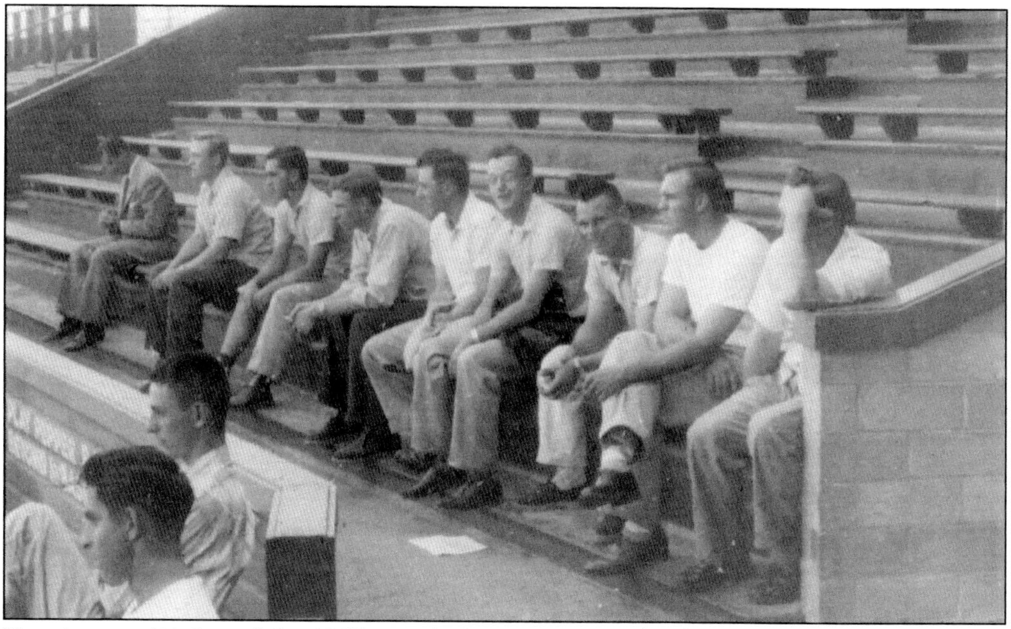

Here is a candid shot of the 1955 team before a game at Aberdeen. From left to right: (front row) Don Jaber and Bob Botz; (back row) Joe Just, Roger Jongewaard, Frank Benevides, Don Edinger, Pete Marashio, Don Gordon, Virgil Tieken, Bill McColly, and Charles Hoffses. (Photo courtesy of Virgil Tieken.)

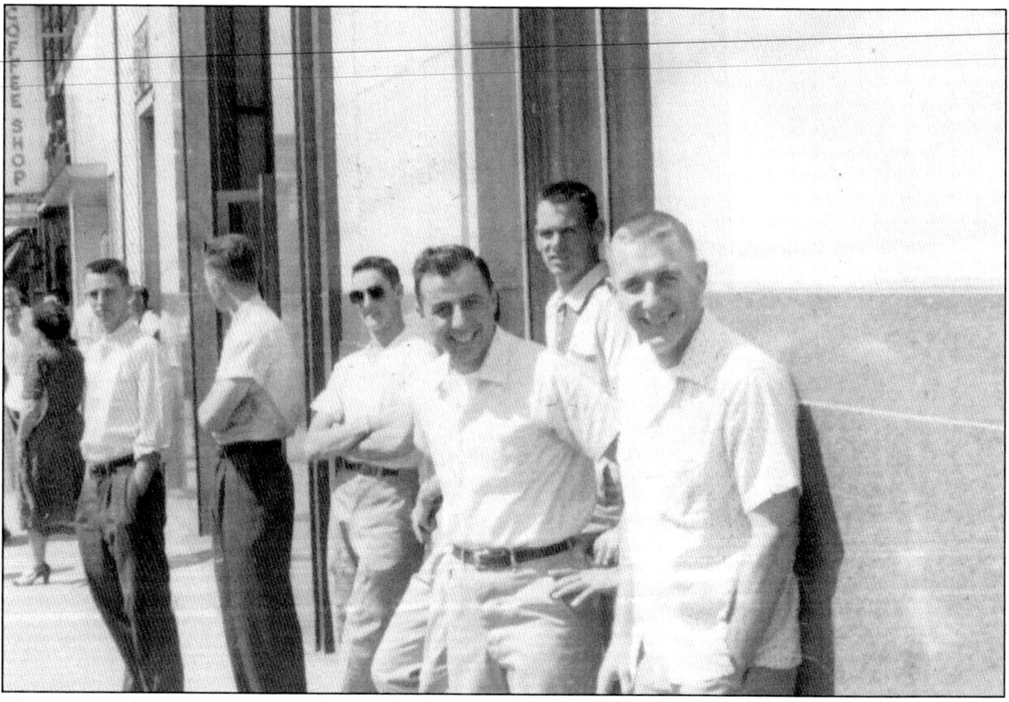

Watching a holiday parade in front of a bank in beautiful downtown Eau Claire are members of the 1955 team. From left to right are Dick Phillips, Pete Marashio, Frank Horan, Virgil Tieken, Ed Banach, and Bob Botz. (Photo Courtesy of Virgil Tieken.)

Bob Botz signed his first contract for $3,999 per year. According to the rules, had he signed for one dollar more he would have had to spend two years on a major league roster. His first stop on the way to the majors was Eau Claire in 1955. He thought the playing field at Carson Park was the best in the Northern League, but had one complaint: "The clubhouse was small and we ran out of hot water really quick, so after a game you'd have to race in and take a quick shower or you'd end up in the cold." (Author's collection—*1961 Milwaukee Braves Yearbook.*)

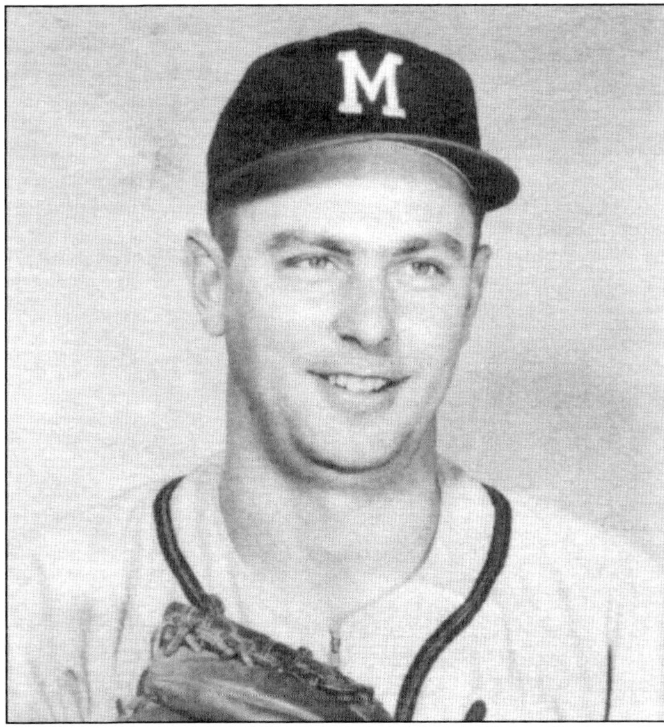

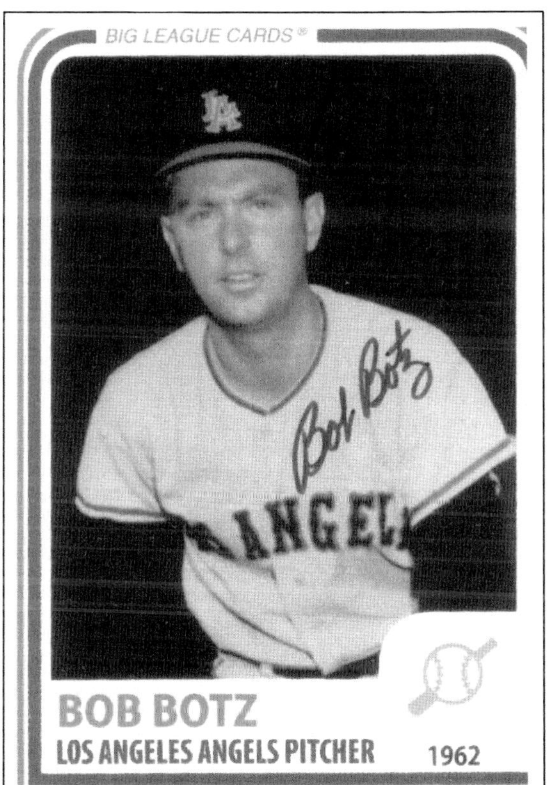

Wisconsin's own Bob Botz used his pinpoint control to make it to the majors in 1962 with the fledgling Los Angeles Angels. He did an outstanding job in his only Big League season, pitching in 35 games, all in relief, going 2-1 with a 3.43 ERA. He struck out 25 and walked only 11 in 63 innings. (Photo Courtesy of Bob Botz.)

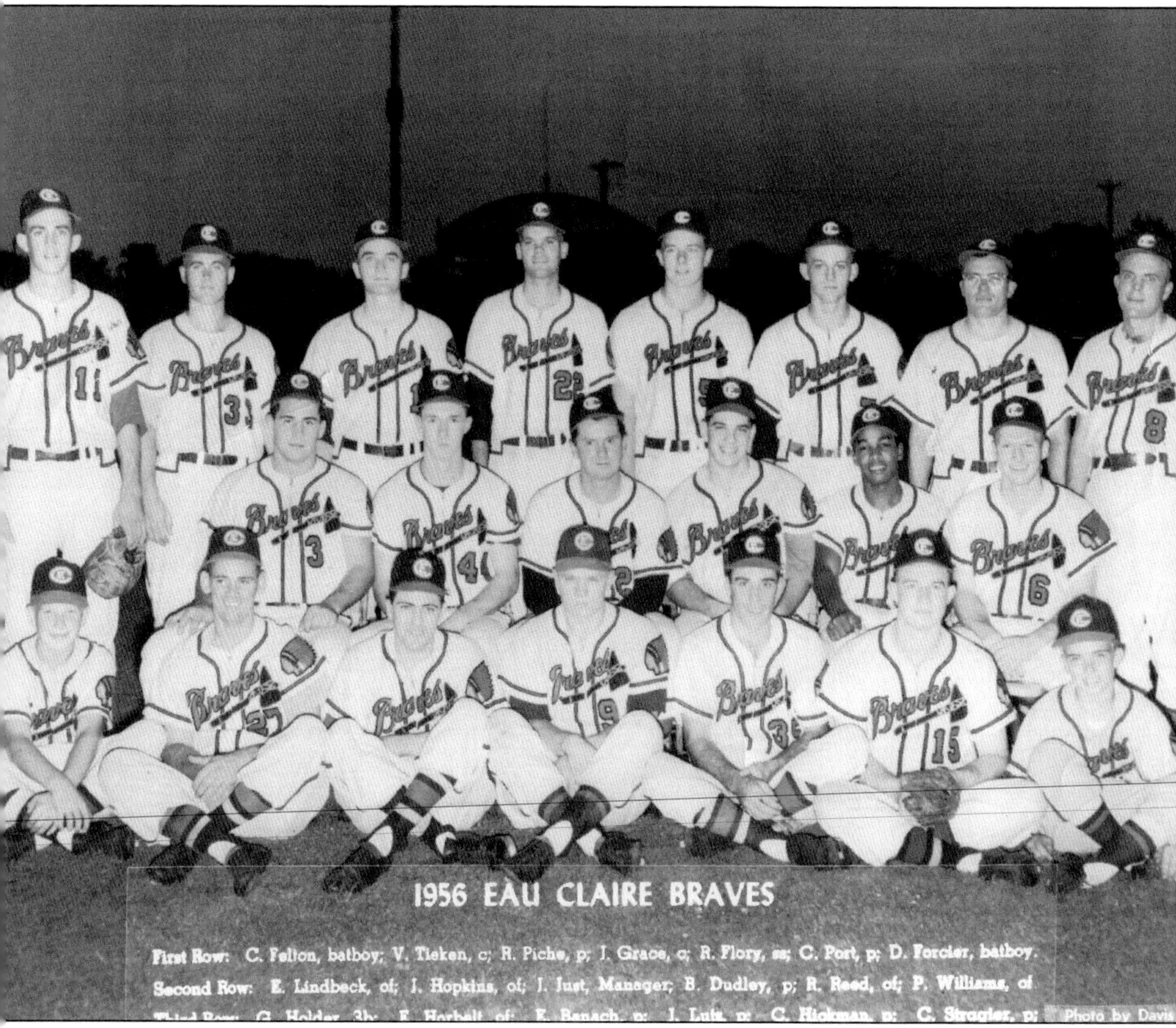

Joe Just led the 1956 team to the Northern League pennant as the Braves finished 70-52 before falling to Duluth-Superior in the playoffs. From left to right: (front row) ? Felton (bat boy), Virgil Tieken, Ron Piche, John Grace, Ralph Flory, Chalmers Port, and Dan Forcier (bat boy); (middle row) Emerit Lindbeck, Jim Hopkins, Joe Just, Bob Dudley, Ray Reed, Phil Williams; (back row) George Holder, Ed Horbelt, Ed Banach, John Lutz, Clair Hickman, and Bob Stragier. (Photo Courtesy of Virgil Tieken.)

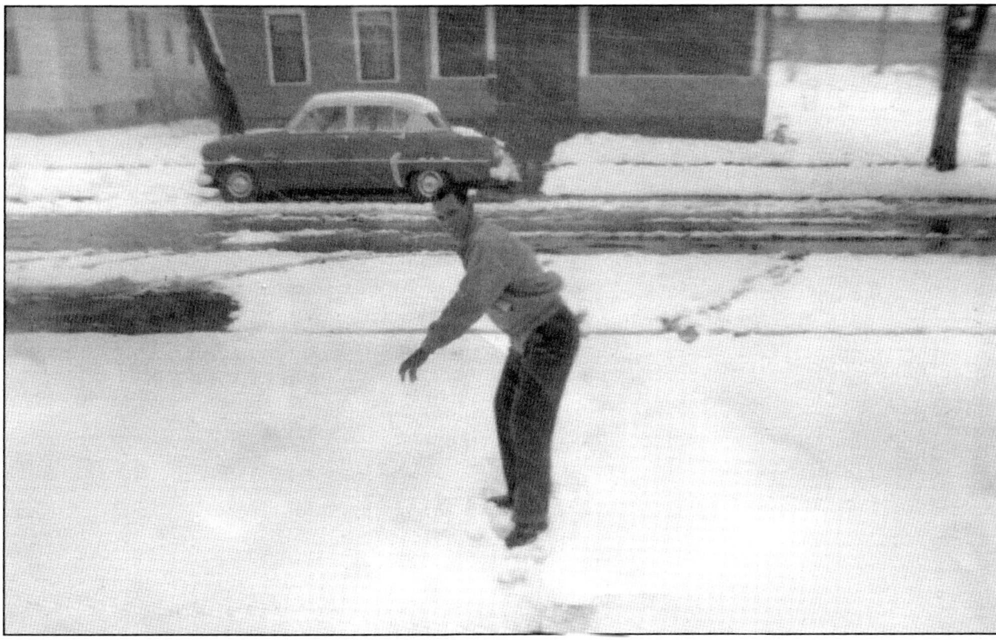

Virgil Tieken is "warming up" with a snowball on April 28th 1956—Opening Day. A heavy spring snow storm halted many Northern League games and postponed the start of the season. Near the end of the season, Tieken was voted "Most Popular Player" by the fans and given a watch as a prize. (Photo courtesy of Virgil Tieken.)

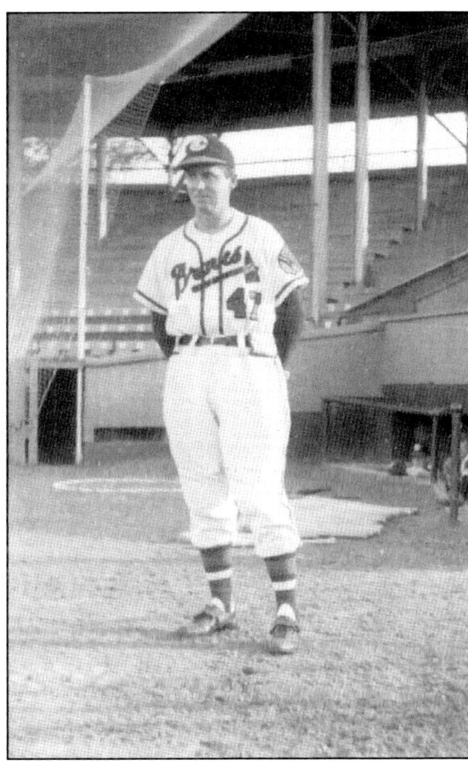

Joe Just was a catcher briefly for the Cincinnati Reds in 1944 and 1945, hitting .156 in 25 career games. He managed the Braves in 1955 and 1956, both seasons resulting in Northern League pennants for Eau Claire. (Photo courtesy of Virgil Tieken.)

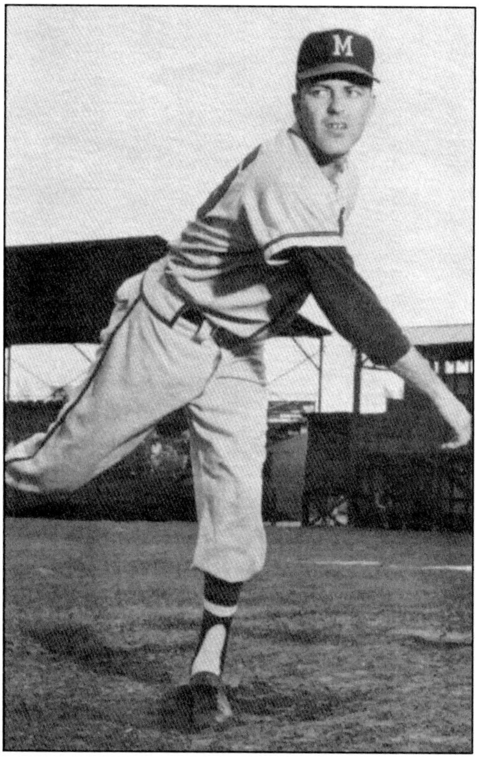

Canadian pitcher Ron Piche (pronounced "peesh") allegedly was assigned his position from his first manager, who asked where he played. Piche, still grasping English as a second language, thought the manager was asking his name, so he replied, "I Piche." Piche was a starter with Eau Claire in 1956, leading the team with a 16-7 mark and a 2.84 ERA. That season, he set a career high for innings pitched with 212. Piche found his niche (pronounced "nitch") as a reliever and played six seasons in the majors before closing out his pro career back in his home province of Quebec. (Author's collection—*1961 Milwaukee Braves Yearbook*.)

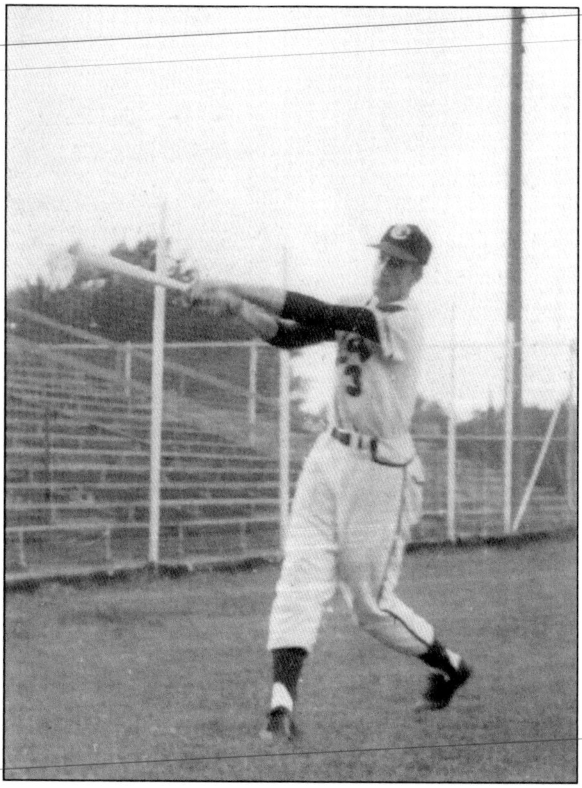

Ed Molasky played two professional seasons, both in Eau Claire. In 1955, he hit .265 with six homers and 48 RBI, and came back in 1956 to go .250/1/36 at the plate. (Photo courtesy of Virgil Tieken.)

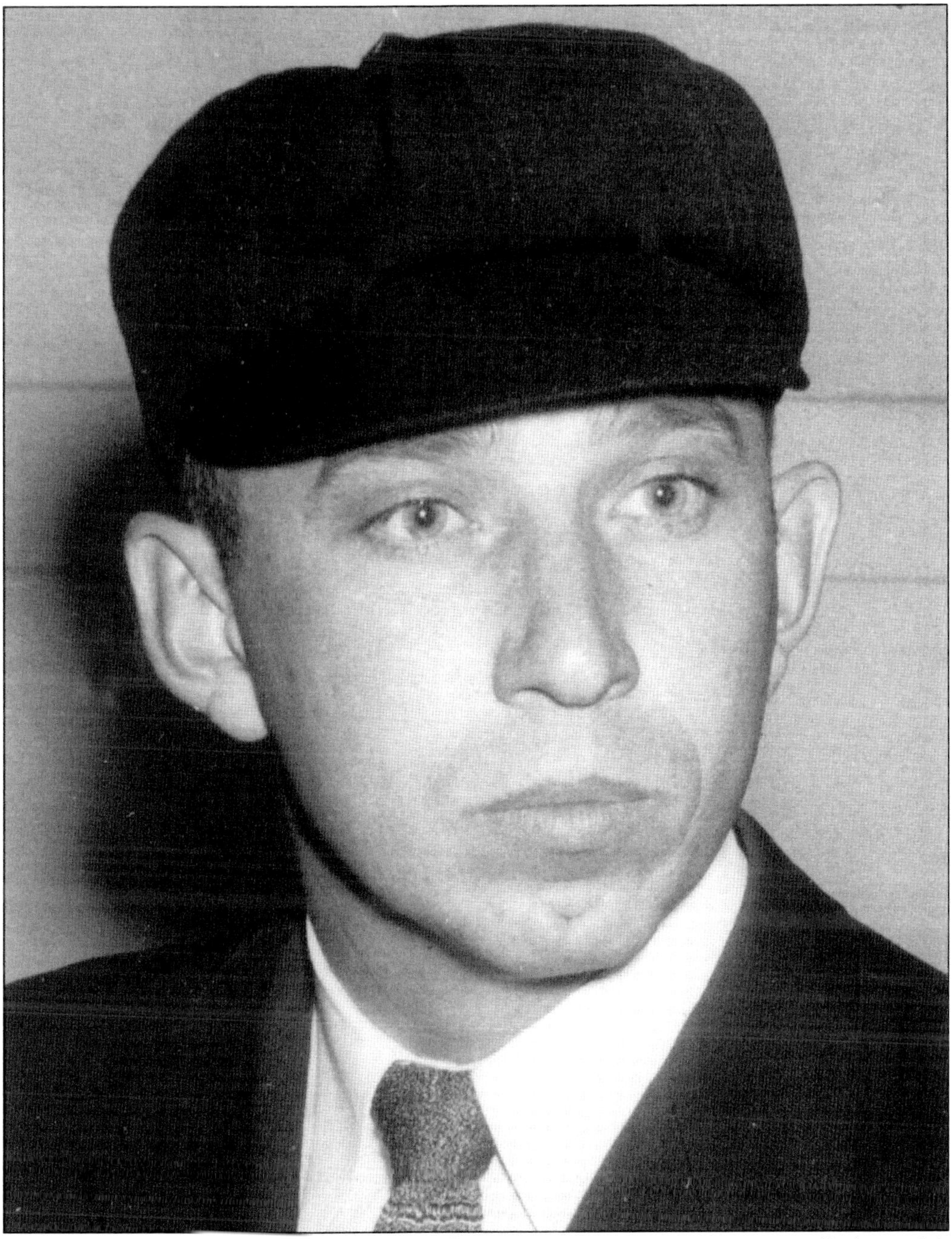

Denver Howard was an umpire in the Northern League in 1956. Umpires usually live a life of obscurity, but on June 15, 1956, EVERYBODY in Eau Claire knew Denver Howard. An appealed ruling against the Braves began the affair. Ralph Flory was the first to be ejected. Howard picks up the story: "The Eau Claire players wouldn't shut up! In the fourth I ejected Joe Just and three pitchers and Mack (McPherson Crum, the other umpire) got Ed Molaskey." Later on, Howard tossed Virgil Tieken. "I preferred Bob (Uecker) as a catcher, but he was playing second base because Flory was ejected," recalled Howard. (Photo Courtesy: Eau Claire Leader-Telegram. Quote from Howard's unpublished book *Twenty-Twenty Was Not Enough.*)

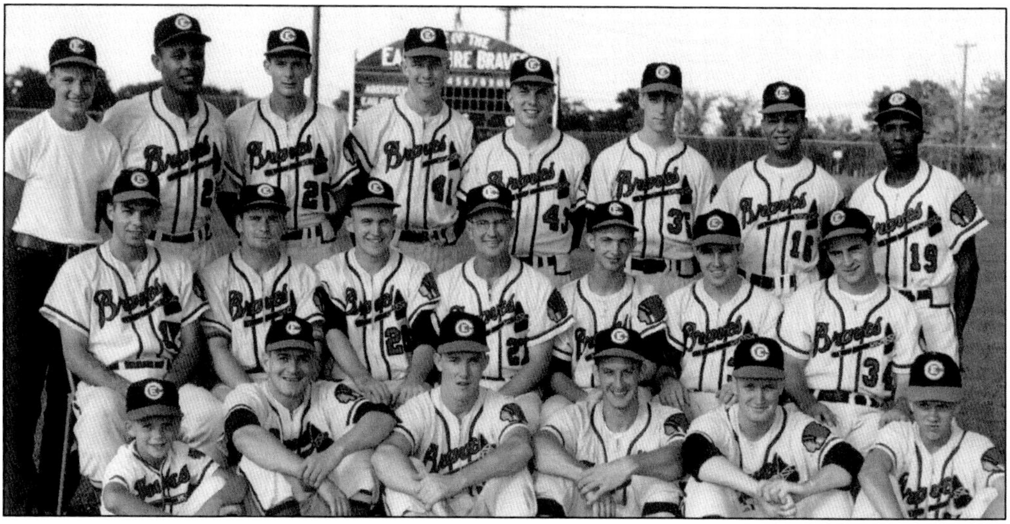

Gordon Maltzberger began his Eau Claire managerial tenure in 1957, leading the team to a 70-55 mark and third place, a mere half game from second place and a trip to the playoffs. Shortstop Juan Guzman was selected to the All-Star game on the strength of his .323 average, while Florida native Ross Carter led the staff with a 14-9 record, throwing most of the season to a young catcher named Bob Uecker, whose 12 homers were second on the team. From left to right: (front row) P. Moehle (bat boy), Fred Hoffman, Jim Hopkins, Bob Uecker, Ross Carter, and L. Taylor (bat boy); (middle row) Don Carter, Doug Smith, Bill Hamilton, Gordon Maltzberger, Bob Fleer, Ed Rynn, and Emerit Lindbeck; (back row) Jerry Baader (clubhouse boy), Howard Rouse, Dan Staniec, Clair Hickman, Bill Walsh, Bob Lee, Roberto Barbosa, and Frank Ensley. (Photo courtesy of the Chippewa Valley Museum, Eau Claire, WI.)

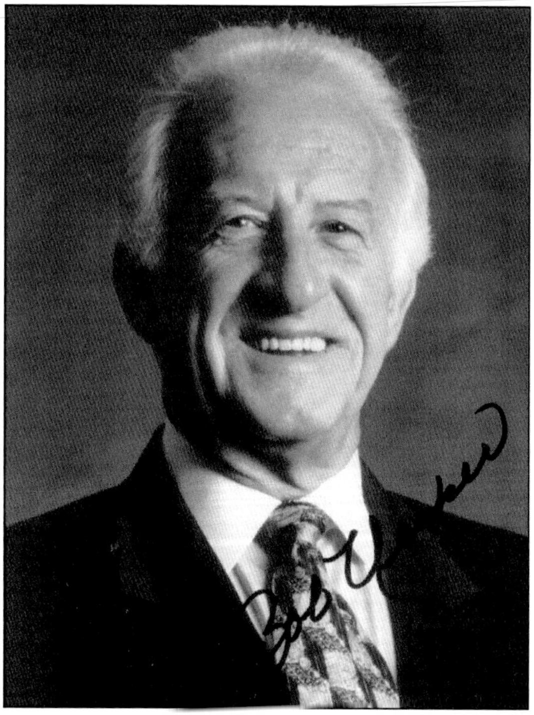

His own worst critic, Bob Uecker was always looked on favorably by his contemporaries. Especially the ones who weren't his teammates! Seriously, Uecker's .200 career batting average unfairly overshadows his ability to call and catch a great game. He began broadcasting Milwaukee Brewers baseball in 1971 and is still going strong. In 2003, he was honored with the Ford Frick Award for Broadcasting Excellence, which lands this former Eau Claire Brave in the Hall of Fame. (Photo courtesy of the Milwaukee Brewers.)

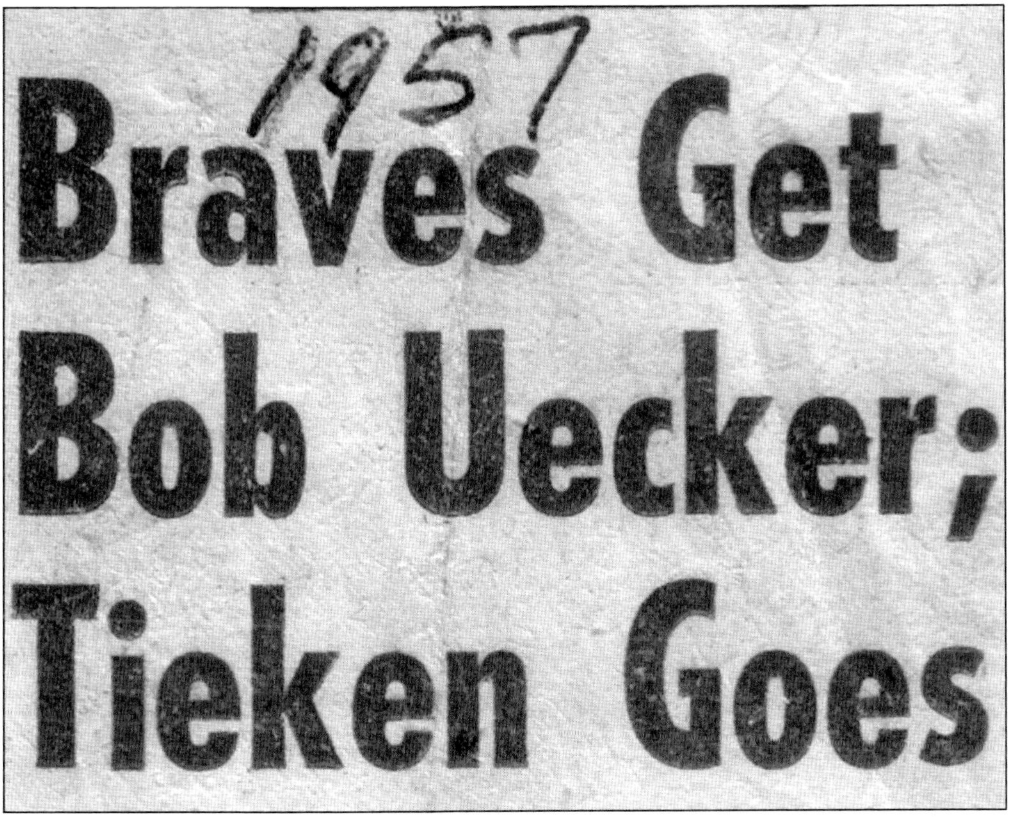

1957

Braves Get Bob Uecker; Tieken Goes

The unkindest cut of all for Virgil Tieken? Not really—Uecker would hit .284 with 12 homers for Eau Claire in 1957. (Photo Courtesy of the *Eau Claire Leader-Telegram.*)

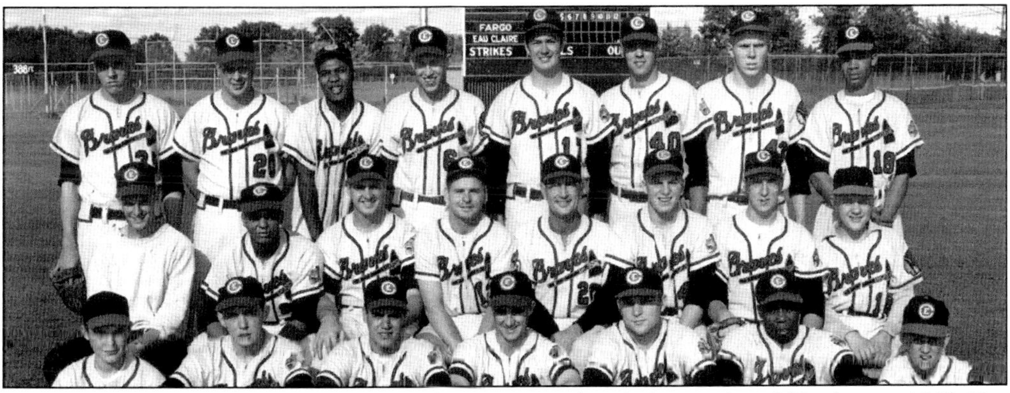

With a record of 65-56, Eau Claire could have expected to do better than fifth place in 1958. But that's exactly what they got. Ernie Christoff led the pitchers with a 15-4 record and a 2.80 ERA, while outfielder Manny Jimenez, the only All-Star selection for the team, led the loop with a .340 average. From left to right: (front row) Jim Burgess (ball boy), Steve Ryder, Chico Perez, Gayle Moore, John Matta, Tommie Aaron, and Tim Reilly (bat boy); (middle row) Jerry Baader (clubhouse boy), Roberto Barbosa, Bruno Terilli, Doug Smith, Gordon Maltzberger, Bob Warner, Bob Lee, and Scott Roberts (ball boy); (back row) Hud Gelein, Pete Peterson, Manuel Jimenez, Paul Poole, Ernie Christoff, Rich Ramont, Larry Maxie, and Cal Henry. (Photo courtesy of the Chippewa Valley Museum, Eau Claire, WI.)

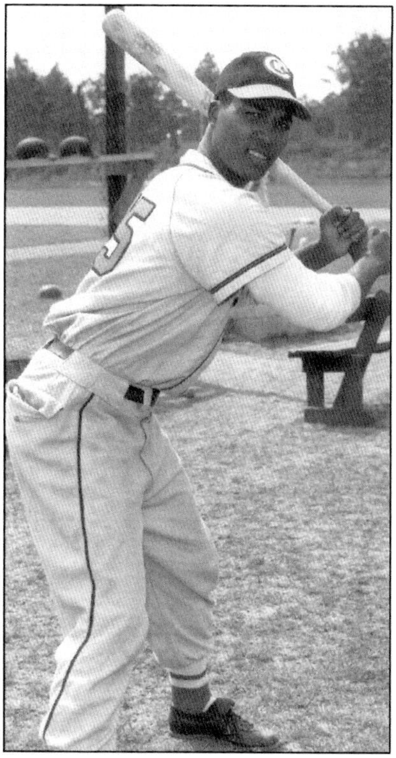

Outfielder Manuel Jimenez was a hitting machine for Eau Claire in 1958, clubbing the ball at a .340 clip with 15 homers and 71 RBI. As it was for several other players, Eau Claire was Jimenez's first stop on the way to the majors. The Braves organization traded him to the Kansas City A's and he admittedly was upset the team had given up on him. He used that treatment as motivation in his first year in the majors, and he put together a .301 average in 1962, good enough for ninth in the American League. He would play until 1969, making stops with the Pirates and Cubs along the way but never recapturing the magic of his rookie season. (Photo Courtesy of the *Eau Claire Leader-Telegram*.)

Tony Cloninger received $100,000 to sign with the Braves, so his stay in Eau Claire was short (2-2 in six games) in 1958 before moving on to Midland. But the money wasn't the reason everybody knew he would eventually make the major leagues. Catcher Wayne Jinske, who worked with Cloninger at spring training and would be in Eau Claire himself in 1962, complained that Cloninger would "kill your hands. I used to use a new mitt and two 'falsies' to catch him! He'd tear your hand off!" (Author's collection.)

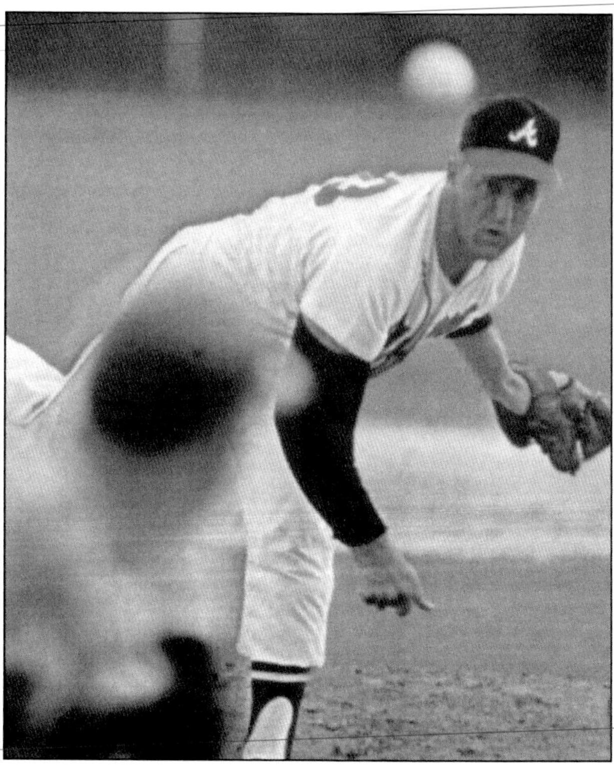

Tony Cloninger liked to hit. In his 12-year major league career, his batting average doesn't look all that impressive (.192) but he was much more than the automatic out expected from the nine slot in the order. On July 3, 1966, Tony hit a home run with the bases loaded. Later on in the game, he did it again! It was the first time any player, let alone a pitcher, hit two grand slams in the same game. (Author's collection—*1961 Milwaukee Braves Yearbook.*)

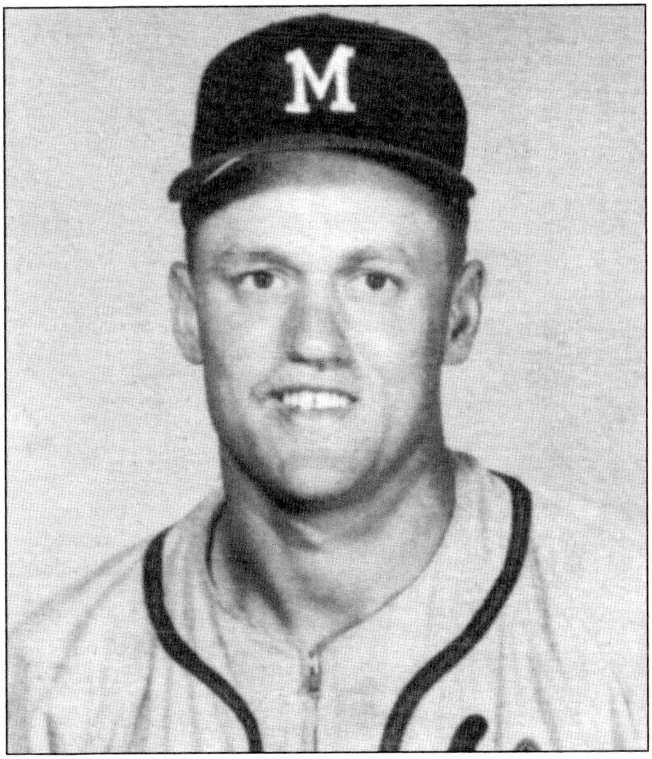

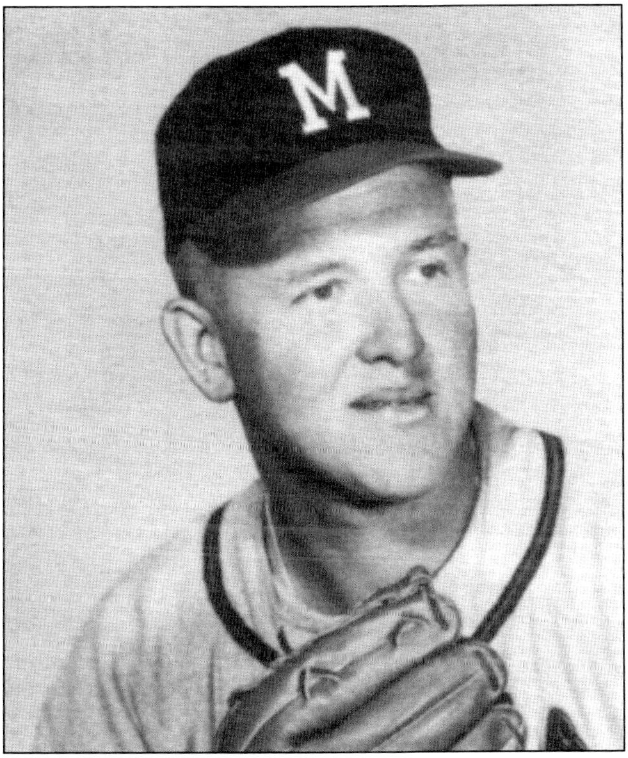

Denver LeMaster appeared in only six games for Eau Claire in 1958, but that was enough for him to register two complete games, a 4-2 record, and a nifty 2.82 ERA. LeMaster progressed through the Braves' minor league system, impressing Milwaukee's top brass all along the way, before finally making his major league debut in 1962. Unfortunately, he developed a sore arm in 1965 that troubled him for the rest of his career. Still, he was an All-Star for the Atlanta Braves in 1967 and he finished his career in 1971 with a sparkling 3.58 career ERA. (Author's collection—*1961 Milwaukee Braves Yearbook.*)

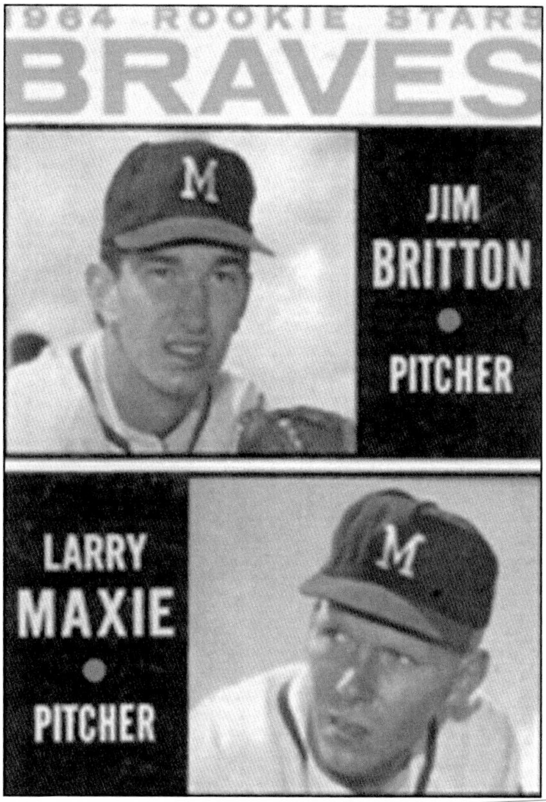

Larry Maxie toiled in the minors for eleven seasons before finally making his major league debut in August of 1969. He would pitch three innings for Atlanta before returning to the minors, where he would remain until he retired in 1972 (going 13-6 with a 1.54 ERA his final season). Like so many others, his journey to the majors began in Eau Claire. Maxie's 3.61 ERA was among the best on the 1958 staff and a better indicator of how he pitched than his 1-5 record. (Photo courtesy of The Topps Company, Inc.)

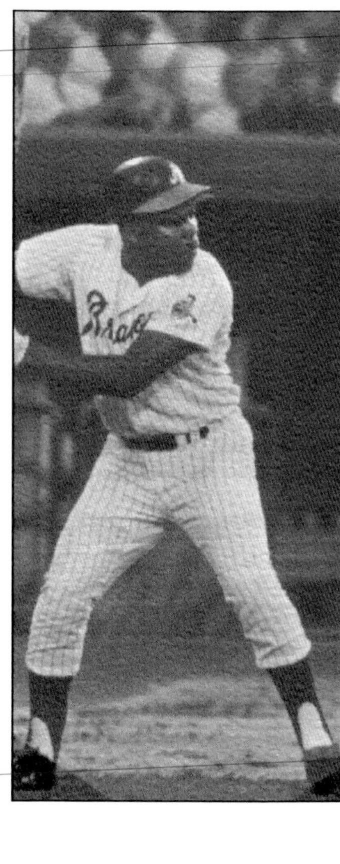

In his book A *False Spring*, Pat Jordan wrote of Henry Aaron's younger brother Tommy: "Tommy was bigger than Hank and looked stronger. He had Hank's quick wrists, too, only every time Tommy swung a bat and hit the ball firmly, the ball hooked foul into the left field stands." In what was likely both wonderful and difficult all at the same time, Tommy Aaron lived in the shadow of his brother. After hitting .274 with three home runs and 33 RBI in his first pro season for Eau Claire in 1958, he came back in 1959 to wallop 26 homers—the single season professional record in Eau Claire. (Author's collection.)

A rare find—an unused ticket from an Opening Day game in Eau Claire. The downtown area would typically close up shops for Opening Day. This particular ticket is from 1959, and since the team finished in seventh place, 26 games out of first, it's quite possible the holder of this ticket had more fun by *not* going to the game! (Author's collection.)

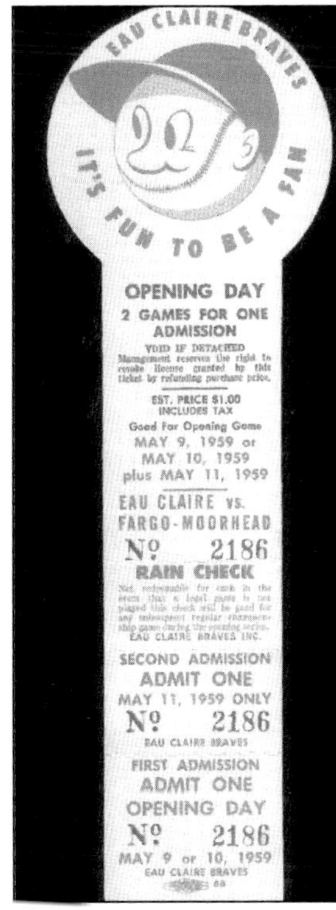

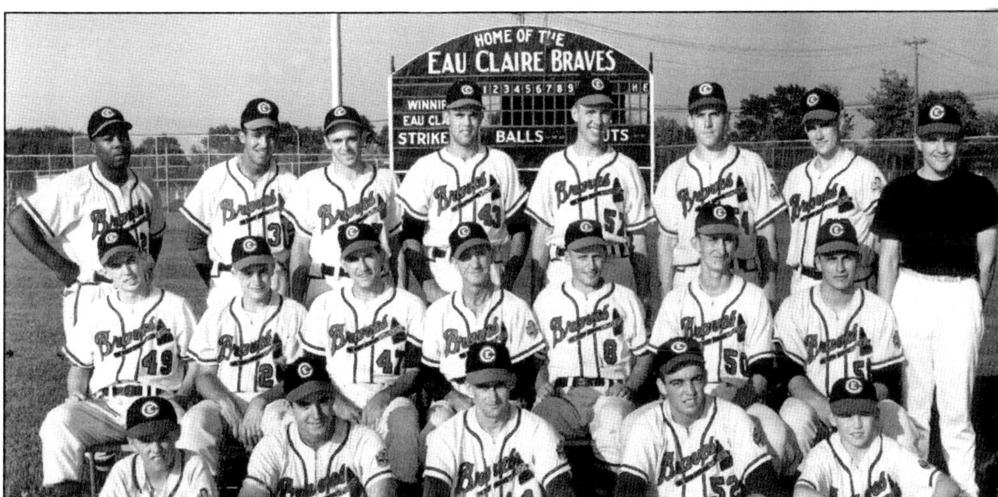

The 1959 Braves, as seen very early on in the season (notice the traces of optimism in the players' faces, a look which would erode away quickly as the team finished 26 games out of first place). Actually, the reason this is identified as an early season photo is the fact that Travis Jackson is the manager. He was replaced by Robert Dudley for a short while, and then Gordon Maltzberger returned by season's end. From left to right: (front row) John Melby (bat boy), Doug "Ty" Clayton, John Huda, Hank Fischer, and Connie Bradison (bat boy); (middle row) Steve Ryder, Wayne Wilson, Jim Davins, Travis Jackson, Orie Wolf, Chuck Duren, Larry Huebner, and Scott McRoberts (clubhouse boy); (back row) Tommie Aaron, Ed Lawrence, Gene Johnson, Rich Ramont, Bill Marnie, Joe Shields, and Jack Redway. (Photo courtesy of the Chippewa Valley Museum, Eau Claire, WI.)

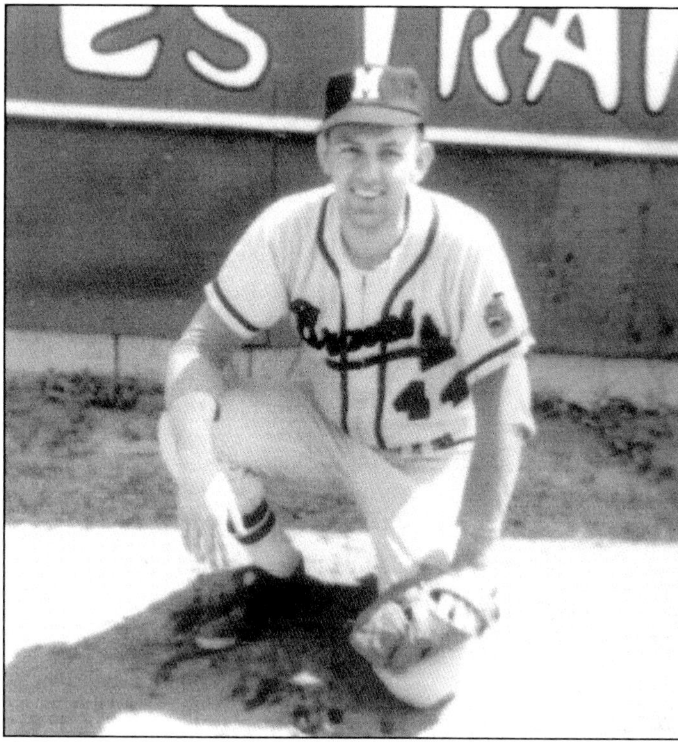

Although his professional baseball career lasted only three seasons, Ted Budzik made the most of that time. The Ohio native won eleven games for Batvia in his first season in 1957, and ten more for the same club the following year. Budzik went 4-4 for Eau Claire's tumultuous 1959 squad. (Photo Courtesy of Ted Budzik.)

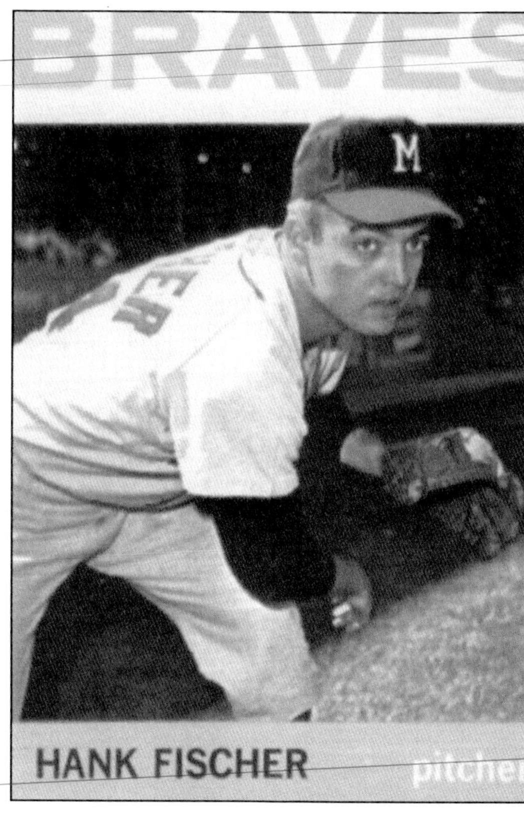

Nicknamed "Bulldog", Hank Fischer was fast-tracked to the Milwaukee Braves, appearing in only twelve games and going 1-2 for Eau Claire before moving on to Cedar Rapids in 1959. Armed with a good fastball and decent curve, he struck out 217 for Cedar Rapids to lead the 3-I League in 1960. Fischer made it to Milwaukee in 1962 and threw five shutouts for the Braves in 1964. Bulldog retired with Boston in 1967 with a career major league record of 30-39 and a 4.23 ERA. (Photo Courtesy of The Topps Company, Inc.)

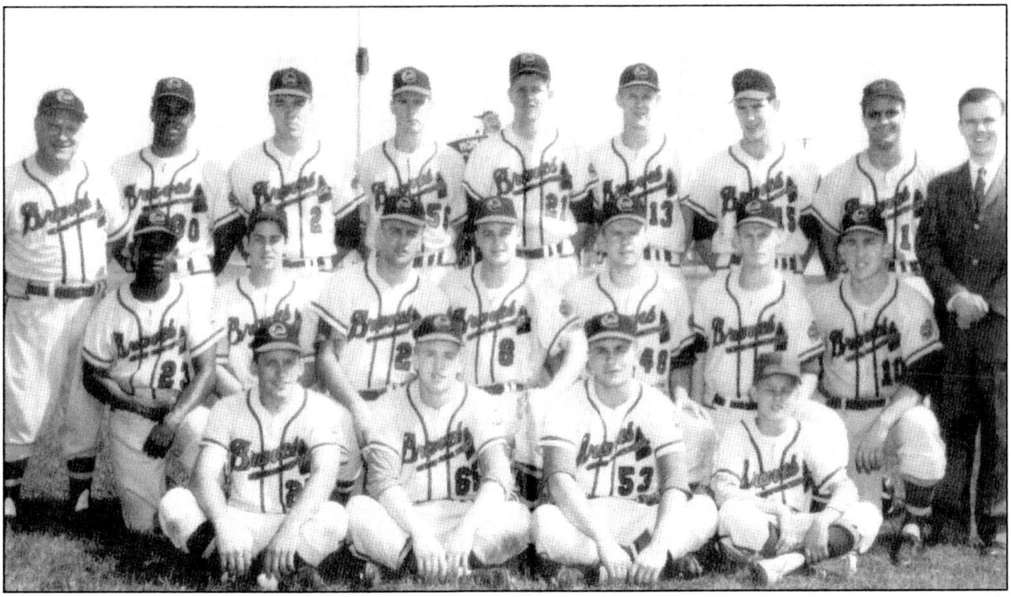

The 1960 Braves finished in a tie for sixth place with Fargo Moorehead with a 58-66 record. Winnipeg won the pennant that year and didn't lose a game in the playoffs. From left to right: (first row) Orie Wolf, Dan Newman, Larry Huebner, and ? Johnson (bat boy); (middle row) Rafael Gomez, Mario Diaz, Ron Liptak, Bob Jacoby, Ron Ross, Charles Carlan, and Paul Chenger; (back row) Bill Steinecke, Bill Stevens, Harold Gelein, Bob Healey, Paul Roof, Garnet Steubing, Larry Alander, Joe Torre, and ? Quinn (business manager). (Photo courtesy of Bob Healey.)

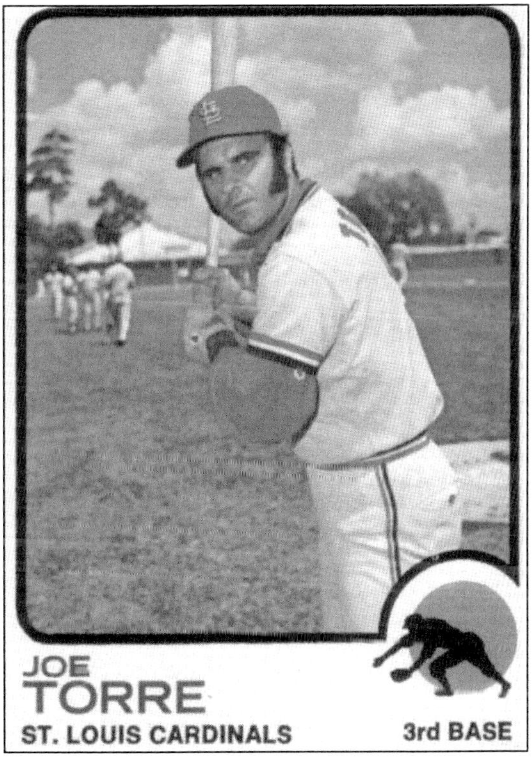

Joe Torre's rise to the major leagues was meteoric. He blistered the Northern League in 1960, hitting .344 for Eau Claire and joining first baseman Roger Morgan as Eau Claire's All-Star representatives. Torre would be called to the parent Milwaukee Braves and, on September 25, hit a single off of Pittsburgh's Harvey Haddix in his first major league at-bat. He would go on to win the National League MVP Award in 1971, and he became a successful manager after his playing career ended. (Photo courtesy of The Topps Company, Inc.)

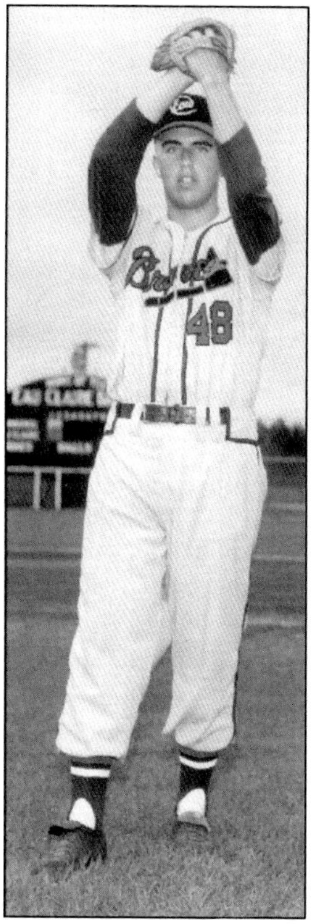

Bruce Brubaker pitched in the minors for eight years, including a brief stop in Eau Claire in 1960, before finally getting a shot at pitching in the majors. Hurling for Los Angeles, Brubaker made his debut on April 15, 1967, and the appearance was taxing. In one and a third innings, he gave up three runs and was sent back to the minors. He would return for one inning of work with the fledgling Milwaukee Brewers in 1970, giving up another run to finish his major league career with an ERA of 13.50. (Photo Courtesy of the *Eau Claire Leader-Telegram*.)

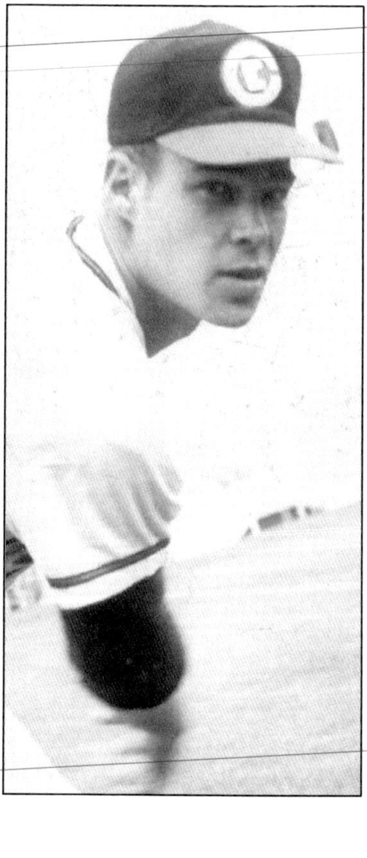

As the son of Daffy and nephew of Dizzy, Paul Dean, Jr. had some large shoes to fill. Perhaps the weight of expectation was too great, as Dean's baseball career never really got on track. With Eau Claire in 1960, he pitched sparingly and compiled a record of 2-6 with a 5.65 ERA. He would play three more years but never attained major league status. (Photo courtesy of the *Eau Claire Leader-Telegram*.)

Bob Healey had one of his best games as a professional at Carson Park in 1960. It was a one-hitter—against the Braves. It left an impression on the club, and when Minot released Healey a few weeks later, Eau Claire snapped him up. The steady Healey was mainly used out of the bullpen in 1960 and 1961 for the Braves. He was credited with two wins in the Braves' first ten games in 1961, and was among the league leaders in ERA for the first two months of that season. (Photo courtesy of Bob Healey.)

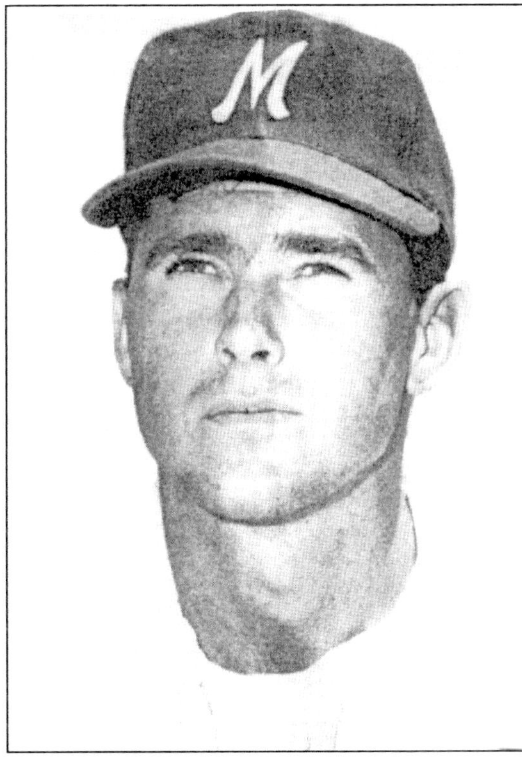

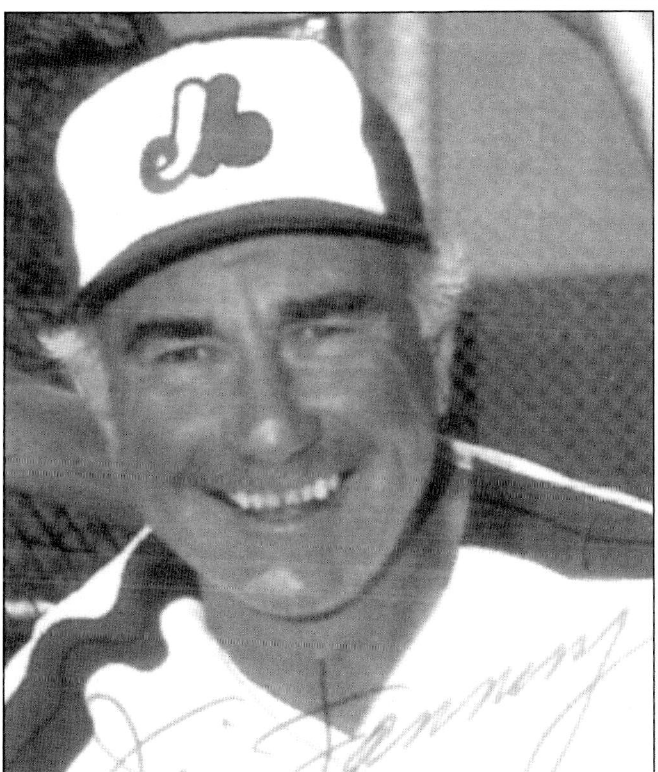

Jim Fanning was only 33 years old when he was tabbed the manager of the Braves in 1961. Though his major league playing career was short (64 games), he would stay in professional baseball into the 1990s, including a 25-year stint with the Montreal Expos. (Photo courtesy of Jim Fanning.)

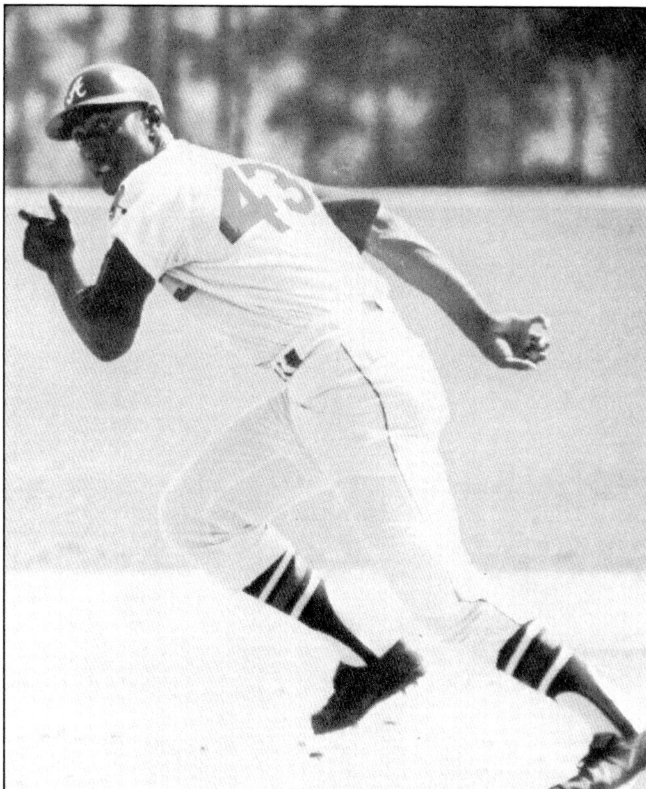

Rico Carty came to Eau Claire in 1961 after hitting just .233 for Davenport (Midwest League) in 1960. He turned it around with the Braves, hitting .298 with 11 homers and 39 RBI while playing catcher (he would later move to the outfield). "The Big Boy," as he called himself, was on his way to stardom. He led the majors in batting average in 1970, swinging at a .366 clip. Despite serious health and injury problems, he would go on to play professionally until 1979. (Author's collection.)

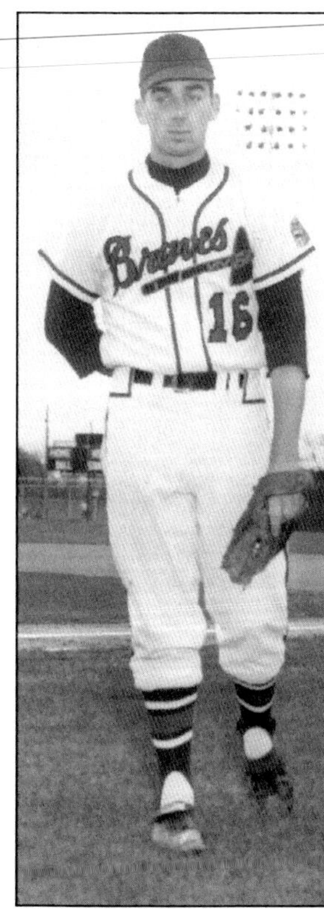

Pat Jordan's baseball career began with a lot of promise as he was signed to a $35,000 bonus by scout Jeff Jones. Immediately after signing, he was whisked to Milwaukee to have some promotional photos taken with long-time Braves ace Warren Spahn. Injuries and an inexplicable loss of control sent Jordan's career spiraling, and he was on his way out when he came to Eau Claire in 1961. The problems continued with the Braves, and eventually he was sent down to Palatka (Florida State League), where he would play out the season before retiring. The once-promising young hurler compiled a minor league career record of only 12-22. But don't cry for him: Jordan became a successful writer and has penned at least nine books (including one on his baseball career and another about a comeback attempt) to go along with freelancing for magazines such as *Sports Illustrated.* (Photo Courtesy of the *Eau Claire Leader-Telegram.*)

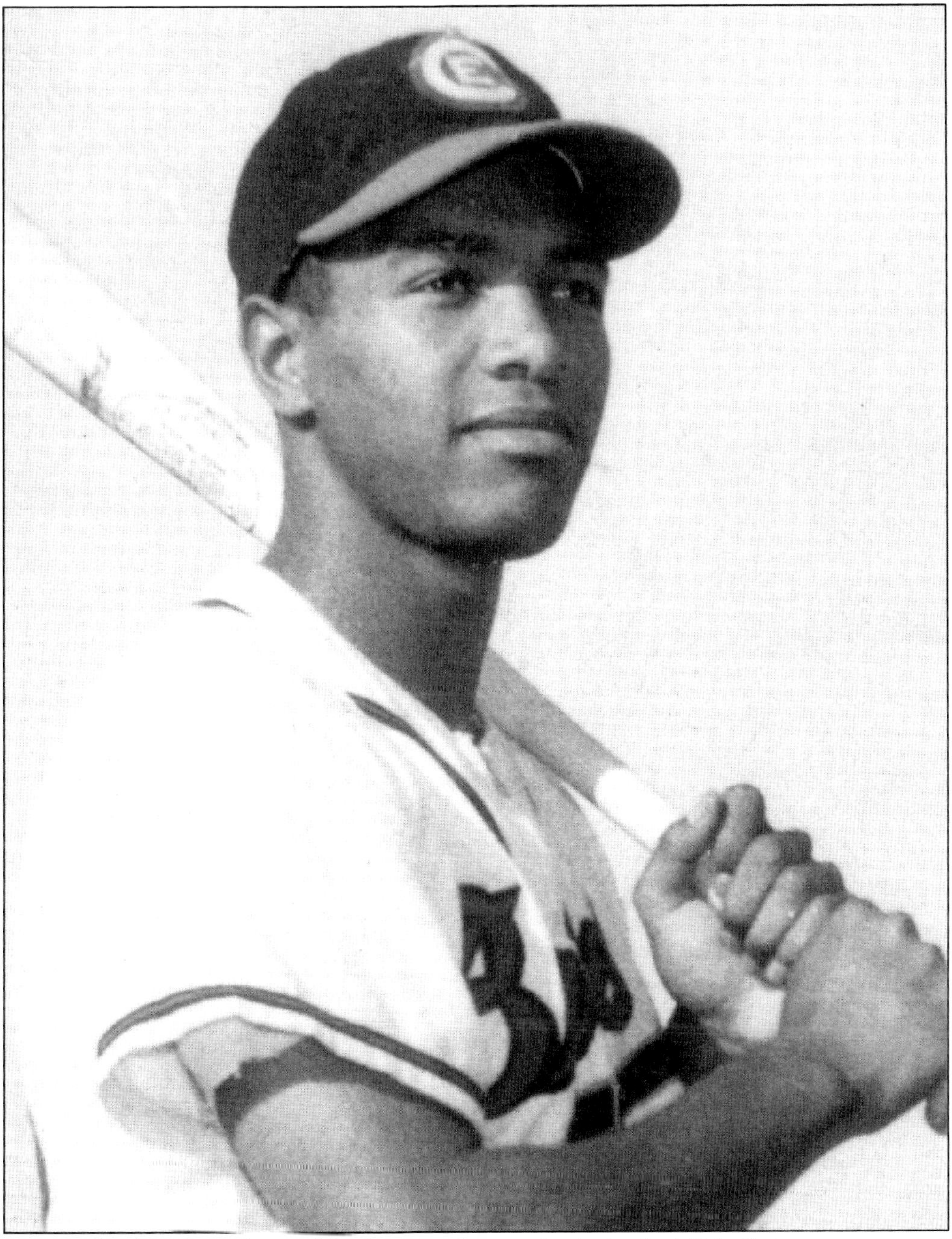

Hermond Hubbard was destined for the major leagues. In the book, *A False Spring*, teammate and future author Pat Jordan compared Hubbard to one of the all-time greats of the game. "[Hubbard was] of uncommon grace and power. Hubbard played center field like a young Willie Mays. He ran the bases like Mays, too. A lengthening, effortless, ground-consuming, greyhound's stride." Hubbard was the prototypical five-tool player, and his 1961 season for the Braves displayed that. He batted .321 with six homers and 37 RBI, and he was stellar in the outfield. Tragedy struck the following year, though, as Hubbard and his fiancé were accidentally asphyxiated in the garage of their home in Delaware. (Photo courtesy of the *Eau Claire Leader-Telegram*.)

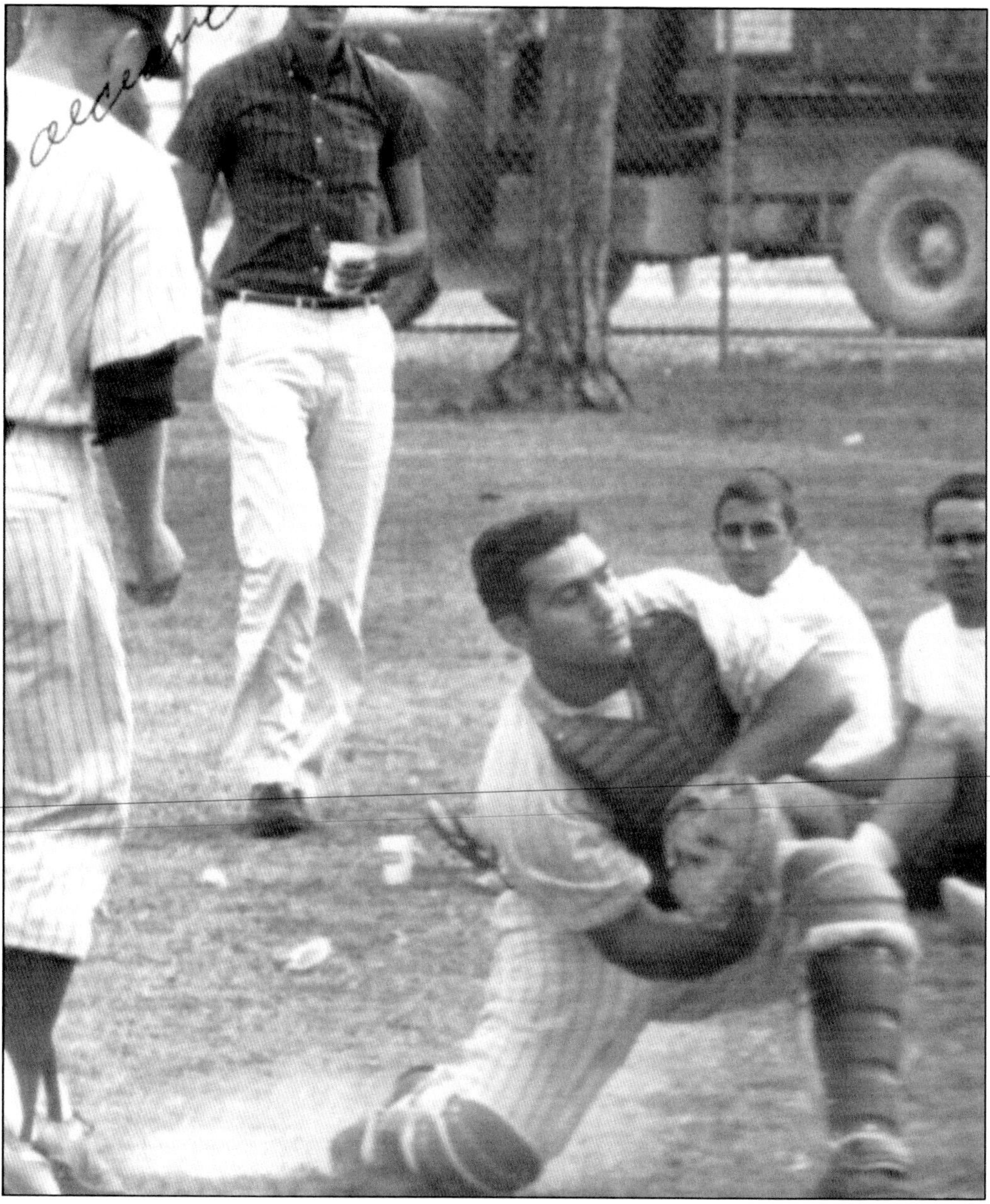

Many people don't know that former Heavyweight Champion Rocky Marciano wasn't the only athlete in the family. Rocky's younger brother Peter left college early to play with the Braves organization. He was assigned to Eau Claire in 1962 and handled most of the catching duties. He only hit .222 but was solid defensively and trusted by the pitching staff. Marciano was thrilled to be following in the footsteps of Joe Torre—Peter even stayed in the same room as Torre had previously! Marciano had one regret, though: "We were playing to get into the championship series. (Duluth-Superior's) Ike Brown, who was known as sort of a hot dog, was on third base and was trying to steal home. He came up really high, on the very last game of the year, and caught me over my shinguard, making a tremendous gash in my knee. As a result, I was out and couldn't play in the playoffs." Marciano would play one more season, in Boise in 1963, before retiring from pro baseball. (Photo courtesy of Peter Marciano.)

THREE
The Modern Era

When the Braves pulled up stakes and left Eau Claire after the 1962 season, there was a huge baseball void that needed to be filled. Sure, there was still Babe Ruth, Connie Mack, and American Legion Leagues, but nothing higher than that for local ballplayers.

Five friends—Gene Koupal, Roger Bohlig, Joe McCauley, Dick Gannon, and Glenn St. Arnault—got together to discuss a potential new amateur baseball program. Koupal suggested the name "Cavaliers" because of the French origin of Eau Claire, and "Cavalier" being a French Warrior. The problem? None of the local sporting goods stores had a Cavalier logo for the team to use! They ended up getting a copy of the ABA's Cleveland Cavaliers logo. The team affiliated with the National Baseball Congress (NBC) and began operations with a 29-8-1 record in 1971 under the leadership of St. Arnault.

Though the affiliations would change over the years, the success on the field experienced that first season has lasted for over three decades. St. Arnault managed the team for the first four years, then came back after a brief hiatus (as a coach of the team) for two more years (1977 and 1978). He finished with a record of 244-62-1, an astounding winning percentage of nearly .800!

In 1979, local baseball hero Harv Tomter took over the reigns from St. Arnault. The winning ways of the Cavaliers continued. The rookie manager, who was the team's pitching coach in 1978, led the club to a then franchise record for wins with a 68-12 record. Tomter, too, has won nearly 80% of the games he has been in the dugout for, peaking in 1987 with a monstrous 77-8 (.906) campaign. Maybe the level of success can be measured better by seeing the worst team the Cavaliers ever put on the field, winning percentage-wise. The year was 1985. The Cavaliers "limped" to a horrific 46-32 (.590) record. That kind of winning percentage could win pennants in the majors, but is only good enough for last place in the 30-plus seasons of Cavaliers baseball.

The Cavaliers have won so many state, regional, invitational, and national titles that it is difficult to keep track of them all. Eau Claire has dominated the Continental Amateur Baseball Association (CABA) in recent years, winning five CABA World Series crowns under Tomter's tutelage, the most recent being in 2001. The CABA loves Eau Claire and Carson Park has been the host for the World Series for several years, a tradition that will come to an end in 2003. The Cavaliers will host their own invitational tournament, bringing in many of the same teams they would have faced in the CABA sanctioned event anyway. Given the talent on the Cavalier squad in any given year, teams may want to think twice before accepting that invitation!

With the seemingly never-ending stream of talented area baseball players combined with strong management and a community-oriented attitude, the Eau Claire Cavaliers figure to be the focal point of Eau Claire baseball for many years to come.

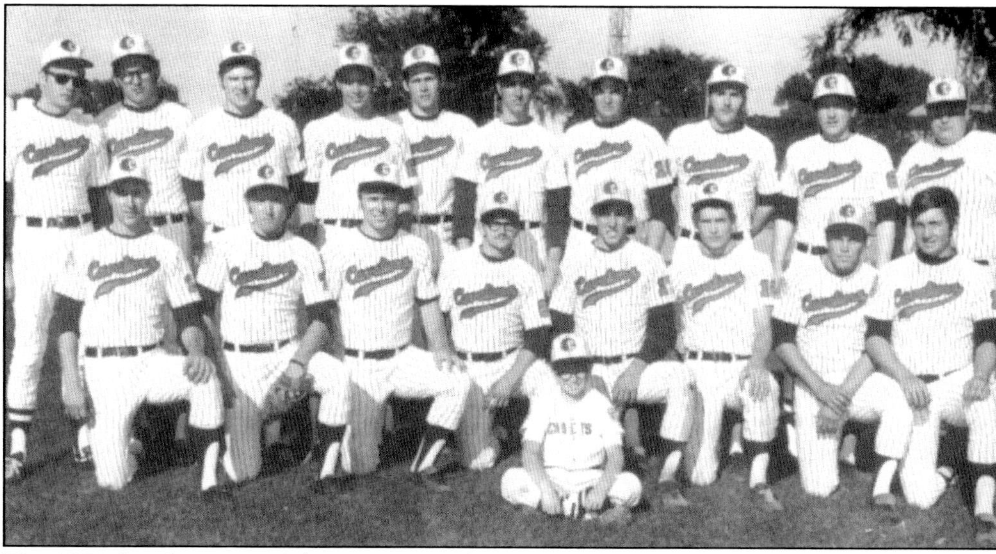

The 1971 Cavaliers started the winning tradition for local amateur baseball. From left to right: (front row) Scott Maske, Randy Millis, Tom Knutson, Dave Johnson, Pete Koupal, Gregg Bohlig, Dick Woletz, and Tom Steele; (back row) Dick Gannon, Connie Bradison, Dick Gust, Kirk Heimstead, Stan Morley, Mike Fern, Larry Bugher, Tim Tyler, Mike Bauer, and Glenn St. Arnault. (Photo courtesy of the Eau Claire Cavaliers/Dave Hanson collection.)

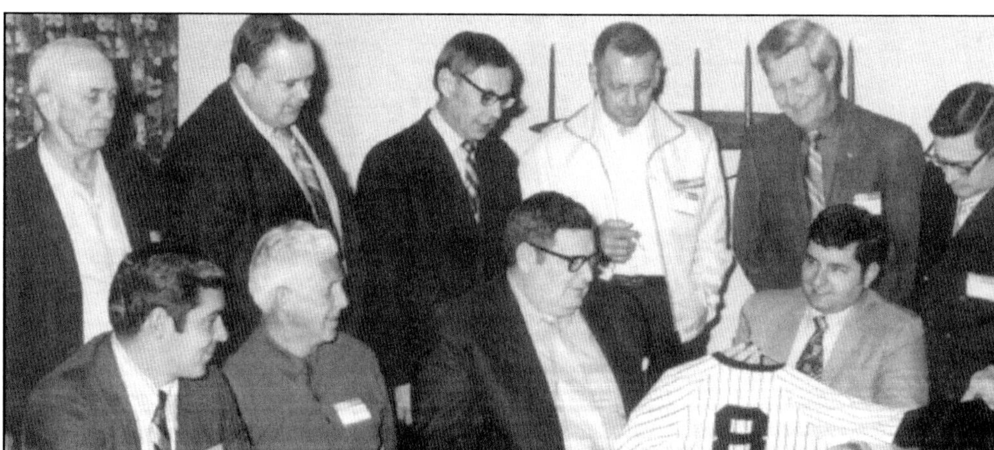

The Cavaliers had (and continue to have) a large, diverse and, most importantly, active Board of Directors. Here is the original Board from 1971, from left to right: (front row) Buzz Mahler, Frank Wrigglesworth, Joe McCauley, and David Anderson; (back row) George Farmer, Glenn St. Arnault, Gene Koupal, Bill Keeton, Bob Dawson, and Roger Bohlig. Dick Gannon is not pictured. (Photo courtesy of the Eau Claire Cavaliers/Dave Hanson collection.)

No one player epitomizes the winning spirit of the Cavaliers like Dave Johnson. Johnson, an original Cavalier, held down the shortstop position through the 1986 season. His 1,070 career hits will likely stand as the Cavalier record for eternity. Though a wizard at getting on base and making things happen while on the bases (200 career steals, also a club record), he only led the team in hitting once—his rookie year of 1971! (Photo courtesy of the Eau Claire Cavaliers/Dave Hanson collection.)

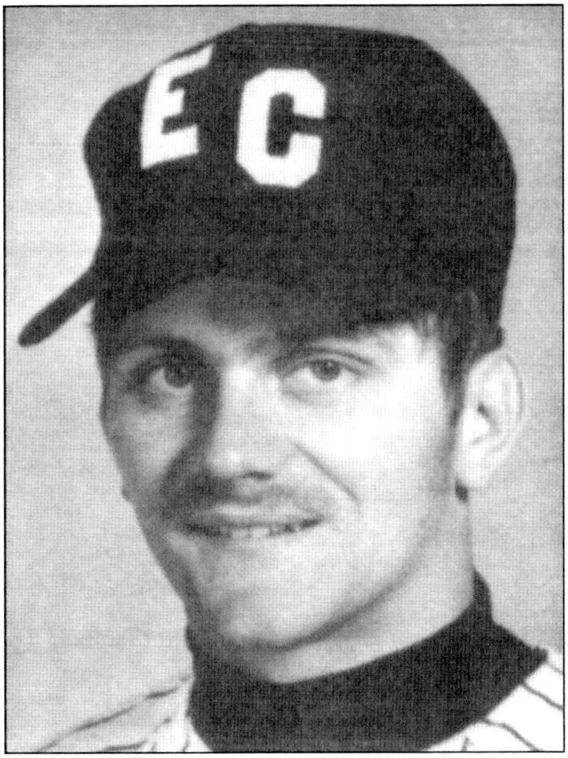

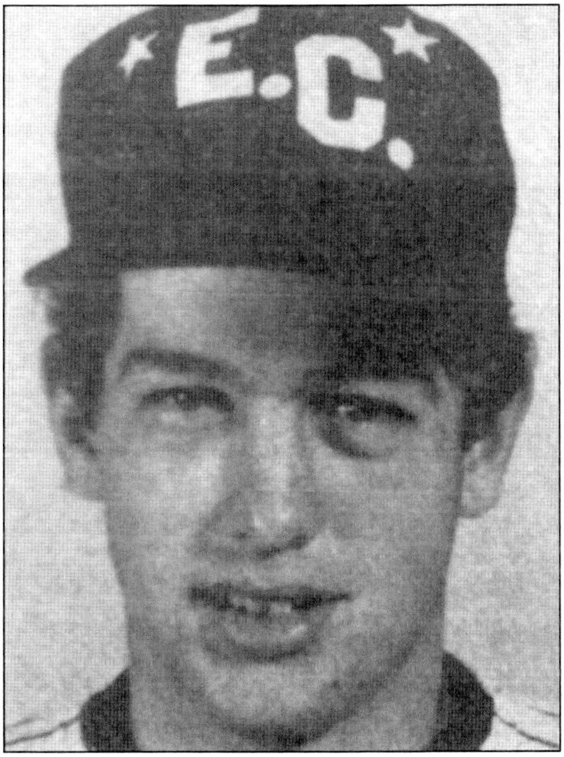

Dennis Barneson, who spent two years in the Angels farm system, put together a phenomenal season for the Cavaliers in 1972. He struggled in his first appearance of the year, giving up two earned runs in his first two-thirds of an inning. It's safe to say he settled down after that. He gave up two more earned runs—in the remaining 60 innings of his season! The 0.59 ERA is still the best single season mark in Cavs history. Barneson's greatest claim to fame? Possibly the time he spent as the author's Little League coach in the 1980s. He could still bring the fastball! (Photo courtesy of the Eau Claire Cavaliers/Dave Hanson collection.)

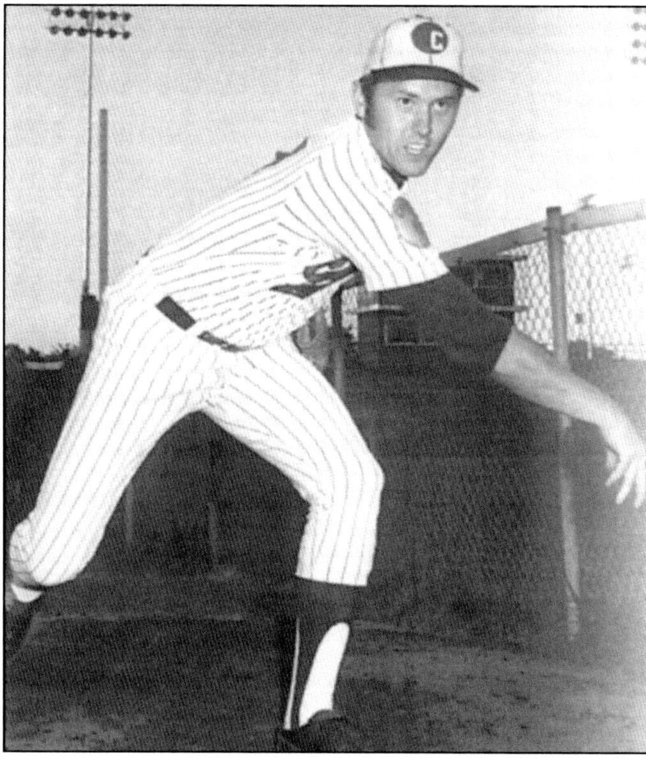

Voted to the 25th Anniversary Team, Randy Millis pitched from 1971 to 1977. His 51 career wins was the most of any Cavalier at the time he retired, but has since been eclipsed by four others. Millis is now pitching for the Cavaliers in a different way—as team president. (Photo courtesy of the Eau Claire Cavaliers/Dave Hanson collection.)

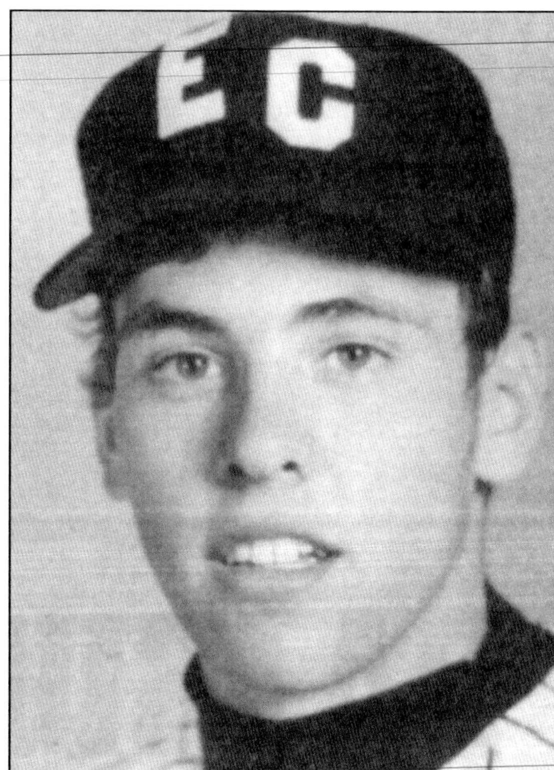

Pete Koupal, a star catcher and second baseman for the powerhouse program at UW-Oshkosh, played for his father Gene's team in the summers. He played for the team through 1980 (long after his days with the Titans were over), and was voted by the fans to the 25th Anniversary Team as a utility player. (Photo courtesy of the Eau Claire Cavaliers/Dave Hanson collection.)

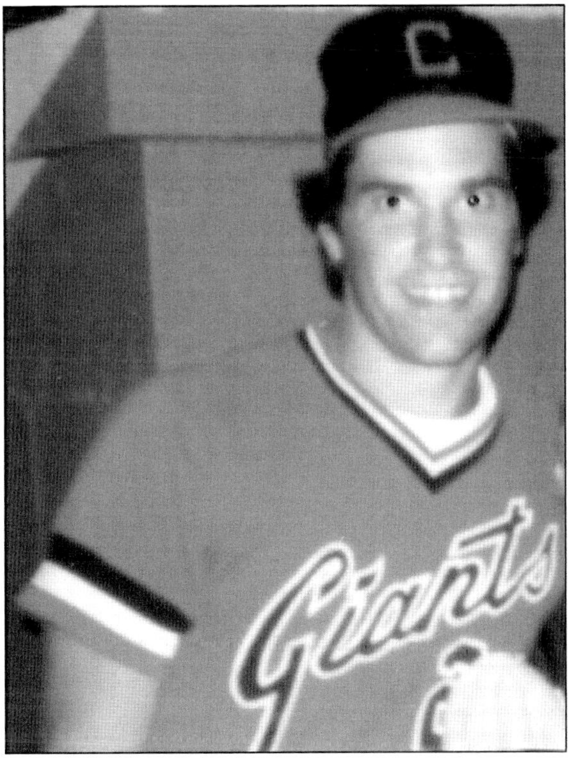

Bob Barron dominated so much for the Cavaliers in 1980 that he earned a cup of coffee with the Clinton Giants in the Midwest League. That didn't pan out, so he came back to Eau Claire in 1981, and became the team MVP. (Photo courtesy of Eunice Whipple.)

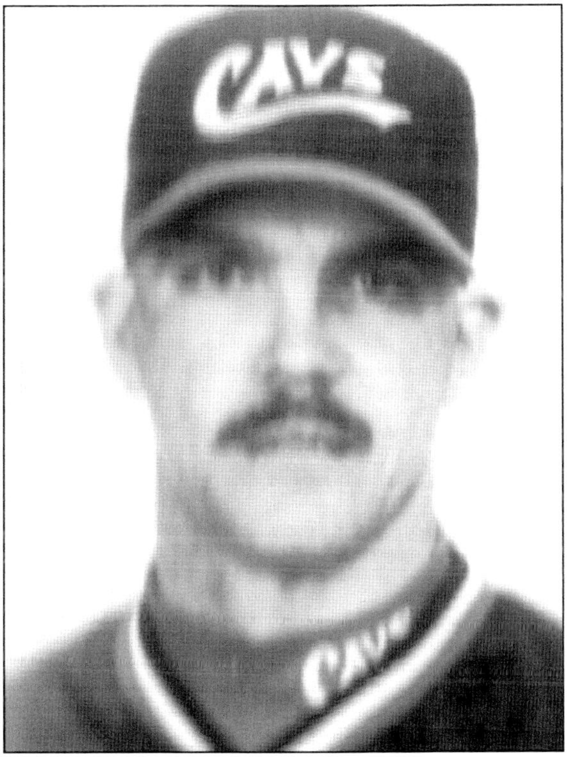

Craig Walter was the iron man of the Cavaliers for most of the 1980s and 1990s. He holds the single season record for wins (22) and his 38 career saves is the team's all-time high water mark. (Photo courtesy of the Eau Claire Cavaliers/Dave Hanson collection.)

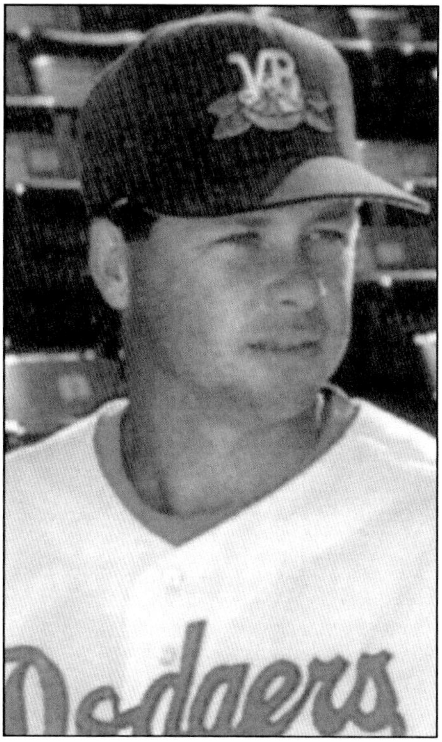

Joe Vavra hit .374 for the Cavaliers in 1981 and .547 in a shortened 1982. Although he wouldn't play in the majors, he has been a successful coach and instructor in the Dodgers and Twins organizations. (Photo courtesy of the Eau Claire Cavaliers/Dave Hanson collection.)

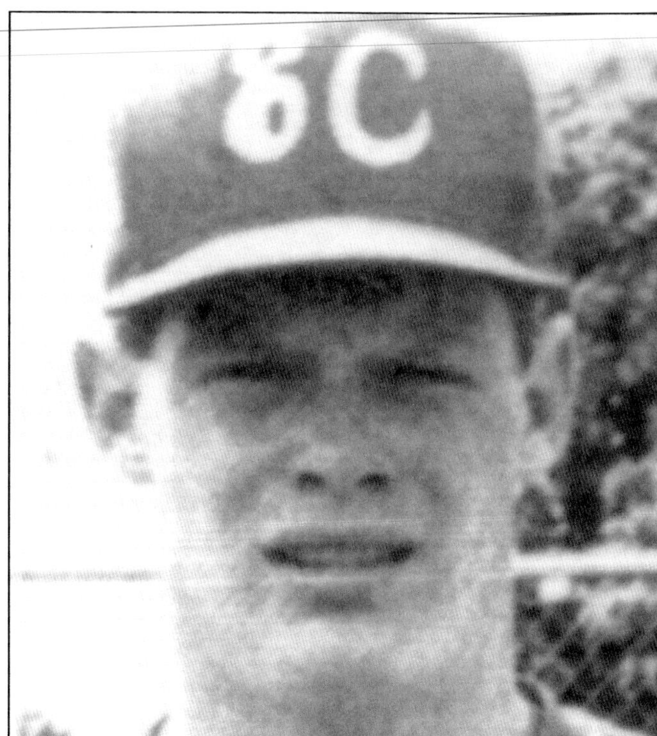

Stan Royer was a standout for the Cavaliers in 1985 and 1986. While he was making his way to the major leagues with the Cardinals and Red Sox (a .250 career hitter in parts of 1991-1994), his younger brother Rick was taking his turn to star with the Cavs. (Photo courtesy of the Eau Claire Cavaliers/Dave Hanson collection.)

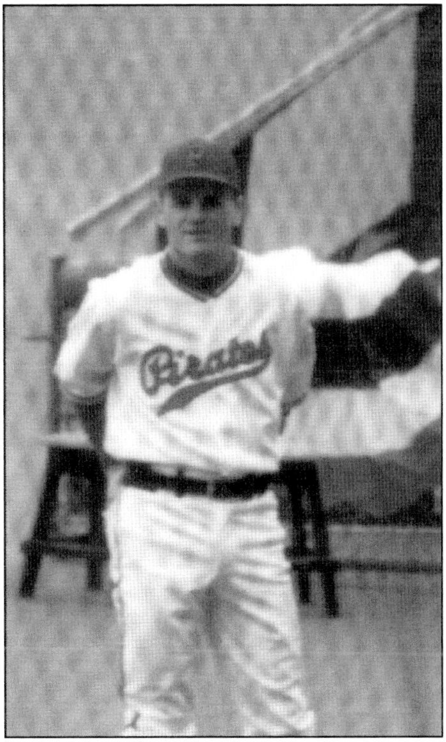

When Gary Varsho (above) made his debut with the Chicago Cubs in 1988, he became the first Cavalier to make it to the major leagues. Younger brother Dale (below) also enjoyed a fine career with the Cavaliers. (Photo courtesy of Eunice Whipple.)

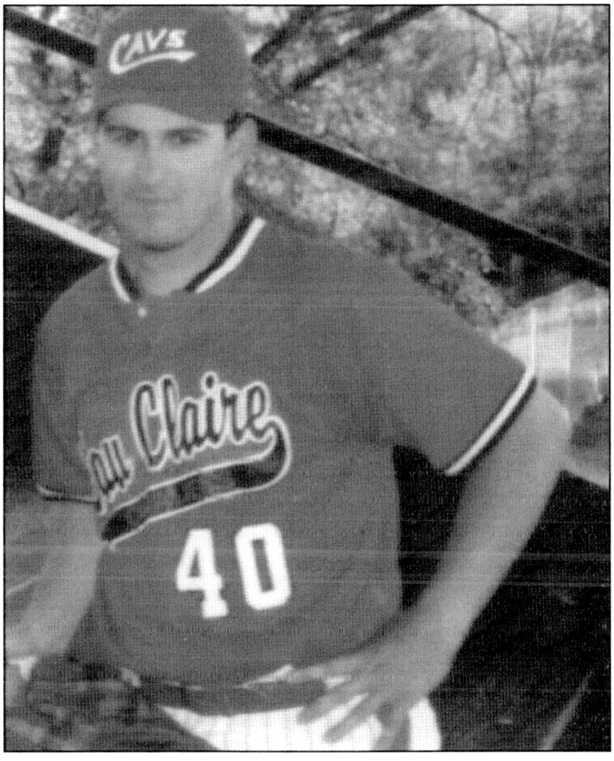

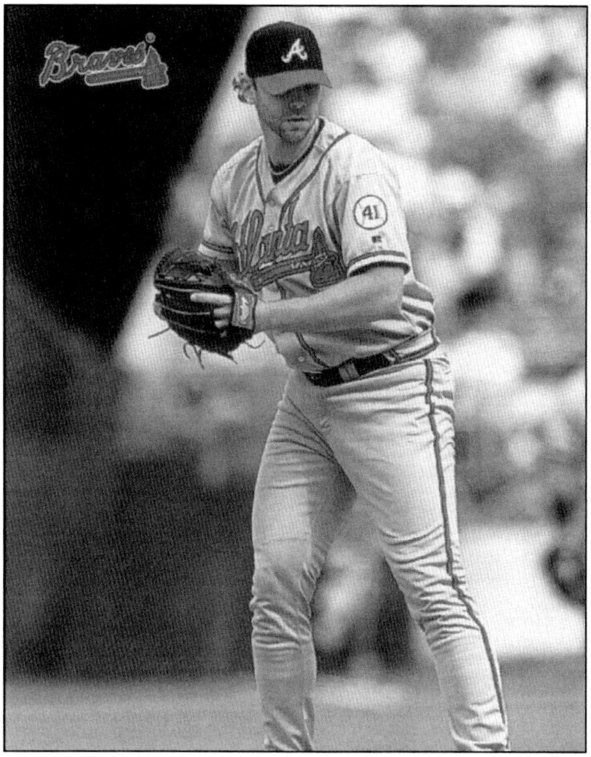

Kerry Lightenberg dealt for the Cavaliers in 1992, which probably seems like a long, long time ago for him since he has been a key reliever for the last several years for Atlanta and now Baltimore. Forgive him for not remembering much about Eau Claire—he appeared in one game! (Photo courtesy of The Topps Company, Inc.)

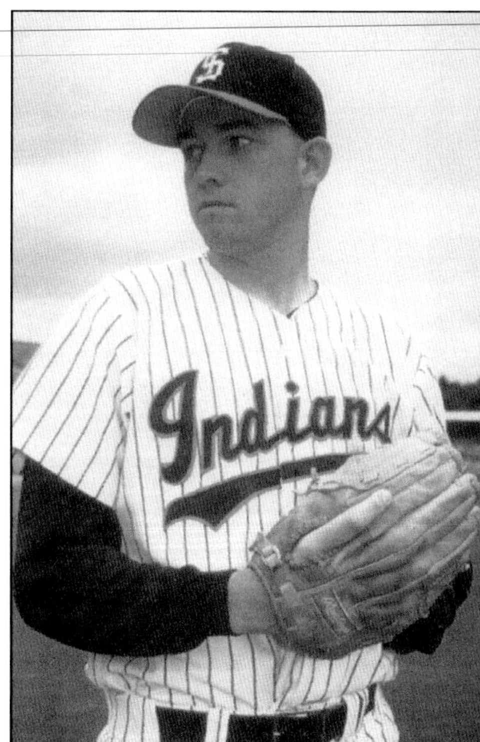

Steve Prihoda pitched well enough in 1993 and 1994 to get noticed by the Cleveland Indian organization. He led the Cavs in 1994 with a 15-3 record and 13 complete games. (Photo courtesy of Eunice Whipple.)

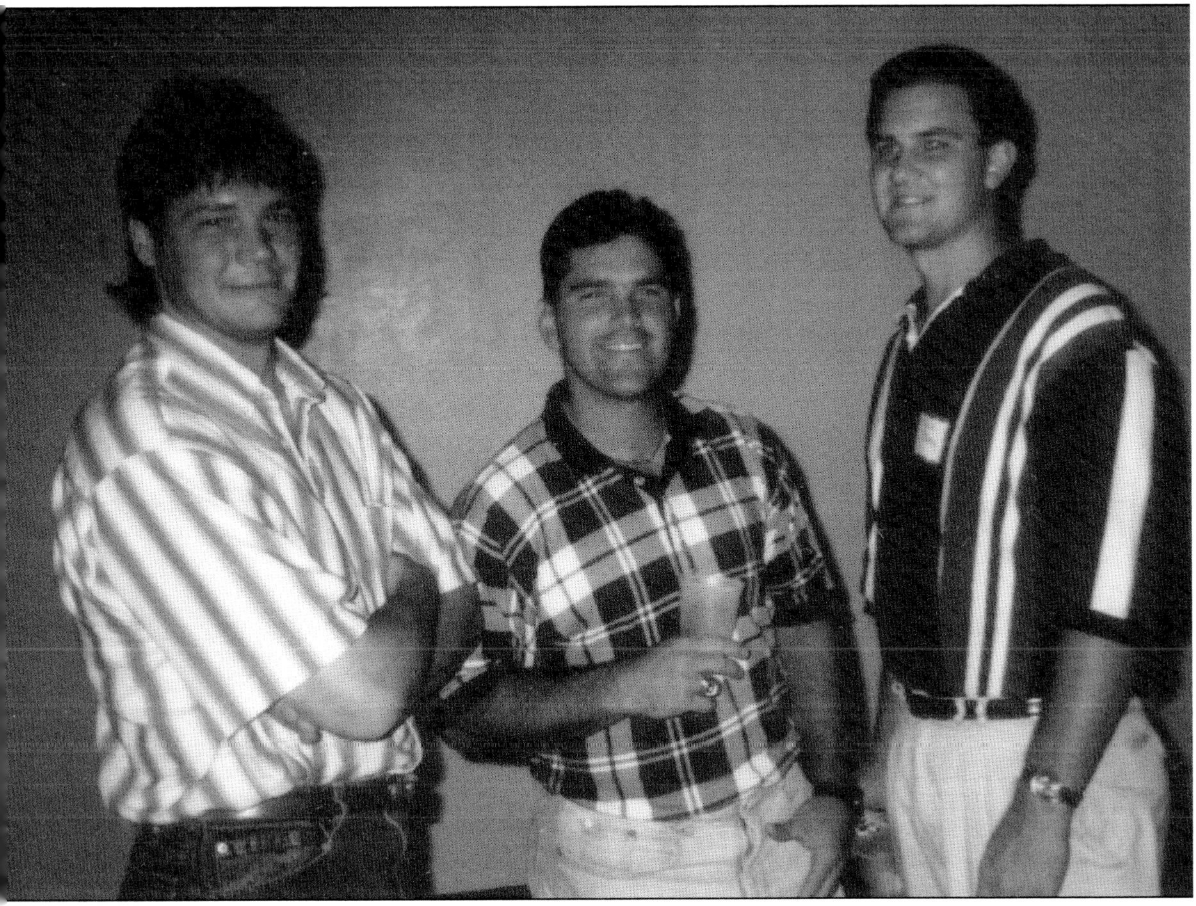

Taken at the 25th Anniversary celebration, this photo is of (left to right) Vic Cable, Chris Malinowski, and Darin Blang. Cable is one of the most prominent hurlers in team history, and as of 2003 is still throwing for an amateur team in the area. Malinowski had a brief stint in the Expos organization as a second baseman. Blang, an Eau Claire native, was a dominating pitcher for the team from 1989 to 1991. (Photo Courtesy of Eunice Whipple.)

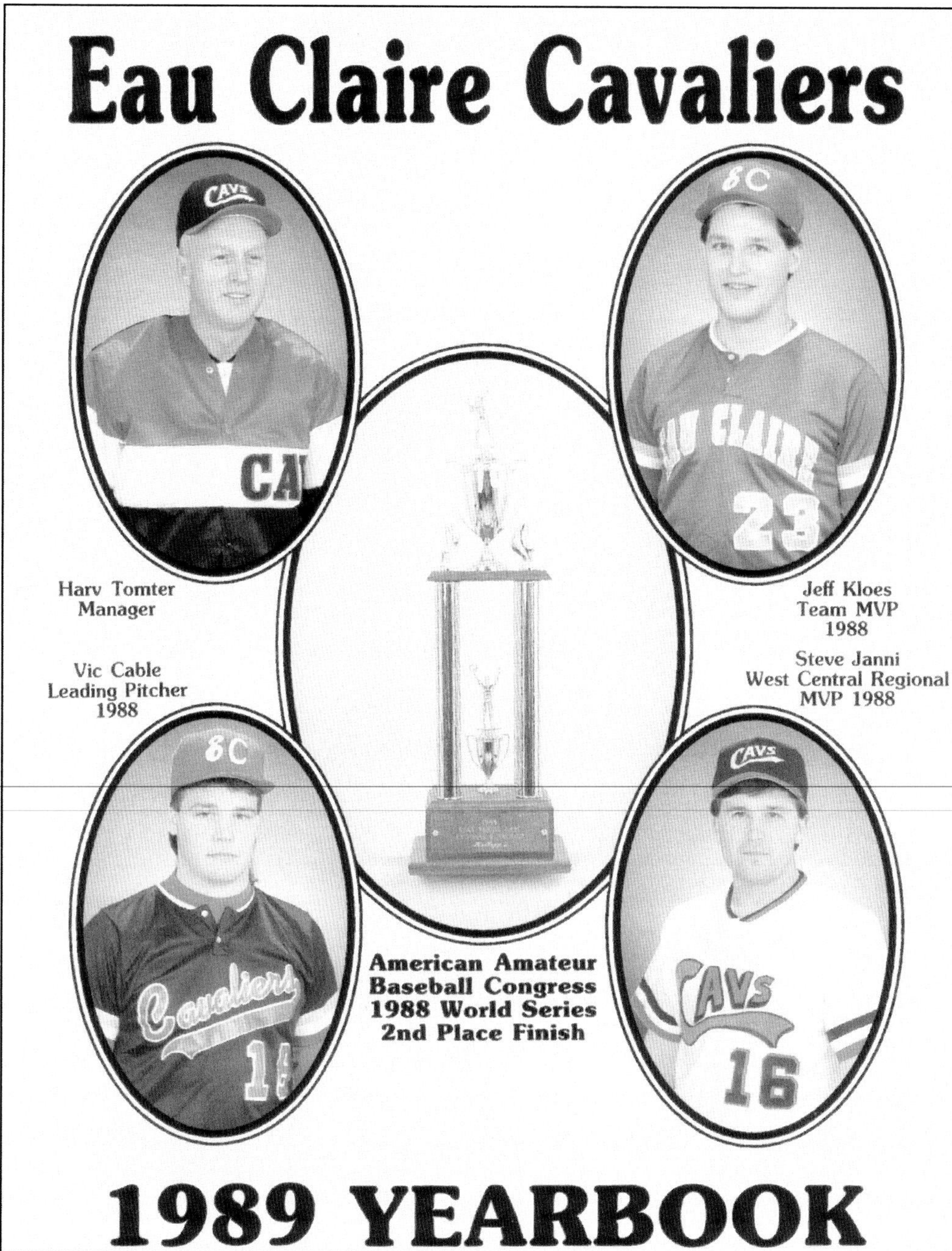

This 1989 Cavalier program features four of the most recognizable Cavaliers ever. Longtime manager Harv Tomter is on the top left. The other three, all voted to the Anniversary Team, are Jeff Kloes (top right), Vic Cable (bottom left), and Steve Janni (bottom right). Kloes is second all-time in career home runs with 131 and holds the RBI mark with 606. Janni is nearly Kloes' equal: third in homers (130) and second in RBI (581). Kloes won team MVP honors each year from 1987 through 1990. Janni then won it the next three years! Cable holds basically every pitching record, and given his love of the game, he may just come back and extend those marks some day. (Photo courtesy of the Eau Claire Cavaliers/Dave Hanson collection.)

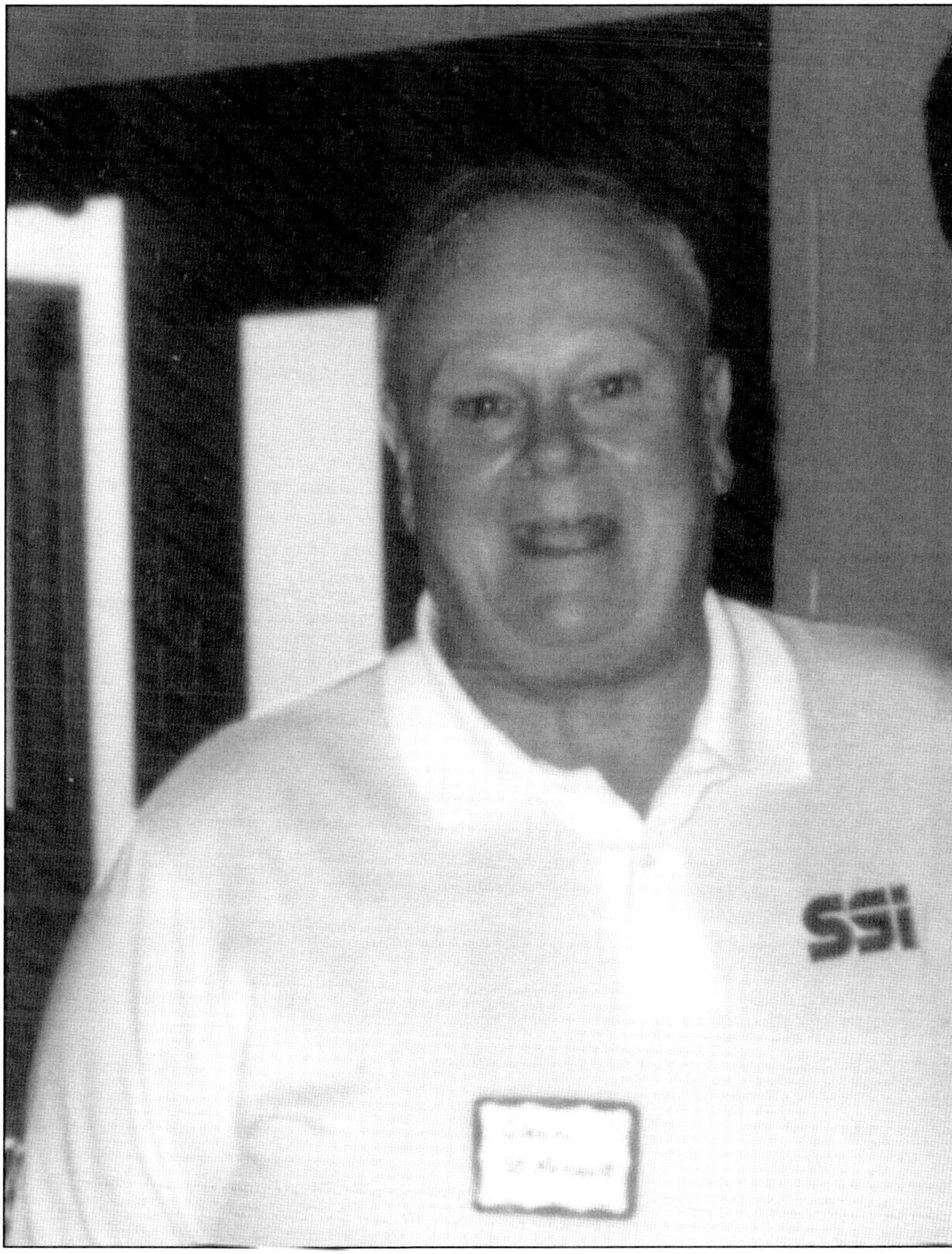

Pictured here is Glenn St. Arnault, one of the founding fathers of the team. He is shown here at the 25th Anniversary celebration. (Photo Courtesy of Eunice Whipple.)

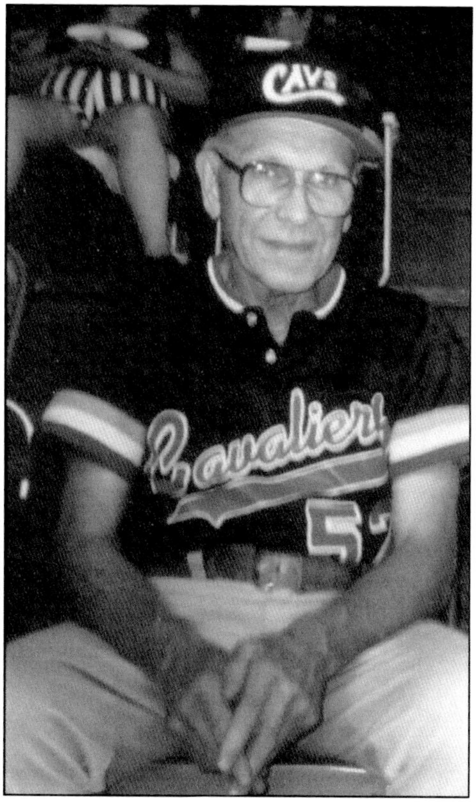

First base coach Don Zaspel has been with Harv Tomter's club since 1987. So devoted to the game is Don that he drives from his home in Rice Lake for every game—about an hour from Carson Park. (Photo Courtesy of Eunice Whipple.)

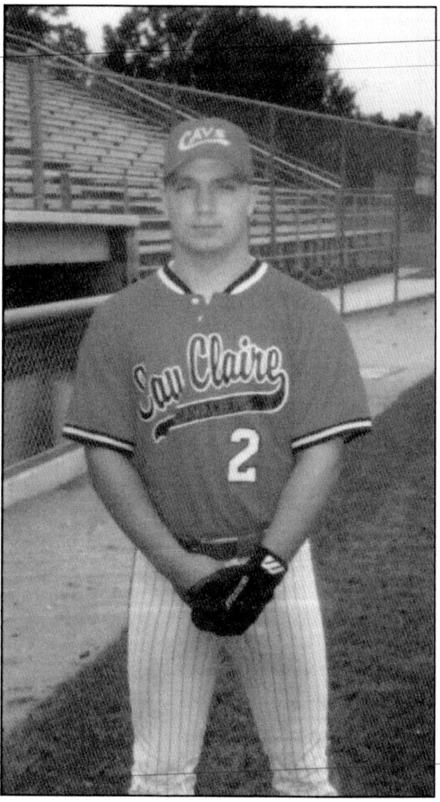

A great all-around player, Collin Sanders was rewarded for his hard work with team MVP honors in 1999. He ranks fifth all-time in homers and seventh in stolen bases. (Photo Courtesy of Eunice Whipple.)

Anybody who has attended Eau Claire Cavaliers games over the last decade-plus knows "Billie." Billie Voss is the ball boy for the Cavaliers, and a darn good one. It's almost eeric that he seems to know when a ball "sounds" foul and out of play. He springs into action in full sprint until the ball is retrieved. Here he is shown taking a popcorn break with a fan. But he's ready to pounce! (Photo courtesy of the Chippewa Valley Museum, Eau Claire, WI.)

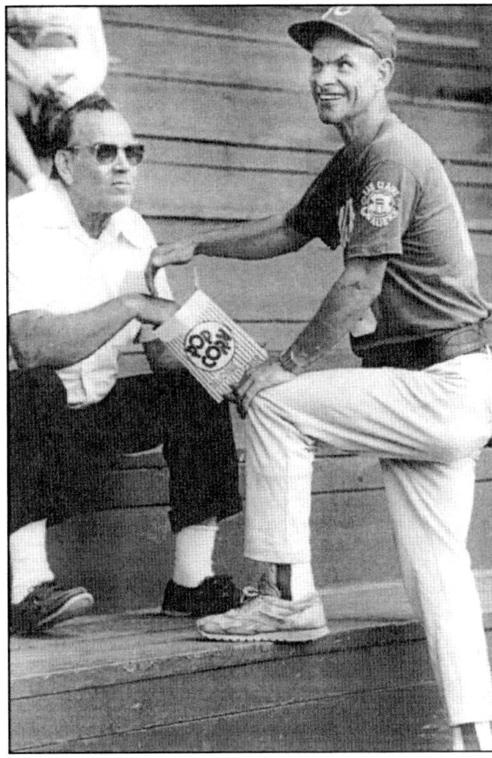

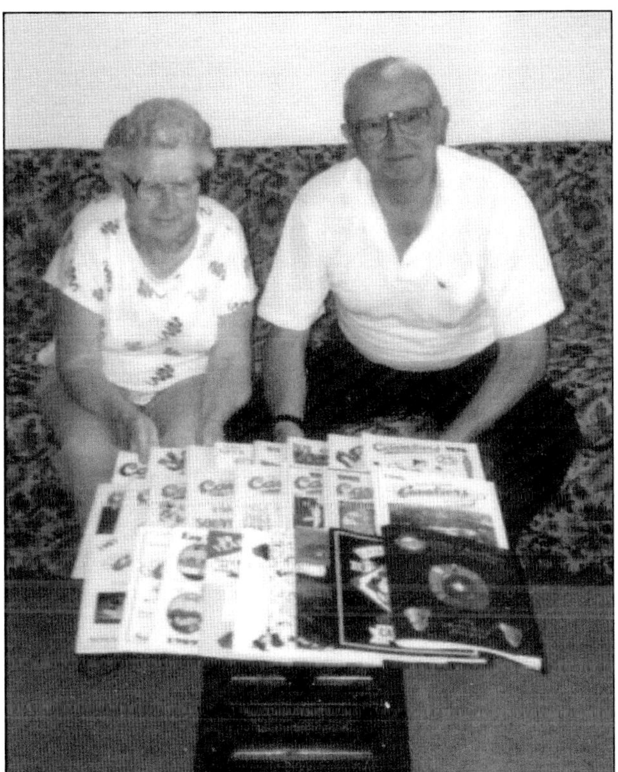

Eunice and Lloyd Whipple both defined the term "superfan." They went everywhere with the Cavaliers, rarely missing even road games. Here they are shown with their complete collection of Eau Claire Cavalier yearbooks. Though Lloyd sadly has passed away, Eunice is still going strong, and talking baseball with her is an absolute treat. Her baseball loyalty now rests with the Chicago Cubs.

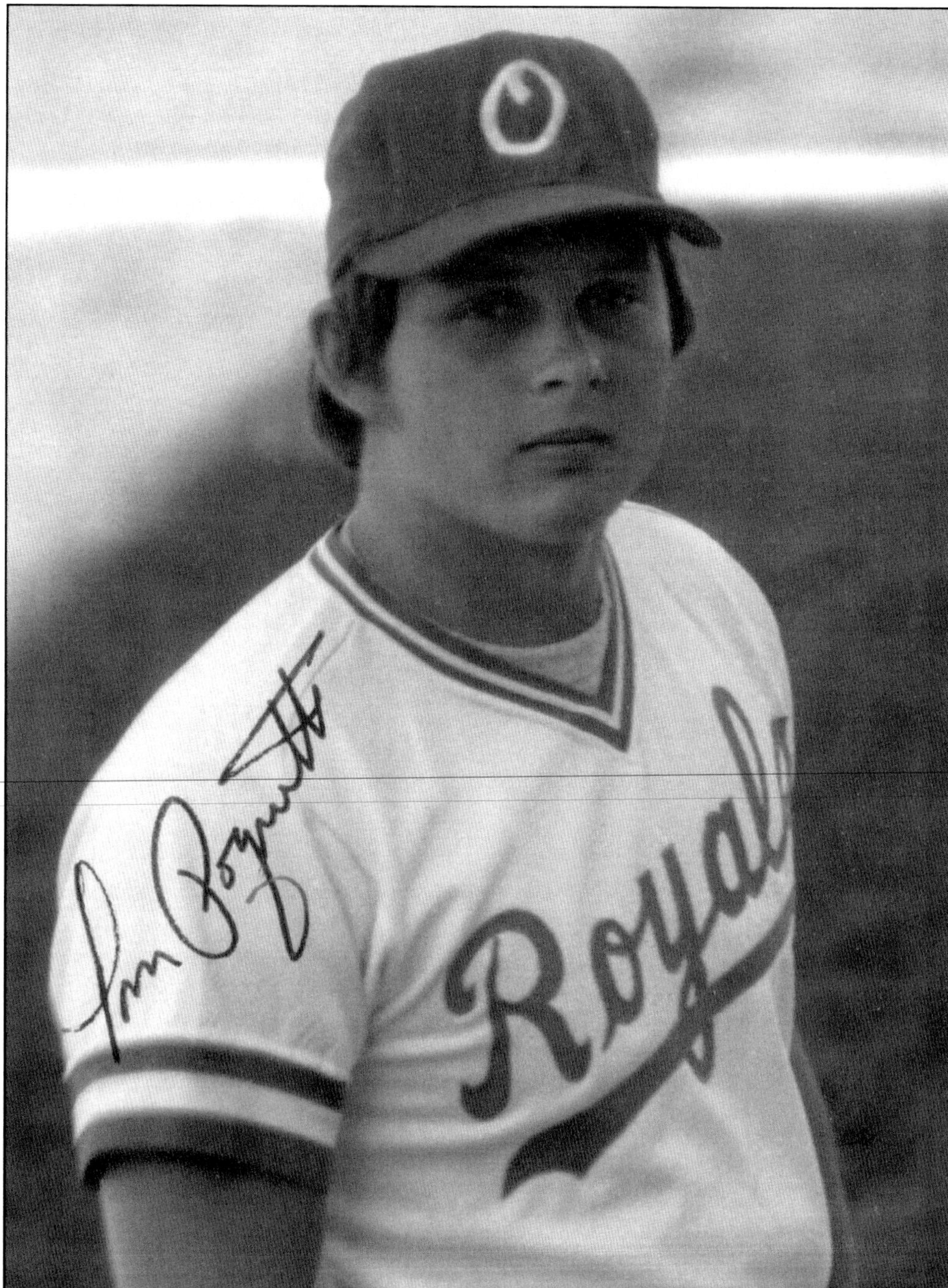

Though technically not a member of the Cavaliers, Tom Poquette was the local hero for the people of Eau Claire in the 1970s. Fans had watched Poquette shine throughout Little League and in high school for the Eau Claire Memorial team. Shown here with Omaha in 1973, he would also make his major league debut that year with Kansas City. He played until 1982 with the Royals, Rangers, and Red Sox organizations, and is currently a coach in the Royals organization. (Author's collection.)

FOUR

Carson Park

Majesty. Beauty. History. Carson Park personifies all of these words.

It is very hard to describe just how lovely Carson Park is. If you are reading this book in the Eau Claire area, and even if you have seen the park a million times, take the short drive downtown to Carson Park and just try to soak it all in.

It isn't easy!

The field is essentially at the highest point of the park, a horseshoe-shaped island donated to the people of Eau Claire by lumber barron William Carson. Along with the baseball field, the park houses a football field (used by the University as well as the city's high schools as their home field), two handsome and meticulously cared for softball fields, a large play area for kids of all ages, and thousands of "perfect" spots for a quiet picnic. Statues of Paul Bunyon and Babe the Big Blue Ox stand guard at the Paul Bunyon Museum, and the Chippewa Valley Museum, the cornerstone for research in Western Wisconsin, is also tucked in the confines of the spacious park. In order to fit in with the beauty of the rest of the park, a baseball stadium needed to be something special.

It is.

The sandstone grandstand looks just like it did the day it opened. And that day happened on May 4, 1937. President Franklin Roosevelt could be considered the Founding Father of the baseball stadium at Carson Park. His brilliant idea of creating the Work's Progress Administration (WPA) to help America emerge from the Depression was directly responsible for the field. The City of Eau Claire proposed a 1500-seat stadium to the WPA, and while completion was hoped for in 1936, delays forced the debut of the park to be pushed back until the following year. A $500,000-plus renovation, completed in 1998, restored the field to its original beauty.

Walk inside the main doors and up the small ramp. You are now looking down on a perfectly manicured playing surface. Even early on in the Spring, the grass is a brilliant green. Now, head up the grandstand and choose your favorite spot to view a game. It's general admission—don't be shy. Maybe you want the panoramic view from Bob Uecker's famous "front row", or maybe you want to be down so low you can hear the catcher yelp if he doesn't catch that new pitcher's fastball just right. Or maybe you want to go to the side and catch some sun in the metal bleachers running along the infield. Grab a hot dog and a beer for under $5 total—try to do THAT at Miller Park. Be sure to say "hi" to Billie (see page 111) while you're there.

Now sit back, watch the pitcher fling his warm ups, and settle in for a couple hours of baseball the way it is supposed to be.

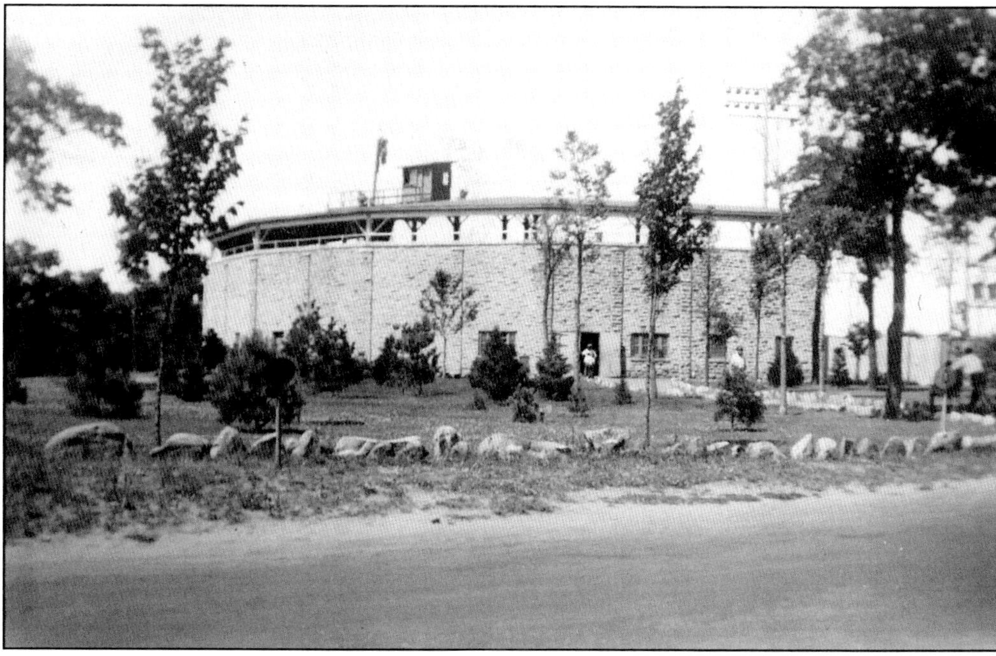

Picturesque Carson Park has been home to dozens of professional, amateur, school, and youth teams for generations. This photo is from the late 1930s. (Author's Collection.)

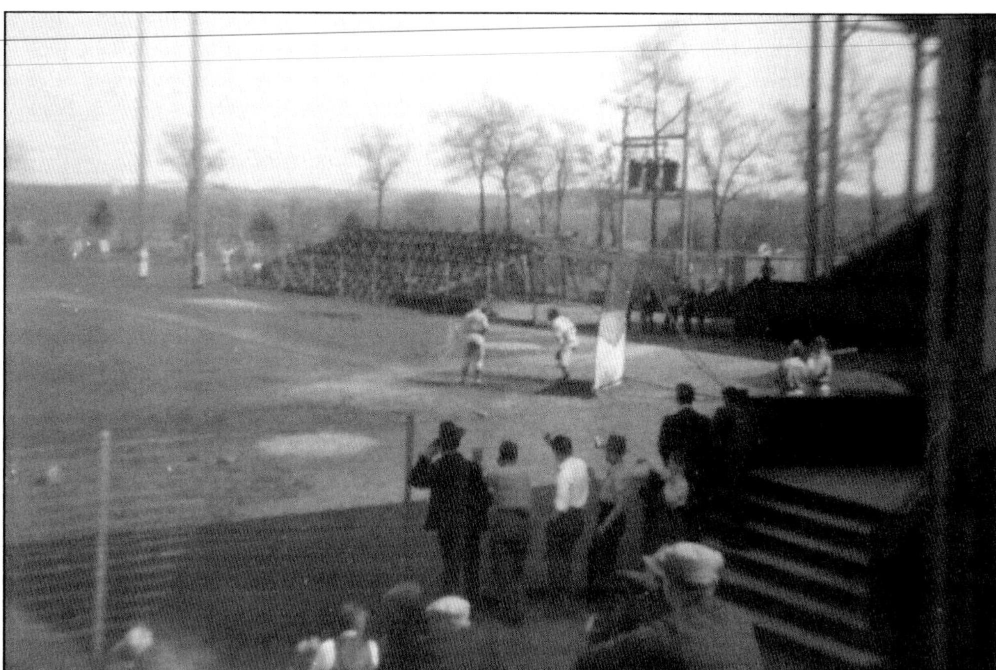

Here is another early shot of Carson Park, as seen from the third base bleachers. (Photo courtesy of the Chippewa Valley Museum, Eau Claire, WI.)

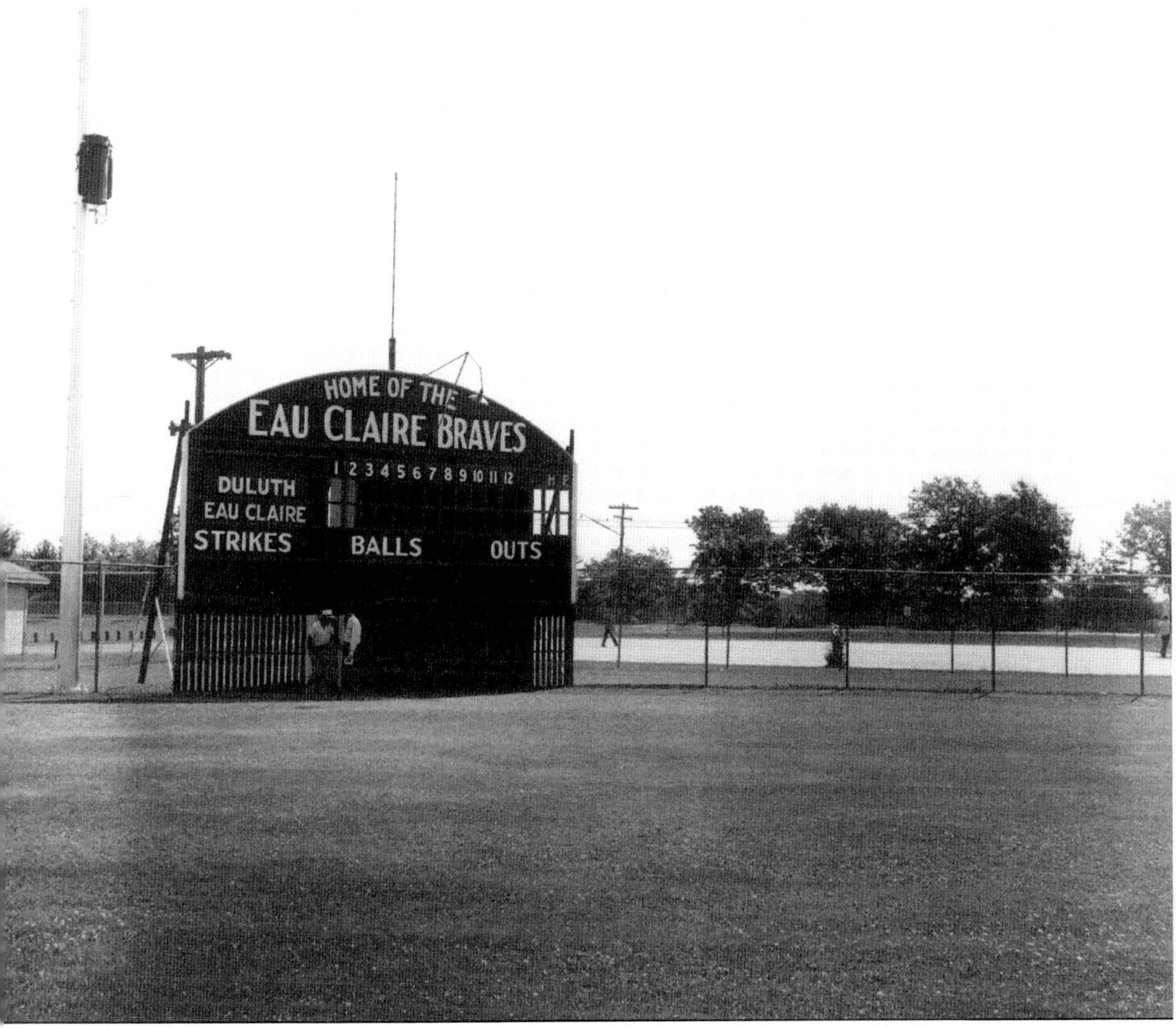

This scoreboard was a staple in right-center field at Carson Park for essentially the entire time Eau Claire was in the Northern League. It was moved to a local softball field after the team left town in 1962. (Photo courtesy of the Chippewa Valley Museum, Eau Claire, WI.)

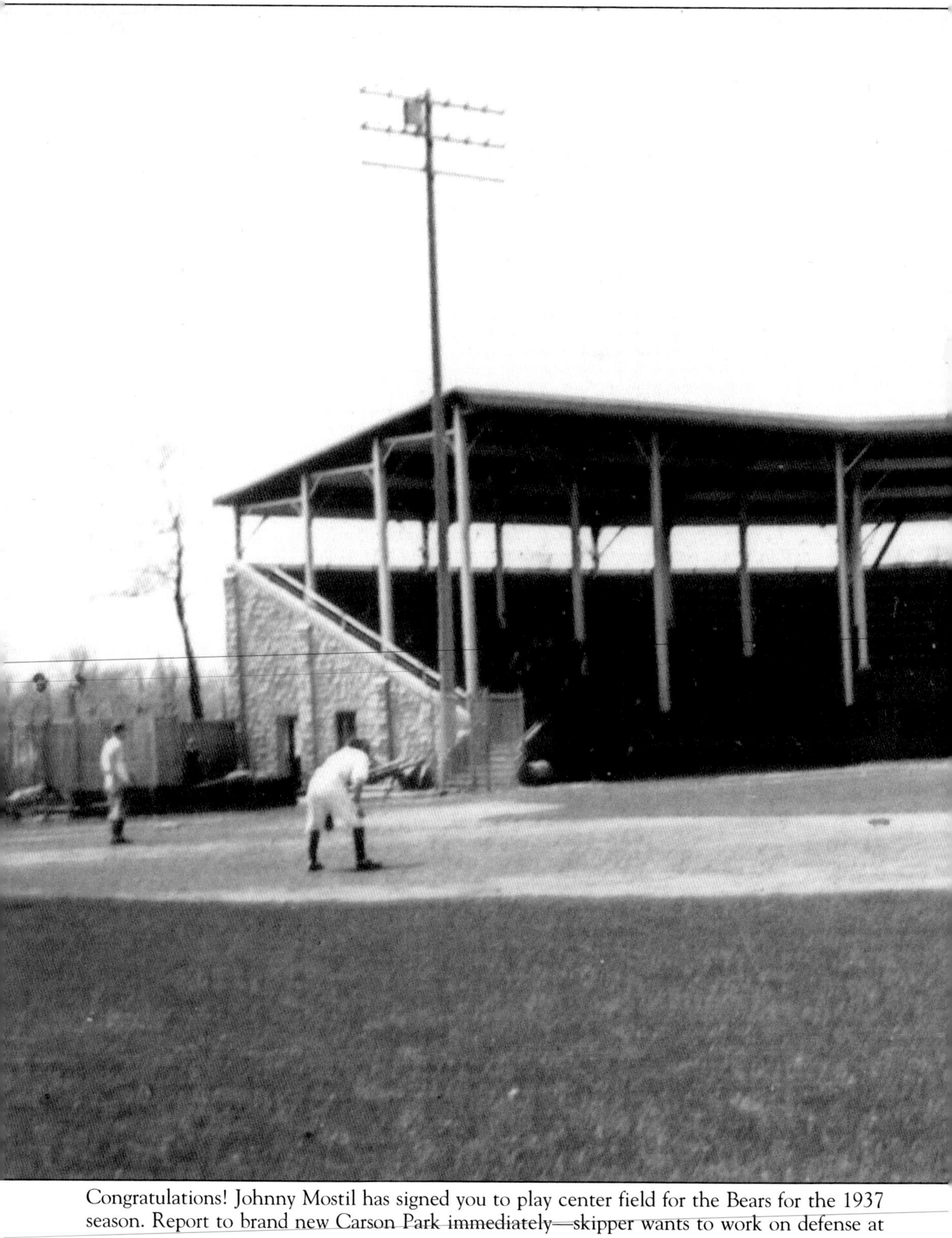

Congratulations! Johnny Mostil has signed you to play center field for the Bears for the 1937 season. Report to brand new Carson Park immediately—skipper wants to work on defense at

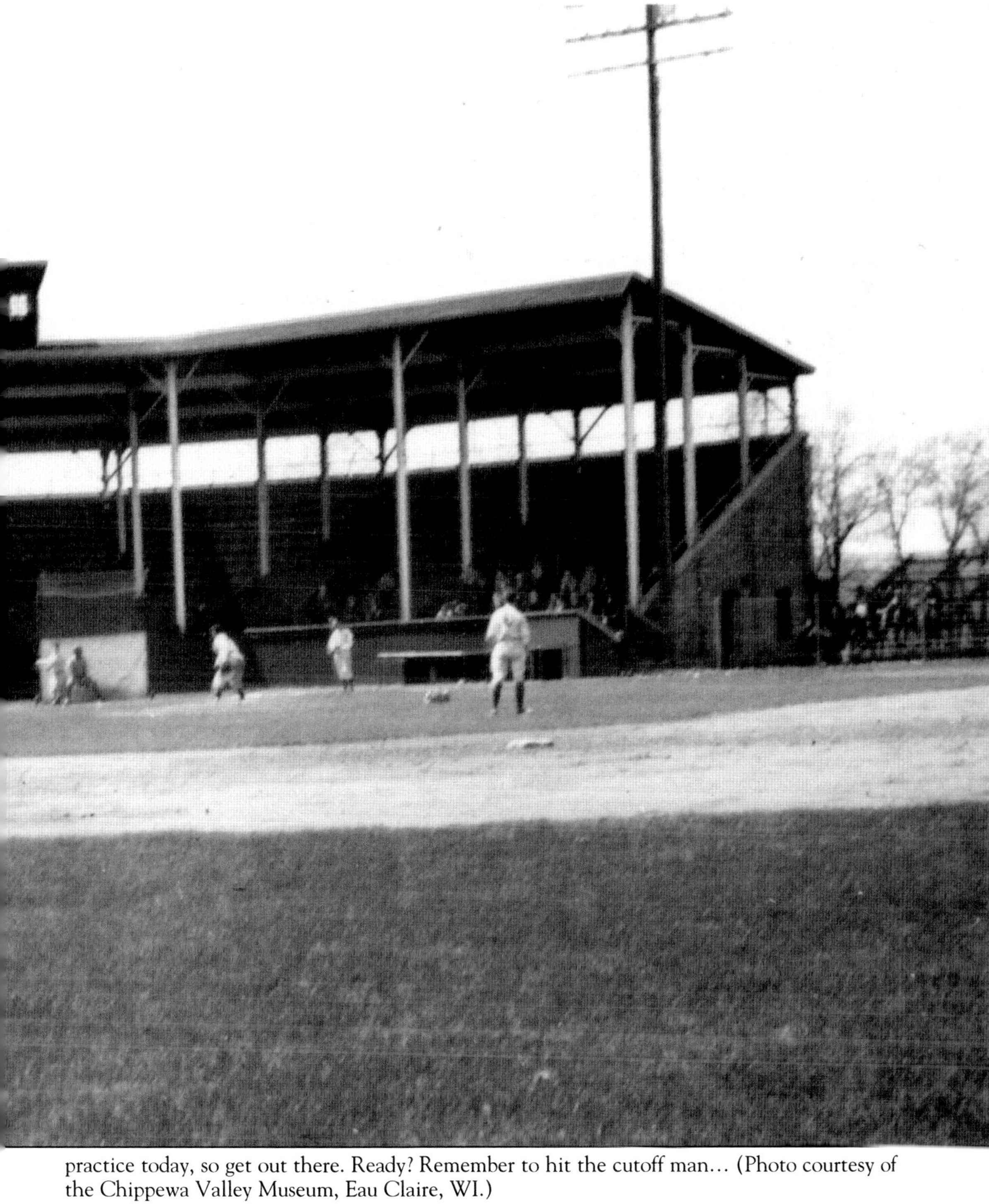

practice today, so get out there. Ready? Remember to hit the cutoff man… (Photo courtesy of the Chippewa Valley Museum, Eau Claire, WI.)

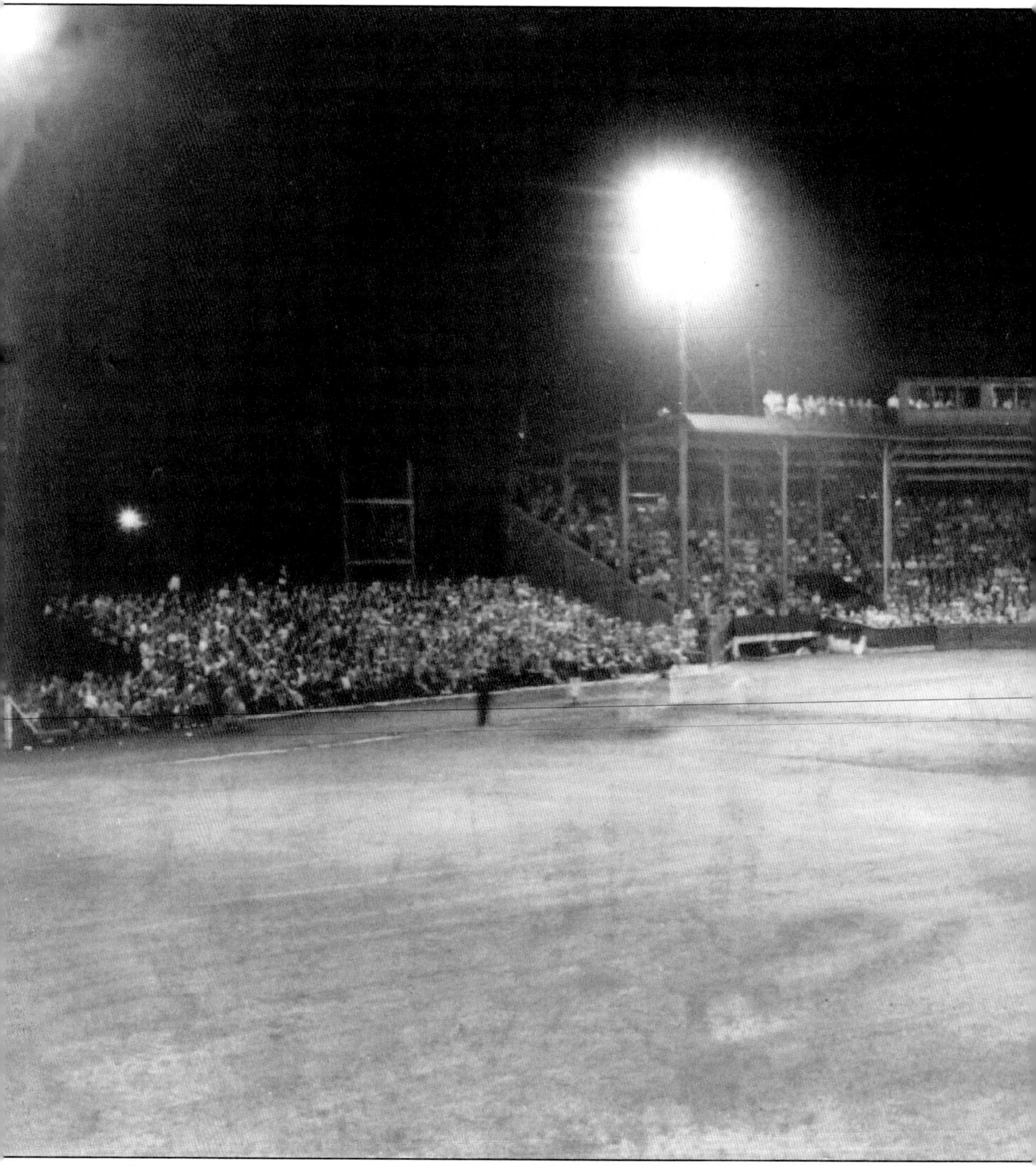

A glorious evening was the backdrop for the 1951 Northern League All-Star Game, hosted by

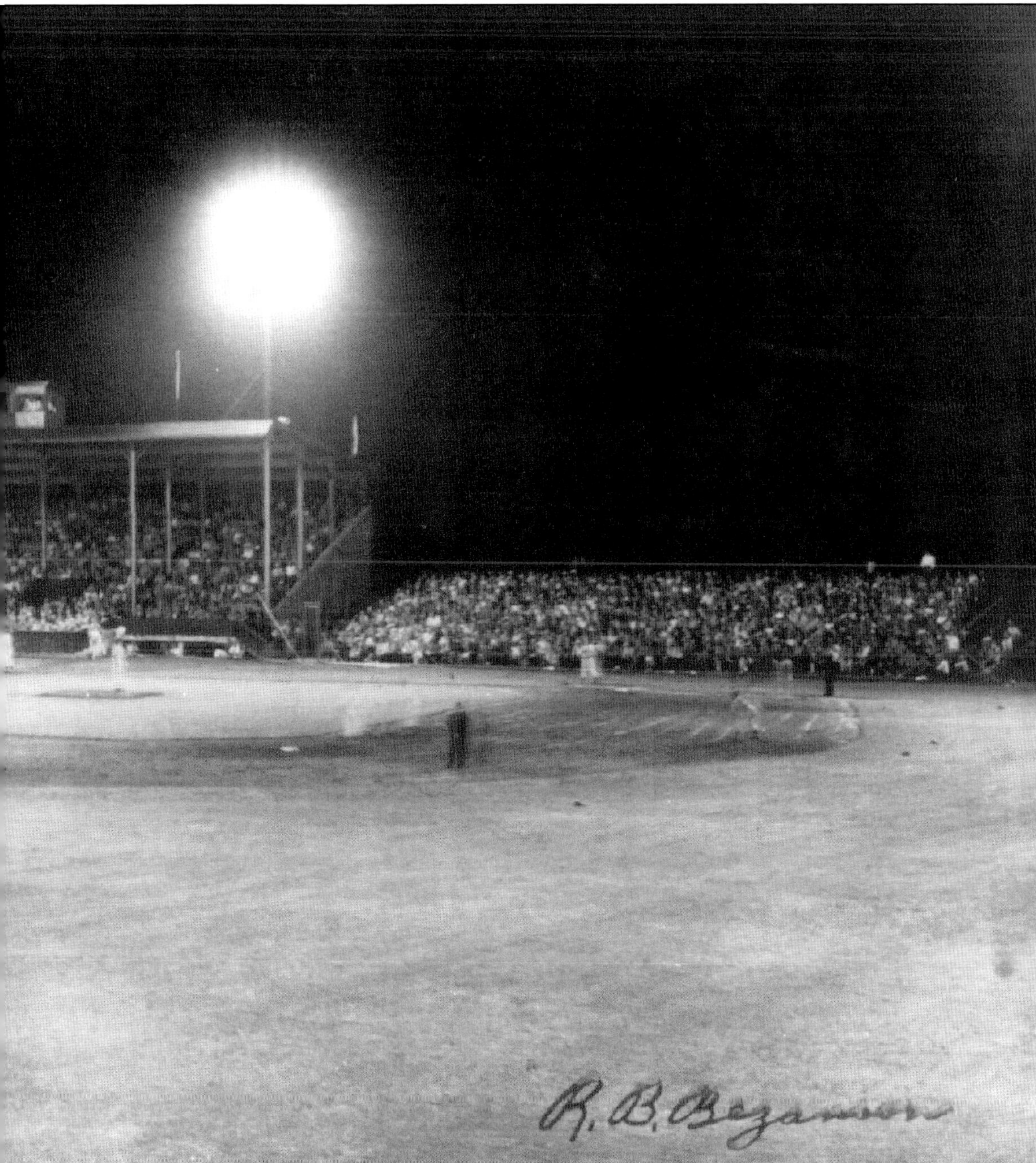

the Bears at Carson Park. (Photo courtesy of the Chippewa Valley Museum, Eau Claire, WI.)

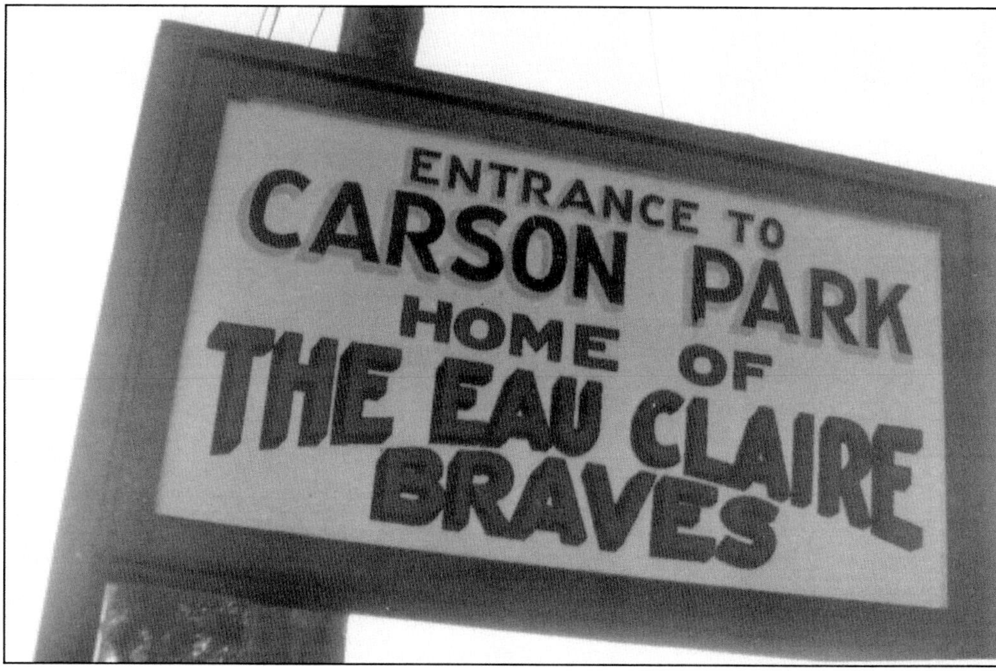

This sign was for benefit of the out-of-towners. By 1955, when this shot was taken, EVERYBODY in Eau Claire knew how to find good baseball! (Photo courtesy of Bob Botz.)

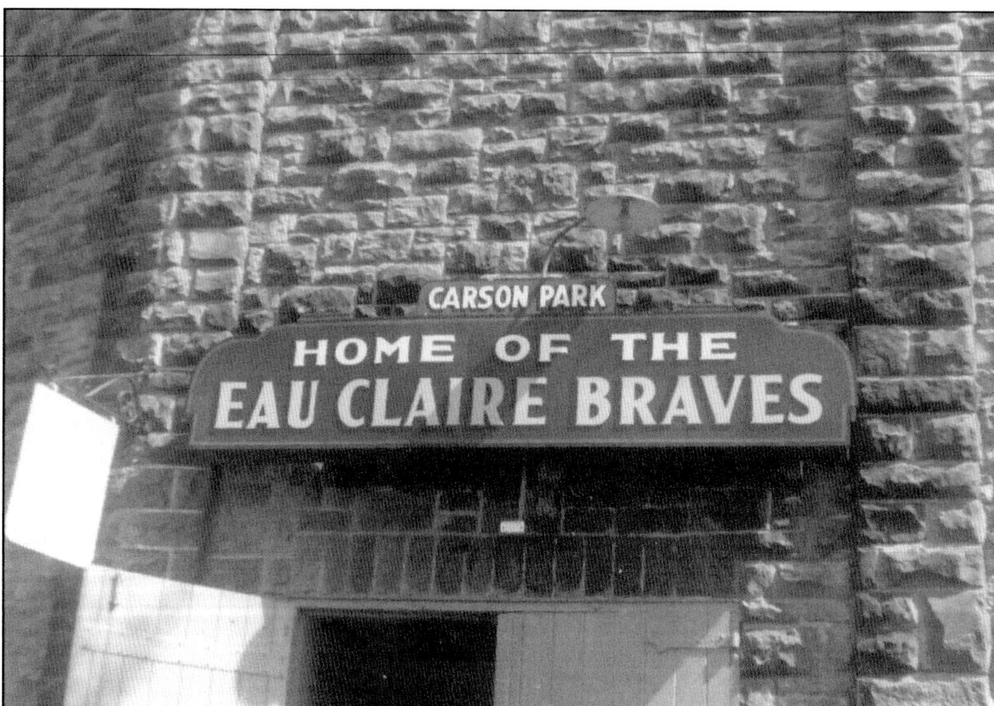

This was the view for fans as they entered the stadium to see the Braves play in 1955. (Photo Courtesy of Bob Botz.)

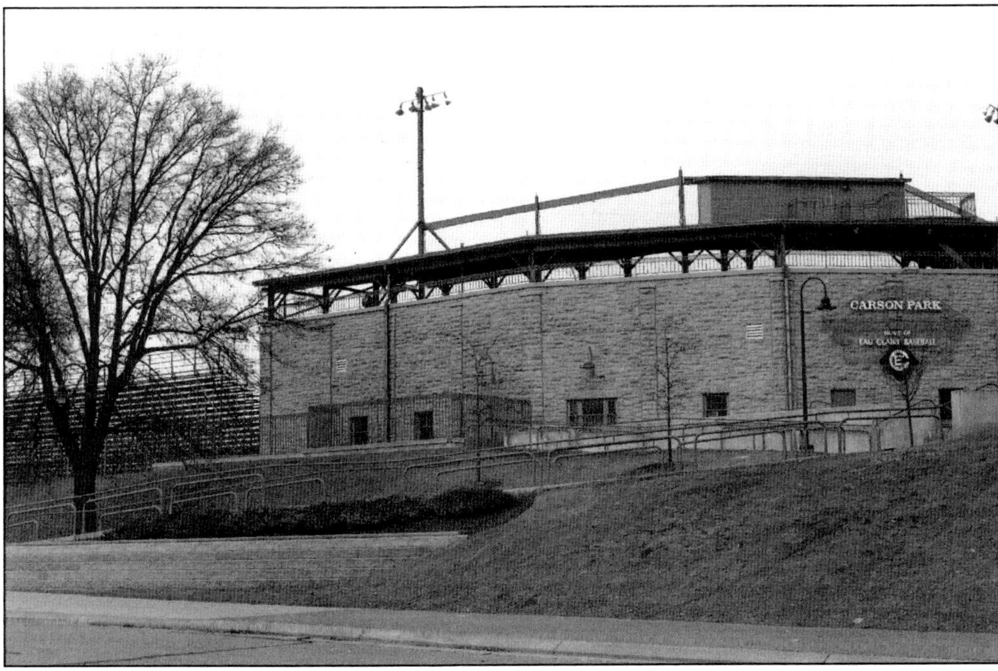

A major renovation project, to the tune of $560,000, was completed in 1998. The work resulted in a stunning face-lift for the aging Carson Park stadium and in many ways restored the park to the level of beauty it had when it opened. Some would argue it is even better now than it ever was! (Photo Courtesy of Ted Snider.)

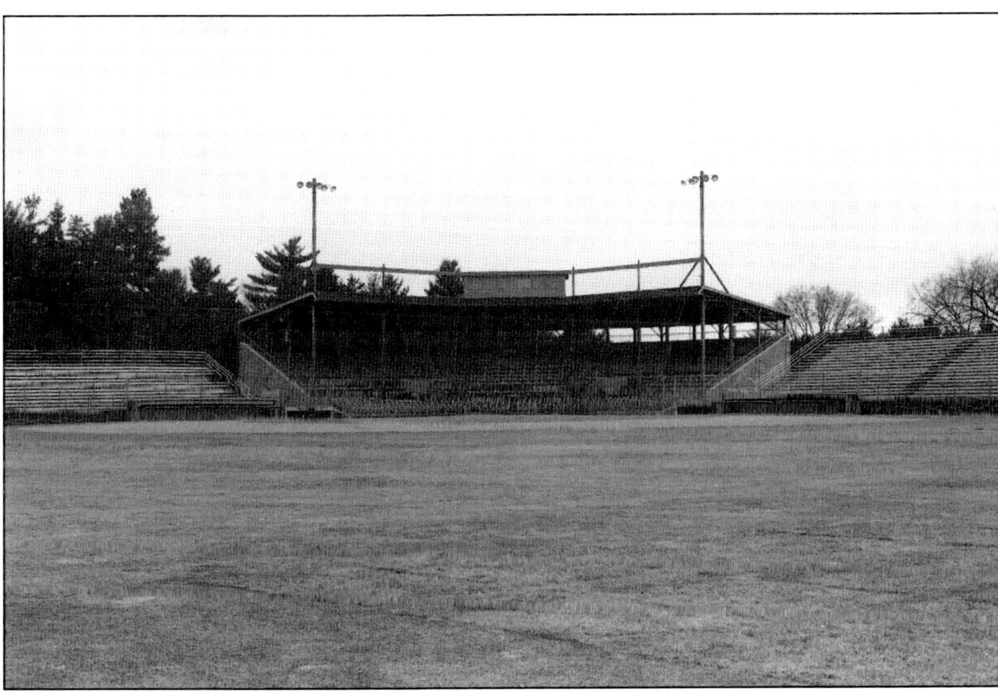

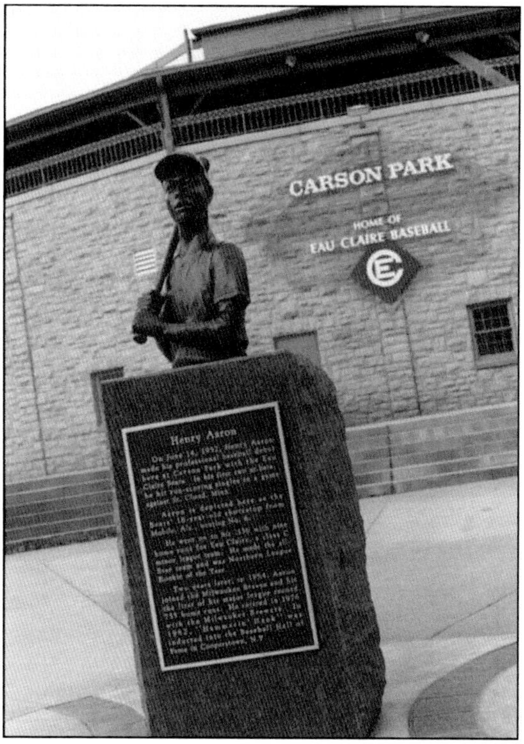

Jerry Poling, a writer for the *Eau Claire Leader-Telegram*, urged the City to somehow permanently recognize Henry Aaron for his baseball accomplishments that began in Eau Claire in 1952. As a result, a committee was formed in 1993 to erect a statue of Aaron in front of Carson Park. Kenneth Campbell was chosen to create the piece. After hundreds of hours of delicate work, but still a month ahead of schedule, Campbell delivered the young Aaron to a foundry in Utah to be bronzed. Sadly, the gorgeous work would be his last. Campbell passed away days later. The statue was put in place in 1994 and Aaron himself came back to the city later on in the summer to unveil it. "It was a great occasion, but I was sad in a way," Aaron said later. "I started thinking about playing for a little city like Eau Claire many, many years ago. I wished I could turn the clock back." (Photo Courtesy of Ted Snider. Quote from September 1, 1994 *Leader-Telegram*.)

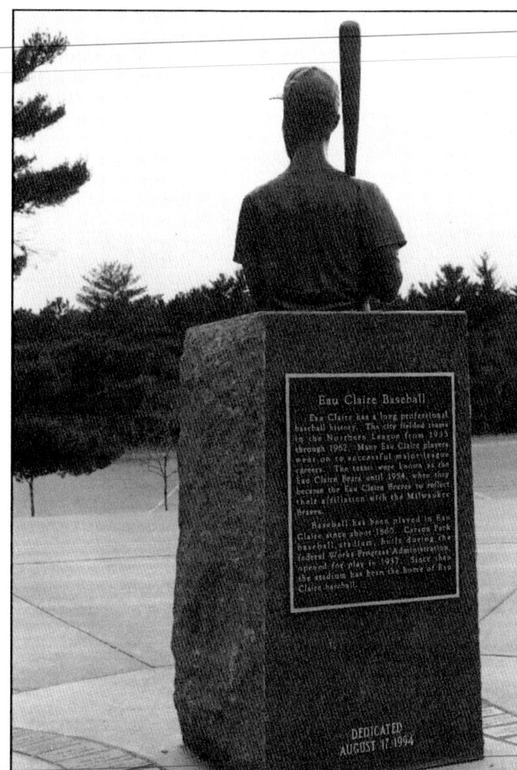

APPENDIX A

Eau Claire's Major Leaguers

A total of 62 former Eau Claire players from the Northern League went on to play in Major League Baseball, while several others (such as Dave Garcia, Roger Jongewaard, Paul Snyder, and Sheldon Bender) went on to the majors in other capacities such as managing, scouting, or working in the front office. Below is a listing of all the professional ballplayers who played in Eau Claire and also in the "The Show." For reference, statistics from the player's time in Eau Claire and his career numbers are also included. This list is believed to be complete, but the author would like to be notified if there are any omissions. Please send correspondence to jschris@triwest.net or N49175 Tracey Valley Rd., Osseo, WI 54758.

LAST NAME, FIRST NAME	ML YEARS	CAREER BA	CAREER HR	CAREER RBI	YEAR(S) WITH EAU CLAIRE	SEE PHOTO(S) ON PAGE(S):
Aaron, Henry	23	.305	755	2287	1952	65, 66–67, 68, 69
Aaron, Tommie	7	.229	13	94	1958, 1959	87, 90, 91
Bruton, Bill	12	.273	94	545	1950	57, 59
Carty, Rico	15	.299	204	890	1961	96
Castino, Vince	3	.228	2	23	1937, 1938, 1939	No Photo
Covington, Wes	11	.279	131	499	1952	66–67, 71, 72
Daniels, Jack	1	.187	2	14	1947	50
Delsing, Jim	10	.255	40	286	1946	65, 67, 68
Fanning, Jim	4	.170	0	5	1961	95
Gharrity, Ed "Patsy"	10	.262	20	249	1938	31
Goryl, John	6	.225	16	48	1952, 1954	66–67, 71
Griffin, Ivy	3	.257	0	39	1939, 1940	32
Hanebrink, Harry	4	.224	6	25	1948	53
Hartung*, Clint	6	.238	14	43	1942	42
Hriniak, Walt	2	.253	0	4	1961	No Photo
Jimenez, Manuel	7	.272	26	144	1958	87, 88
Lafata, Joe	3	.229	5	34	1941	35, 38, 41
Lindbeck, Emerit	1	.000	0	0	1956, 1957	82, 86
Linden, Walt	1	.400	0	0	1946	45
Littrell, Jack	4	.204	2	17	1962	No Photo
Majeski, Hank	13	.279	57	501	1935, 1936	28
Masi, Phil	14	.264	47	417	1936	28
Maye, Lee	13	.274	94	419	1955	79
Mostil, John	10	.301	23	376	1933–1937	22, 26, 28
Pafko, Andy	17	.285	213	976	1940	33, 34
Phillips, Dick	4	.229	12	60	1955	75, 80
Queen, Bill	1	.000	0	0	1951	62–63
Robinson, Bill	16	.258	166	641	1962	No Photo
Samuel, Amado	3	.215	3	25	1958	No Photo
Sanford, Jack	3	.209	0	11	1953	No Photo
Spence, Stan	9	.282	95	575	1935	No Photo
Sperry, Stan	2	.255	0	31	1933, 1934	23
Tanner, Chuck	8	.261	21	105	1947, 1948	53
Torre, Joe	18	.297	252	1185	1960	93
Uecker, Bob	6	.200	14	74	1956, 1957	86
Westrum, Wes	11	.217	96	315	1941	35, 36
Wheeler, Don	1	.240	1	22	1941, 1942	35, 42, 43
Whisenant, Pete	8	.224	37	134	1947	No Photo

*Hartung also pitched in the Major Leagues, going 29–29 with a 5.02 ERA.

Last Name, First Name	# ML Years	Career Wins	Career Loses	Career ERA	Year(s) with Eau Claire	See Photo(s) on page(s)
Anderson, Arnold	3	5	8	4.35	1933	No Photo
Bain, Loren	1	0	0	7.88	1941	35
Botz, Bob	1	2	1	3.43	1955	75, 77, 80, 81
Braun, John	1	0	0	0.00	1961	No Photo
Brubaker, Bruce	2	0	0	13.5	1960	94
Butland, Bill	4	9	3	3.88	1937	No Photo
Clark, Otis	1	4	4	3.07	1941	35, 39
Cloninger, Tony	12	113	97	4.07	1958	88, 89
Eilers, Dave	4	8	6	4.45	1962	No Photo
Epperly, Al	2	2	0	4.00	1936	27, 28
Fischer, Hank	6	30	39	4.23	1959	91, 92
Handrahan, Vern	2	0	2	5.31	1960, 1961	No Photo
Hardy, Frank "Red"	1	0	0	6.75	1942	42
Johnson, Vic	3	6	8	5.06	1942	42
Lemaster, Denver	11	90	105	3.58	1958	89
Maranda, Georges	2	2	7	4.52	1954, 1955	74, 75
Maxie, Larry	1	0	0	3.00	1958	87, 90
Piche, Ron	6	10	16	4.19	1956	82, 84
Rudolph, Ernest	1	1	0	5.19	1941	No Photo
Ryan, Wilfred "Rosy"	10	52	47	4.14	1941, 1942	35, 36, 42
Sproull, Charlie	1	4	10	5.94	1939, 1940	32
Thiel, Bert	1	1	1	7.71	1947	52
Trowbridge, Bob	5	13	13	3.95	1950	57, 59
Umbach, Arnold	2	1	2	3.12	1962	No Photo

Note: Two others who played for Eau Claire, Marion "Bill" Adair and Dave Garcia, did not play in the Major Leagues but did manage at that level.

Appendix B

Eau Claire All-Time Professional Roster

Below is a "liquid" listing of all the ballplayers that appeared professionally for Eau Claire during the city's Northern League run. As with nearly all minor league roster projects, there are likely some omissions. If you know of one (or, heaven forbid, SEVERAL), please e-mail the author at jschris@triwest.net or N49175 Tracey Valley Rd., Osseo, WI 54758.

Aaron	Henry	1952
Aaron	Tommie	1958, '59
Abraham	Mike	1933, '34
Adair	Marion "Bill"	1951–52
Aguilar	Bob	1962
Alander	Larry	1960
Allen	John	1948, '49
Alomar	Demetrio	1960, '61
Alworth	Fred	1961
Anderson	Arnold	1933
Anderson	Dick	1961
Anderson	Don	1939–'41
Anthony	George	1948
Augustoni	Bill	1954
Auten	Don	1952
Bain	Loren	1941
Baity	Don	1951
Ballantine	Fred	1950
Ballinger	Tom	1953, '54
Banach	Ed	1955–'58
Barbosa	Roberto	1957, '58
Barnes	Charlie	1935
Barnett	Lowell	1936, '37
Barney	Charles	1937, '38
Bass	Earl	1948,'49, '52
Bastien	Ed	1940
Bauch	Ron	1933, '34
Bauer	Bob	1951
Beckman	Steve	1957, '58
Bekeza	Lew	1938
Belardi	John	1953
Belinsky	Fred	1953
Bell, Jr.	Fred	1941, '42
Bench	John	1949
Bender	Sheldon	1941
Benevides	Frank	1954, '55
Bennett	Al	1948
Berbeck	Marv	1962
Bergstraesser	Bill	1958
Betenz	Bill	1940
Bickett	Jack	1955
Bielke	Carl	1934
Billows	Ralph	1940
Binder	Bob	1954

Blackdeer	Wilmer	1934, '35
Blaney	Lantz	1952–'54
Blatz	Ralph	1933
Boehm	Herb	1933
Bonine	Ben	1954
Booton	Lowell	1941
Bortz	Ray	1949, '50
Botkin	Del	1962
Botz	Bob	1955
Bowers	Bill	1953,'54
Brandreth	John	1951
Brann	Ray	1937
Bratkowitz	Andy	1950
Braun	John	1961
Brodahal	Don	1936
Brown	Levi	1962
Brown	Bob	1951, '52
Brown	Dick	1953
Brubaker	Bruce	1960
Bruhn	Ed	1940
Bruton	Bill	1950
Budzik	Ted	1959
Bullock	Howard	1942
Burgess	Ed	1938
Burke	Delvan	1946
Burse	Dick	1938
Butkis	Tony	1933
Butkovich	Ed	1939, '40
Butland	Bill	1937
Byerly	Bob	1959, '62
Byers	Paul	1951
Cadario	Charles	1954
Calo	Frank	1954
Campbell	Ray	1937
Carlan	Charles	1960
Carmichael	Dick	1950
Carr	Rex	1953
Carr	Charlie	1953
Carter	Don	1955–'57
Carter	Ross	1957
Carty	Rico	1961
Caruso	Pete	1962
Casellas	Orlando	1952
Casey, Jr.	Bill	1950
Castino	Vince	1937–'39
Catto	Paul	1962
Chenger	Paul	1960
Christensen	ElRoy	1941
Christoff	Ernie	1956, '58
Clark	Otis	1941
Clayton	Doug	1959
Cloninger	Tony	1958
Cochran	---	1935
Colby	Bill	1953, '54
Collins	Dan	1933–'35
Conroy	Bill	1952
Conton	Alfredo	1961
Cosgrove	Francis	1942
Couch	Max	1948, '49
Covington	Wes	1952
Cox	Barry	1949
Cross	Don	1953
Cross	Don	1934
Crowe	Don	1934
Crowl	Ken	1951
Cruthers	Hal	1938
Cullum	Ken	1960, '62
Cusack	Walt	1952, '53
Dailey	Gil	1950, '53
Dalton	Mike	1958
Dandurand	Tom	1955
Daniels	Jack	1947
Daublender	Jim	1946
Davins	Jim	1959
Davis	Wendell	1953
Dawley	Russ	1935
Dawson	Don	1946
Dean, Jr.	Paul	1958
Decker	Roy	1934, '35
DellaMonica	Joe	1947
Delliosa	Pete	1953
DelPiano	Mike	1953
Delsing	Jim	1946
DeMars	Harold	1957, '61
Diaz	Mario	1960
Dickinson	Joe	1936
Dickson	Dick	1955, '56
Dietz	Bob	1933
Dinges	Jim	1955
Doehler	Charles	1952
Dolley	Gordon	1941
Douglas	Leon	1960
Dowie	Gene	1954
Dowling	Al P. "Pete"	1937
Downs	Ben	1948
DuBrava	Bill	1954, '55
Dudley	Bob	1956, '59
Duren	Charles	1959
Dvorak	Jerry	1938
Dziura	John	1938, '39
Ebel	Walt	1939
Edinger	Don	1954, '55
Edwards	Bill	1940, '46, '47
Edwards	Howard	1953
Edwards, Jr.	George	1953
Eilers	Dave	1962
Eisenach	Bob	1946, '47
Ekern	Alvin	1947
Ellis	Bob	1955
Ellison	Len	1937, '38
Emerson	Ralph	1936
Engquist	Dick	1952
Ensley	Frank	1957
Epperly	Al	1936
Erickson	Mel	1937, '39
Essex	Bob	1939, '40
Everson	Lynn	1938
Facchini	Al	1949, '50
Fairchild	Jim	1952
Fanning	Jim	1961
Feret	Leo	1937
Ficek	Ed	1935–'37
Figueroa	Bill	1954
Fischer	Dick	1947
Fischer	Hank	1959
Fitzgerald	Tom	1957
Fleer	Bob	1957
Florian	Herman	1941
Flory	Ralph	1956
Floyd	Marion "Jake"	1946
Flynn	Jim	1962
Foell	John	1941
Fontaine	Roy	1941, '42
Ford	Don	1953
Ford	Erv	1953
Ford	---	1938
Forthmann	Al	1954
Fossen	Manley	1950
Foy	Ceferino	1959, '61, '62
Franiak	Walt	1946–'48
Frank	Red	1936
Franko	Tony	1939
Frederickson	Les	1941
Fuhrman	Mike	1946
Fuscoe	John	1953
Gabryck	Gene	1940
Ganus	Don	1957
Garcia	Dave	1941, '42
Garner	Horace	1951
Garner	Oatis	1959
Garofalo	John	1961
Gelein	Harold	1958, '60

Gendreau	Ron	1952
Gerlach	Charles	1939
Geske	Art	1947
Gharrity	Ed "Patsy"	1938
Gierek	John	1952
Gilski	---	1938
Gilstad	Burton	1938
Gittens	Ed	1940
Glor	Henry	1941
Godfredson	Don	1937, '38, '46
Golich	---	1936
Gomez	Rafael	1960
Goryl	John	1952, '54
Gozdzialski	John	1938
Grace	John	1956
Graham	Charles	1954
Granley	Les	1936
Graziano	Tom	1962
Green	Andy	1946
Greene	Bob	1936
Griffin	Ivy	1939, '40
Grimes	Glenn	1939
Groth	---	1933
Guzman	Juan	1957
Haas	Elmer	1949
Hady	Chester	1935
Hamilton	Bill	1957
Hamilton	Marv	1939
Handrahan	Vern	1960, '61
Hanebrink	Harry	1948
Hansen-Snipe	Roy	1936
Harbaugh	Ray	1953, '54
Harden	Bob	1946, '47
Hardy	Frank "Red"	1942
Hartung	Clint	1942
Hasson	Jim	1956
Hayworth	George	1962
Healey	Bob	1960, '61
Heath	Les	1935
Hendricks	John	1939
Hendrix	Ralph	1939
Henning	Al	1938, '39
Henrichs	Russ	1961
Henry	Calloway	1958
Henry	Charles	1948
Henze	Rex	1947
Herich	Charles	1938, '39
Herman	Rawling	1940
Hickman	Clair	1956, '57
Hicks	Bill	1949
Hinman	Charles	1955
Hitt	Bob	1948
Hoard	Royce	1939
Hoepner	Harold	1942
Hoff	Bob	1941, '42
Hoffman	Fred	1957, '58
Hoffses	Charles	1955, '56
Hogan	John	1939
Holder	George	1956
Holton	---	1937
Hopkins	Jim	1956, '57
Horan	Frank	1955
Horbelt	Ed	1956
Hough	Percy	1950
Howard	Art	1952
Howard	Hugh	1953
Howe	Bill	1939
Hriniak	Walt	1961
Hrovatic	Carlos	1951
Hubbard	Hermond	1961
Huda	John	1959, '60
Huebner	Larry	1959, '60
Hughes	Francis	1962
Hummitzsch	Jerome	1961
Hunt	Tom	1958
Infante	Manuel	1958

Jaber	Don	1955
Jacobs	Ed	1946
Jacoby	Bob	1960
James	Teofilo	1962
Janda	Willis	1933
Janes	Marv	1936, '39
Javerick	---	1940
Jimenez	Manny	1958
Jinske	Wayne	1962
Johnson	Gene	1959
Johnson	George	1959, '60
Johnson	Lorne	1959, '62
Johnson	Rufus	1954
Johnson	Ted	1941
Johnson	Wallace	1942
Johnson	Earl	1935
Johnson	Vic	1942
Johnston	Paul	1950
Jones	Lew	1954
Jongewaard	Roger	1955
Jordan	Don	1951, '52, '55
Jordan	Pat	1961
Juntenen	Ensio	1933–34
Jusits	Charles	1937, '38
Kanter	Ed	1937, '38
Karpinski	John	1950
Kash	Mike	1937
Kasmier	Frank	1934
Kelly	Bill	1936
Kenyon	Art	1949
Keohane	Dick	1948
Kern	Dan	1962
King	Jim	1958
Kirkleski	Ed	1938
Kirmer	Mike	1956
Klim	Curtis	1935
Kmet	Stan	1946
Knutson	Ken	1940
Kornack	George	1952
Kraus	Ed	1935
Krug	---	1935
Kubiszak	Henry	1937
Kwak	Karol	1949, '50
Lafata	Joe	1941
Lague	Ray	1954
Lakars	John	1940
Larsen	Vic	1942
Lawrence	Ed	1959
Lebida	Joe	1951
Lee	Bob	1956–58
Leeper	Dale	1947
Lemaster	Denver	1958
Lemmer	Clarence	1935
Levan	Clarence	1937
Lindbeck	Emerit	1956–57
Linden	Walt	1946
Linehan	Jim	1948, '49
Liptak	Ron	1960, '62
Litman	---	1937
Littrell	Jack	1962
Long	Sam	1953
Lotzer	---	1936
Louman	Jack	1942
Lucas	Bob	1955
Luddy	Harold	1949, '50, '53
Lukart	George	1959
Lund	Dick	1942
Lutz	Joe	1942
Lutz	Carl	1954
Lutz	John	1953, '56
MacConnell	Bob	1952, '56
MacLeod	Don	1962
MacPherson	Jim	1959
Maderrich	Marv	1938
Magula	Steve	1946
Majeski	Ed	1937

Majeski	Hank	1935, '36
Maranda	Georges	1954, '55
Marashio	Pete	1953, '55
Marciano	Pete	1962
Marnie	Bill	1959
Masi	Phil	1936
Mathews	Jude	1938
Matta	John	1955, '58
Maxie	Larry	1958
Maye	Lee	1955
McBride	Tom	1954
McCabe	Bob	1942
McColly	Bill	1955, '56
McFarlane	George	1940
McGarrey	Tom	1961
McGuire	Charles	1953, '54
McKeon	Bill	1953
McLaughlin	Bernard	1953
McManus	Joe	1947, '48
McRoberts	Gordon	1941
Mead	Ralph	1934
Mertlik	Jim	1954
Meyer	Henry	1936
Miller	Dean	1938
Mills	Don	1953
Mish	Pete	1941
Molaskey	Ed	1955, '56
Molden	LeRoy	1953
Moore	Gayle	1958
Moore	Lynn	1962
Morgan	Roger	1960
Morgan, Jr.	Chet	1951, '52
Mostil	John	1933–'37
Mozie	John	1946
Murphy	Roland	1940
Murray	Byron	1939
Nace	Harry	1934, '35
Nance	John	1962
Negri	Pete	1939
Nehring	Bob	1940
Nelson	Don	1940
Nesseth	Frank	1941, '42
Nettles	Hardie	1947
Newman	Dan	1960
Newton	Tom	1960
Nichols	Bob	1946
Nieman	John	1938, '39
Niemiec	Ed	1938
Ninnemann	Paul	1939, '40
Nitz	Ralph	1940
Nixon	Ken	1962
Norbert, Jr.	Ted	1958
Noterman	Dick	1953
Null	Bob	1938
Oddo	Vince	1946
Odom	Liburne	1939
O'Keefe	John	1933
Olson	Terry	1960
O'Melia	Dennis	1953
Orlikowski	Ray	1960, '61
Ozark	Norwood	1949
Pafko	Andy	1940
Palazzini	Julio	1951
Palcek	Joe	1953
Pan	Harry	1941, '42
Patro	Ed	1940
Patterson, Jr.	George	1949, '50, '52
Pellizzer	Pete	1948
Pelosi	Guido	1951
Perez	Joaquin	1958, '59
Peterman	Jim	1939
Peters	Clarence	1948
Peterson	Allen	1958
Petroski	Harry	1933
Pfeiffer	Harold	1951
Phillips	Dick	1955
Piche	Ron	1956
Pizzitola	Vince	1951
Plad	John	1938, '39
Pocan	George	1933, '34
Polglaze	Ed	1938
Poole	Paul	1958
Port	Chalmers	1954, '56
Pottenger	Bob	1949
Potter	Bill	1956
Powers	Bob	1955
Powers	John	1938
Prangel	Lou	1933
Price	Charles	1938
Principe	John	1938
Pupore	Bernard	1959
Queen	Bill	1951
Ramirez	Carlos	1959
Ramont	Dick	1958, '59
Redifer	Cy	1940, '41
Redmond	Ed	1953
Redway	John	1959
Reed	Ray	1956
Rehm	Vic	1954
Reitmeier	Ken	1952, '55
Rendler	Frank	1933–'35
Reynolds	Alfredo	1958
Rezotko	Ed	1935
Ries	Bob	1949
Riley	John	1959
Roach	Gordon	1951, '52
Roberts	John	1956
Robertson	Bill	1954
Robinson	Bill	1962
Robinson	Tyler	1952
Rochford	Bill	1959
Rodriguez	Marcos	1961
Roesler	Ken	1960–'62
Roland	Dick	1938
Ronovsky	Dick	1940
Roof	Paul	1960
Rosato	Frank	1957
Rosenthal	Gerald	1961
Ross	Ron	1959, '60
Rouse	Howard	1957
Rowan	Lee	1939
Rudolph	Ernie	1941
Ruff	George	1936
Rullman	Ed	1947
Russell	Dave	1962
Russell	Delmar	1950
Russo	Anthony	1953
Ryan	Wilfred "Rosy"	1941, '42
Ryder	Steve	1958, '59
Rynn	Ed	1957
Saia	Frank	1960
Samuel	Amado	1958
Samuelson	Sid	1933, '34
Sanford	Jack	1953
Scalise	Frank	1936, '37
Schaack	Francis	1934
Schaefer	John	1934
Schantel	Jim	1941
Schiller	Gene	1954, '55
Schlarb	Jack	1954
Schloessman	Ray	1947
Schohl	Ed	1933–'35
Schumacher	Art	1934
Schuming	Henry	1935
Schwartz	Henry	1938
Schymanski	Jim	1946, '47
Searles	Walt	1938
Seguin	Lou	1938
Seifert	Gene	1946
Sekeres	Bill	1938
Self	John	1961
Sell	Wes	1953, '54

Sentementes	George	1951
Severson	Don	1959
Shafer	Jack	1942
Sherman	Russ	1940
Sherrill	Pat	1961, '62
Shields	Gene	1940
Shields	Joe	1959, '61
Shinn	Jim	1957
Shoffer	Don	1940
Shuck	Larry	1962
Shuryn	Bill	1953
Sibert	Maynard	1934
Siegert	Don	1946
Sielski	Ed	1936
Skogstad	---	1936
Skurski	Joe	1946
Smith	Doug	1957–'59, '62
Snyder	Jim	1961
Snyder	Paul	1959
Sollazo	Ralph	1938
Soquet	Paul	1942
Sorrels	Bill	1949
Soscia	Lou	1951
Sosnouski	Joe	1937–'39
Southworth	Lynn	1950, '53
Spelbrink	Dick	1941
Spence	Stan	1935
Sperry	Stan	1933, '34
Sprague	Earl	1950
Sproull	Charlie	1939, '40
St. John	Bob	1961, '62
Standaert	Al	1937
Staniec	Dan	1957
Statham	Cliff	1951
Stedman	Vaughn	1954
Steffen	---	1938
Steger	Don	1948, '49
Steimling	Derwin	1936, '37
Stemmer	Warren	1941–'42
Sternberg	Don	1938
Steubing	Garnet	1960, '61
Stevens	Bill	1960
Stillings	Gerald	1957
Stokoe	John	1961
Stopa	Joe	1950, '53
Storenski	Ed	1941
Stragier	Bob	1956
Stratton	John	1955
Straub	Don	1953
Strunk	Werner	1942
Surgalski	John	1934
Sweeney	George	1941
Swittel	Tom	1946, '47
Szarzynski	John	1953
Szemczaj	John	1939
Szurma	Stan	1946, '47
Taft	Bill	1951
Tamaska	Joe	1949
Tanner	Chuck	1947, '48
Teeples	Bob	1938
Terilli	Bruno	1958
Terry	Vic	1938
Thiel	Bert	1947
Thompson	Lyle	1936
Thompson	Jerry	1939, '40
Tieken	Virgil	1953, '55–'57
Timm	Ordie	1940
Toraason	Don	1938
Toraason	Goodwin	1935
Torre	Joe	1960
Toth	Elmer	1952
Trowbridge	Bob	1950
Tucker	Ron	1947
Tufano	Lou	1948
Turck	Don	1942
Tuthill	John	1947
Uecker	Bob	1956, '57
Uhle	Stan	1937
Umbach	Arnold	1962
VanHoff	Harold	1946
Vestal	Dan	1961, '62
Vroman	Larry	1956, '57
Wagner	Fred	1953
Walker	Joe	1956
Walsh	Mike	1952, '54
Walsh	Bill	1957
Warmouth	Jim	1951
Warner	Bob	1958
Warner	Harry	1950
Wartmann	Phil	1953
Way	Bud	1958
Webster	Dave	1942
Wedberg	John	1948
Wegner	John	1935
Weiting	Henry	1935–'38
Wendlandt	Elver	1935
West	Ken	1933
Westrum	Wes	1941
Wheeler	Don	1941, '42
Whisenant	Pete	1947
White	Roy	1950
Whitney	Harry	1949, '50
Willard	Ralph	1936, '37
Williams	Phil	1956
Wilson	Wayne	1959, '61
Winn	Jim	1935, '36
Wise, Jr.	Hugh	1954
Wittichen	Florian	1958
Wolf	Orie	1959, '60
Woods	Bob	1935
Worman	Darby	1935, '37, '38
Wright	Bill	1954
Wrinn	Charles	1953
Yank	John	1938, '39
York	Bob	1958
Yorke	George	1948, '49
Young	John	1940
Zajac	John	1949
Zambold	Eric	1935
Zebrowski	Al	1954
Zeihen	Bernard	1958
Zoellick	Fred	1936
Zolinski	Arnold	1946, '47